US Interagency Regional Foreign Policy Implementation

A Survey of Current Practice and an Analysis of Options for Improvement

ROBERT S. POPE
COLONEL, USAF

Air University Press
Air Force Research Institute
Maxwell Air Force Base, Alabama

Project Editor
Jerry L. Gantt

Copy Editor
Andrew Thayer

Cover Art, Book Design, and Illustrations
Daniel Armstrong

Composition and Prepress Production
Vivian D. O'Neal

Print Preparation and Distribution
Diane Clark

AIR FORCE RESEARCH INSTITUTE

AIR UNIVERSITY PRESS

Director and Publisher
Allen G. Peck

Editor in Chief
Oreste M. Johnson

Managing Editor
Demorah Hayes

Design and Production Manager
Cheryl King

Air University Press
155 N. Twining St., Bldg. 693
Maxwell AFB, AL 36112-6026
afri.aupress@us.af.mil

Contents

Illustrations

Figures

CONTENTS

Tables

Foreword

In today's ever-changing world, the United States depends upon a complex, multiagency structure to plan, synchronize, and execute its foreign policy and ensure its national security. The public servants who work to advance US interests and values overseas and keep our citizens safe at home and abroad invariably strive to coordinate with other agencies, the US military, and the intelligence community. But effective communication and coordination within and among the national security and foreign policy bureaucracy can sometimes nevertheless become a casualty of the exuberance and enthusiasm with which many managers and action officers go about their respective missions.

In some ways, the working atmosphere among federal agencies today is similar to what the armed services experienced after the implementation of the landmark Goldwater-Nichols Act in 1986: a steep learning curve on how to work with fellow military officers raised in a different bureaucratic culture. Even if an Army officer and an Air Force officer are superficially more similar than, say, a military officer and Foreign Service officer, it's hard to dismiss the shock that the sudden "jointness" brought to the services—even though it's equally hard not to be impressed with the joint service culture that now prevails at the Department of Defense (DOD).

Today, officials at all levels of State and Defense are going through the same process, albeit more gradually, in learning to speak the other's language. After overcoming a previous Pentagon leadership's exclusion of State from involvement in postwar Iraq, military officers and diplomats went on to build a strong mutual respect on the ground in Iraq, Afghanistan, and elsewhere. This positive trend continues today. Communication between Defense and State—in Washington and around the world—is as strong and regular as I have seen in my 30 years working on political-military issues.

In places like Iraq, Afghanistan, and Pakistan, not to mention the Middle East and the Horn of Africa, we have learned anew—and sometimes the hard way—that the US government must present a solid and united front in its dealings with other nations and its execution of operations in various regions around the world. Strong regional interagency coordination is critical to the success of security cooperation, counterterrorism and counterproliferation engagements, and complex contingency operations, as well as—perhaps most importantly—how foreigners perceive the United States on a day-to-day basis. Globalization and instantaneous, around-the-clock media coverage have only served to underscore this requirement.

In a thoroughly researched and well-documented study, Col Robert Pope has analyzed how we have achieved regional interagency coordination in the past, how various organizations are presently structured toward this goal, what works and does not work, and how we can improve on the system. Enabled by a National Defense Fellowship at the Belfer Center for Science and International Affairs in Harvard University's Kennedy School of Government, he applied his diverse experience as a career Air Force officer to examine various organizational structures—past and present—and analyze them against an exhaustive reading of public policy and administration literature relevant to his subject matter.

By statute, the State Department is the lead agency for US foreign policy. In theory, its merit-based, professional diplomatic service is indispensable to its formulation and implementation. However, in practice, the much larger and better-funded DOD exercises an ever-increasing role in the conduct of US foreign policy activity—sometimes with insufficient coordination with the State Department, overseas embassies, or other relevant agencies.

Over the past two decades, the military's geographic combatant commands have taken an increasing lead in planning and executing foreign policy activities around the world. This trend has often effectively put a military face and voice on US foreign policy, sometimes to the detriment of broader goals and relationships. The key message we seek to send—that security depends upon both strong civilian and military institutions—is often obscured. For example, few recipients of US military assistance are aware that it is provided from the State Department budget because the aid is "delivered"—with high visibility—by the regional military commander.

Competing domestic priorities in an emerging era of renewed fiscal discipline will likely make what critics see as the creeping militarization of foreign policy difficult to sustain. That is mostly a good thing. While certain parts of the military are skilled at retail diplomacy, the effective conduct of US foreign policy requires greater interagency coordination at all levels and a greater role for the State Department as America's lead agency for foreign policy.

Colonel Pope's book examines current interagency structures, with a particular focus on the regional level, to describe and analyze several current or recent shortfalls in interagency unity of effort. He considers not only military operations but also nonmilitary US government responses, often in concert with other nations, to natural disasters around the world. While the US military is often best equipped to be the first agency on the scene with the greatest resources, it may not always be the most appropriate agency to run the show, particularly in regions where the appearance of US military "intervention" would be less than welcome.

Based on his own analysis of existing organization models and critiques presented in the literature, Colonel Pope analyzes several potential reform proposals and recommends a bold new model: a State Department–led regional interagency headquarters. This US regional mission would lead all US foreign policy activities within a region, including those of the relevant geographic combatant command and US embassies. The US regional mission would conduct country-level or subregional crisis operations by creating interagency task forces, which would be headed by a leader from the department or agency most appropriate to the mission.

Sir Winston Churchill once remarked, "You can always count on Americans to do the right thing—after they have tried everything else." While numerous organizational structures have been tried, with varying degrees of success, Rob Pope's insightful analysis seeks to get regional interagency coordination right. He applies more than a dozen goals to his model. These include sensible objectives such as providing a nonmilitary voice and face for US foreign policy, achieving unity of effort in execution by leveraging the unique assets of each agency, establishing clear and authoritative leadership in the region through a well-defined chain of command, balancing responsibilities between State and Defense, and developing interagency expertise among working-level personnel.

As bold as he is in proposing a new model, Colonel Pope is also forthright in describing the obvious (and not so obvious) obstacles to its achievement. He recognizes the need to minimize the financial, personnel, and material costs of his proposal and agency culture shocks resulting from that reform—that's important given the magnitude of the reorganization he is proposing. Superimposing a State-led regional interagency headquarters constitutes a form of shock therapy that could lead to questions about the role of traditional vehicles of US diplomacy such as State, the US Agency for International Development, our embassies, and other agencies.

Change does not occur rapidly in Washington or in the vast bureaucracy that flows outward from its many headquarters. Power
struggles will not become any less intense as agencies compete for
their portion of an ever-shrinking national budget. US foreign policy
becomes more complex and crucial by the moment as tensions rise in
multiple regions, the balance of power fluctuates, and state authority
continues to erode, causing both friends and foes to ask about the
future US role in the world. The same factors that make a return to
diplomacy conducted (at least in large part) by diplomats so vital also
make reforms difficult to implement. How Washington and its myr-
iad outposts respond to Col Robert Pope's analysis and recommendations remains to be seen, but he has made a valiant contribution toward worthwhile and needed change.

TOM COUNTRYMAN
Assistant Secretary
Bureau of International Security
and Nonproliferation
US State Department

About the Author

Col Robert S. Pope, USAF, is deputy chief of the Security Cooperation (SC) Division, Directorate of Strategy, Plans, and Policy (J-5) at Headquarters US Central Command (CENTCOM), MacDill AFB, Florida. In this position, he helps direct military-to-military cooperation and Phase Zero activities in 18 countries across the CENTCOM area of responsibility. Since June 2010, he has served in two previous positions within CENTCOM/J5-SC, most recently as chief of the South Asia Branch and prior to that as deputy chief of the Policy, Plans, and Programs Branch.

Colonel Pope's previous assignments include Air Staff duty as chief of Research and Assessment for the Directorate of Public Affairs and Directorate of Strategic Communication, Office of the Secretary of the Air Force. He has served on an Air Force major command staff as the chief of Long-Range Strategy and Policy and chief of Counterproliferation Plans and Policy at Headquarters, US Air Forces in Europe at Ramstein AB, Germany. His interagency experience comes from three years as the special advisor for nuclear counterproliferation operations at the Central Intelligence Agency in Washington, DC. Other assignments include a tour as a directed-energy weapons analyst at the National Air Intelligence Center, Wright-Patterson AFB, Ohio, and chief of development in the radiochemical division of the Air Force Technical Application Center's Technical Operations Division, developing new scientific procedures to support US monitoring of nuclear weapons treaties.

Colonel Pope was commissioned in 1991 through the Air Force Reserve Officers Training Corps program at Michigan State University, where he received a bachelor of science degree in physics. He also holds a master of military operational art and science degree from the Air Command and Staff College as well as a master of science degree in nuclear weapons effects physics and a PhD in physics from the Air Force Institute of Technology. Colonel Pope is an in-residence graduate of the Squadron Officer School and Air Command and Staff College and an Air War College graduate by correspondence. In 2009–10, he served as a National Defense Fellow in the International Security Program of the Belfer Center for Science and International Affairs in Harvard University's Kennedy School of Government, where he prepared the manuscript for this book.

Preface

The United States has a complex multiagency structure to plan, synchronize, and execute foreign policy. In national security issues, the most significant agencies are usually the Department of Defense, the State Department, the many agencies of the intelligence community, and the national security staff at the White House. Dedicated professionals in each of these organizations are trying hard to develop interagency policies for the tough foreign policy issues we face today including US goals for Afghanistan and Pakistan after 2015, our reaction to the Arab Spring, and what to do about the murderous regime in Syria and a government in Iran apparently intent on developing nuclear weapons. I have had the honor to work with these dedicated professionals from across our government, particularly while detailed to the Central Intelligence Agency from 2000 to 2003—a time that spanned the 9/11 terrorist attacks and the beginnings of the wars in Afghanistan and Iraq—and at US Central Command (CENTCOM) from 2010 to 2013. There, I have spent much of my time focusing on representing CENTCOM's views to the interagency as the United States formulated policies for Afghanistan and Pakistan. This book is dedicated to the professionals across our US foreign policy apparatus who work very hard through a system of drafting policy papers and seeking interagency consensus through an assortment of formal and informal interagency meetings.

I would like to thank the Air Force for giving me a year to research, think, and write about this issue; the International Security Program at the Harvard Kennedy School's Belfer Center for Science and International Affairs for giving me an academic environment in which to do this work; and Dr. Edwina Campbell at the Air Command and Staff College and Dr. Meghan O'Sullivan at the Harvard Kennedy School for their advice along the way. Most of all, I thank my wife for her constant support, patience as I worked on this project, and many helpful comments as she proofread the manuscript.

ROBERT S. POPE
Colonel, USAF

Chapter 1

Introduction

The United States has a complex multiagency structure to plan, synchronize, and execute foreign policy and national security. By statute, the State Department is the lead agency for conducting US foreign policy. However, in practice, the much larger and better-funded Department of Defense (DOD) conducts much of the nation's foreign policy activities—from peacetime engagement to postwar state building and counterinsurgency (COIN)—often with little coordination from the State Department or other relevant agencies. This is particularly true at the regional level—between agency headquarters in Washington and embassies in the various countries—where only the DOD has an effective presence via the military's geographic combatant commands (GCC). This book argues that a more effective US foreign policy requires greater interagency coordination at all levels and a greater role for the State Department as the lead US agency for foreign policy.

The Department of Defense has attempted to improve interagency unity of effort at the regional level through creation of several interagency entities at the GCCs, such as the combatant commanders' political advisors (POLAD) from the State Department, joint interagency coordination groups (JIACG) to attempt to produce regional interagency unity of effort from within the combatant command (COCOM), and joint interagency task forces (JIATF) to bring together several federal agencies to work together at the regional or country level below the COCOM headquarters. However, these mechanisms have only brought the key foreign policy and national security agencies a short way toward true unity of effort and have done little to put a nonmilitary, diplomatic face and voice on US foreign policy.

The US military views the world through a three-level hierarchy: strategic, operational, and tactical. At the top level, the government determines strategic objectives and develops broad policy and plans to achieve these objectives. At the operational level, plans are formulated to translate strategic objectives into tactical actions. Finally, the tactical level focuses on planning and executing individual activities or engagements to achieve operational or strategic objectives.[1] All US foreign policy agencies operate at the strategic level in Washington, and many function at the operational and tactical levels in individual countries through US embassies, but only the military has a substantial operational presence at the regional level—between Washington and the country level.

The regional level is important for both organizational and operational reasons. Organizationally, a regional-level entity facilitates more manageable spans of control for key leaders. National-level structures cannot achieve sufficient day-to-day control over all subordinate foreign policy activities around the globe. On the other hand, country-level structures cannot integrate US activities and messages across multiple countries and cannot effectively share resources between countries. Operationally, a regional-level organization assists US foreign policy planning and execution, because the United States must increasingly deal with regional groups and issues in addition to traditional bilateral relationships. While the United States maintains bilateral diplomatic relations with nearly 200 countries, more than 800 intergovernmental organizations (IGO) around the globe shape issues at a regional level, including the North Atlantic Treaty Organization (NATO), the African Union (AU), the Organization of American States (OAS), and the Association of Southeast Asian Nations (ASEAN), as well as thousands of nongovernmental organizations (NGO) which frequently operate in more than one country.[2] Additionally, many threats and challenges to the United States exist at a regional level, including transnational terrorist, criminal, and narcotics organizations. According to the Hart/Rudman Commission's 2001 report, "Regions will become more important in the emerging world of the 21st century. State borders no longer contain the flow of refugees, the outbreak of ethnic violence, the spread of deadly diseases, or environmental disasters. Humanitarian and military operations will often depend on access rights in many different countries."[3]

As US foreign policy activities have become increasingly regional in nature, the military's GCCs—in the absence of any regional-level State Department or other interagency presence—have taken the lead in planning and executing both military and nonmilitary activities in regions around the world. This has often effectively put a military face and voice on US foreign policy, and this trend has increased since the 9/11 attacks. According to *Washington Post* investigative reporter Dana Priest, "Long before September 11, the U.S. government had grown increasingly dependent on its military to carry out its foreign affairs. The shift was incremental, little noticed, de facto. . . . After September 11, however, the trend accelerated dramatically. . . . Without a doubt, U.S.-sponsored political reform abroad is being eclipsed by new military pacts focusing on anti-terrorism and intelligence sharing."[4]

The primacy of the geographic combatant commands in regional US foreign policy leads to overmilitarization of foreign policy. The commanders of the military's GCCs are four-star generals or admirals with a career-long military outlook and a predominantly military toolkit, leading them to define most problems—and often their solutions—in military terms. Ambassador Robert Komer, who led interagency COIN pacification and development efforts during the Vietnam War, stated, "military men are naturally going to give primary emphasis to the military aspects," and former secretary of defense and Central Intelligence Agency (CIA) director James Schlesinger stated that the military leadership "of course, by definition are for military solutions."[5] Though Komer's and Schlesinger's observations are perhaps less true today after more than two decades of expanding interagency thinking by senior military leaders, it is still true that the GCCs are first and foremost military officers and not primarily professional diplomats.

With the military in the lead for regional foreign policy and the GCC as the public face of US policy, the United States loses the ability to engage many governments, actors within states, NGOs, and IGOs that do not wish to be publicly associated with the US military.[6] A 2006 Senate Foreign Relations Committee investigation concluded, "There is evidence that some host countries are questioning the increasingly military component of America's profile overseas."[7] Assistant Secretary of State for Political-Military Affairs John Hillen stated in 2005,

> If we subvert, however unintentionally, our ability for the lead foreign policy agency of the US government [the State Department] to deliver credible and consistent messages—in the field and at all levels—to those actors whose behavior we are trying to shape and change, we will lose influence and legitimacy. Especially when those messages are inherently about democracy, political pluralism and compromise, the rule of law, civilian control of the military, the importance of institutions in civil society, legitimacy and governance gained through peaceful means and processes, and diplomatic exchange and negotiation as the preferred way of solving differences. These are not inherently military messages, needless to say, but today it is most often the US military that delivers them on the ground.[8]

One of the major reasons for the overwhelming influence of the military in foreign affairs is the massive resource imbalance between the Departments of Defense and State. The State Department is much smaller in terms of both budget and personnel than the Defense Department. The DOD has an annual budget of about $660 billion and a workforce of approximately three million people, while State has an annual budget of about $50 billion and a workforce of fewer than 60,000 people, of whom only 6,400 are Foreign Service officers (FSO).[9] FSOs are commissioned officers of the US Foreign Service. They are the State Department's professional diplomats and fill most of the leadership roles at the headquarters in Washington and at US embassies abroad, including about two-thirds of US ambassador positions (the other third are political appointees). FSOs are selected through a competitive written and oral exam process called the Foreign Service Exam.[10]

After the 1986 Goldwater-Nichols DOD reorganization, which created today's joint military, the GCCs expanded in size and importance. Around the same time, Congress cut the State Department's operating budget and personnel by 20 percent, forcing closure of more than 30 overseas missions.[11] The 9/11 Commission concluded, "State came into the 1990s overmatched by the resources of other departments and with little support for its budget either in Congress or in the President's Office of Management and Budget."[12]

However, instead of being fixed, this imbalance has continued to expand, causing Washington to increasingly rely on the military to execute foreign policy. Assistant Secretary Hillen stated in 2005, "The resources that [combatant commanders] bring to bear in their theaters, in terms of people, money, and logistics support, far outstrip the foreign assistance programs that ambassadors and their country teams can routinely deliver to host governments."[13] Hillen cautions, "When [military-to-military] relationships bear more and better fruit than political relationships can deliver, we run the risk [of] sacrificing our larger foreign policy goals to the exigencies of military priorities with shorter horizons."[14] One US ambassador echoed this, noting, "Foreign officials are 'following the money' in terms of determining which relationships to emphasize."[15]

While it would seem the Defense Department is the bureaucratic "winner" in terms of obtaining the majority of operational resources and funding, many in the DOD would prefer to see the State Department receive additional resources so the two departments can both carry out their core missions abroad. Former secretary of defense Robert Gates several times noted the resource imbalance between the Departments of Defense and State and has argued for increased funding for the State Department. In June 2008, Gates warned against the "creeping militarization" of foreign policy and advocated for more funding for the State Department: "America's civilian institutions of diplomacy and development have been chronically underfunded for far too long relative to what we spend on the military, and . . . the responsibilities our nation has around the world."[16] In July 2008, Gates said, "Our diplomatic leaders . . . must have the resources and political support needed to fully exercise their statutory responsibilities in leading American foreign policy."[17] Continuing this theme in testimony before the Senate Appropriations Committee on 30 April 2009, Gates said, "I believe that the challenges confronting our nation cannot be dealt with by military means alone. They instead require whole-of-government approaches—but that can only be done if the State Department is given resources befitting the scope of its mission across the globe."[18]

In addition to the resource imbalance between the DOD and other US agencies involved in foreign policy, another significant challenge in today's system is how to obtain interagency unity-of-effort without unity of command. For the military, the Goldwater-Nichols Act created a direct chain of command from the president to the secretary of defense to the GCCs, creating both unity of command and unity of effort for the joint military force.[19] However, in the interagency foreign policy arena, no one below the president can direct the efforts of all executive branch agencies or settle disputes among them. Congress created the National Security Council (NSC) in the National Security Act of 1947 to assist the president with interagency coordination and unity of effort in foreign policy and national security, but the system rarely produces true unity of effort. Interagency working groups in the NSC or under a lead agency can set policy but cannot enforce compliance across the interagency. Since the president has no way to delegate his authority over these agencies, issue management for interagency foreign policy is overly centralized in the White House, and the president and his advisors must spend time on crisis management and dispute resolution, leaving little time for the formulation of strategic policy.[20]

In the more than two decades since Goldwater-Nichols created the joint military and increased the effectiveness of the DOD, hundreds of authors have examined the problem of interagency unity of effort and offered various proposals for reform. Some have advocated comprehensive, Goldwater-Nichols type reforms. Military authors and defense-centric think tanks have often focused more narrowly on interagency solutions to the challenges of "complex contingency operations"[21] or postconflict stabilization and reconstruction operations, largely arising out of the challenges the US military has faced in operations over the 21 years from US intervention in Panama to operations in Iraq and Afghanistan.

This book reviews the current interagency structures established by the military, State Department, and White House; describes several cases of shortfalls in interagency unity of effort in peacetime engagements, humanitarian operations, and military operations; surveys the interagency reform literature; and finally, analyzes potential reforms and recommends a new model, focused particularly on the regional level.

Focusing below the national/strategic level considers interagency reform at two levels: operationally across a region and operationally in a subregion or country during crisis operations. Within each of these two levels, the universe of reform proposals can be grouped into four major categories: a military-led organization, a State Department–led organization, an integrated interagency organization, or a parallel structure with no single leader or organization in charge.

This book argues that an improved interagency structure needs to:

1. Provide a nonmilitary voice and face for US foreign policy.

2. Produce fully coordinated planning.

3. Produce unity of effort during execution.

4. Be more efficient and effective than agencies working alone.

5. Give leaders authority commensurate with their responsibility.

6. Provide legitimacy to leaders' decisions.

7. Enable leaders to access necessary resources.

8. Provide a clear chain of command to the president.

9. Avoid overburdening the president with operational or crisis matters.

10. Balance the power and prestige of the Departments of State and Defense.

11. Develop interagency expertise among working-level personnel.

12. Minimize the financial, personnel, and material costs of reform.

13. Minimize agency culture shocks resulting from the reform.

Based on the understanding developed from review of current interagency structures, the shortfalls in unity of effort in several current and recent operations, and the goals for reform above, this book recommends a new structure with a State Department–led regional interagency headquarters. This US regional mission would lead all US foreign policy activities in the region, including those of the geographic combatant command and US embassies in the region. Each US regional mission would conduct subregional contingency operations by creating interagency task forces headed by a leader from the department or agency most appropriate to the mission.

Notes

1. Joint Publication 3-0, *Doctrine for Joint Operations*, 17 September 2006 (incorporating change 1, 13 February 2008), II-1–2.

2. MAJ Brett G. Sylvia, USA, "Empowering Interagency Capabilities: A Regional Approach," monograph (Fort Leavenworth, KS: School of Advanced Military Studies, US Army Command and General Staff College, 25 May 2006), 25.

3. US Commission on National Security/21st Century (Hart/Rudman Commission), *Road Map for National Security: Imperative for Change*, Phase III Report, 15 February 2001, 62, http://govinfo.library.unt.edu/nssg/PhaseIIIFR.pdf.

4. Dana Priest, *The Mission: Waging War and Keeping Peace with America's Military* (New York: W. W. Norton, 2003), 14.

5. Sylvia, "Empowering Interagency Capabilities," 40.

6. Ibid.

7. US Senate, Committee on Foreign Relations, *Embassies as Command Posts in the Anti-Terror Campaign*, 109th Cong., 2nd sess., 15 December 2006, Senate Print 109-52 (Washington, DC: Government Printing Office [GPO], 2006), 2.

8. John Hillen, "The Changing Nature of the Political-Military Interface," remarks, Joint Worldwide Planning Conference, Garmisch, Germany, 30 November 2005), http://2001-2009.state.gov/t/pm/rls/othr/misc/58492.htm.

9. Louis J. Nigro Jr., "The Department of State and Strategic Integration: How Reinforcing State as an Institution Will Improve America's Engagement with the World in the 21st Century," in *Affairs of State: The Interagency and National Security*, ed. Gabriel Marcella (Carlisle, PA: Strategic Studies Institute, December 2008), 258–59; US Joint Forces Command (USJFCOM), *Insights and Best Practices: Interagency,*

Intergovernmental, and Nongovernmental Coordination: A Joint Force Operational Perspective, Focus Paper no. 3 (Norfolk, VA: Joint Warfighting Center, July 2007), 2, http://jko.cmil.org/file/109/view; Secretary of State Hillary Rodham Clinton, "President's Proposed Budget Request for Fiscal Year 2011 for the Department of State and Foreign Operations," testimony before the Senate Appropriations Subcommittee on State, Foreign Operations, and Related Programs, 24 February 2010; and White House Office of Management and Budget, "The U.S. Department of Defense 2010 Budget," fact sheet, 1, http://www.whitehouse.gov/omb/ assets/fy2010_factsheets/fy 10_defense8.pdf.

10. See Harry W. Kopp and Charles A. Gillespie, *Life and Work in the U.S. Foreign Service* (Washington, DC: Georgetown University Press, 2008).

11. Priest, *Mission*, 45.

12. *The 9/11 Commission Report*, 22 July 2004, 94, http://govinfo.library.unt.edu /911/report/911Report.pdf.

13. Hillen, "Changing Nature of the Political-Military Interface."

14. Ibid.

15. Senate, *Embassies as Command Posts*, 12.

16. Defense Secretary Robert M. Gates, quoted in Gabriel Marcella, "Understanding the Interagency Process: The Challenge of Adaptation," in *Affairs of State*, 39.

17. Secretary Gates, quoted in "A Foreign Affairs Budget for the 21st Century," *Foreign Service Journal* 85, no. 12 (December 2008): 54.

18. Secretary Gates, quoted in William I. Bacchus, "Regaining Relevance: Five Steps to Strengthen State," *Foreign Service Journal* 86, nos. 7–8 (July/August 2009): 14.

19. Clark A. Murdock and Michèle A. Flournoy, *Beyond Goldwater-Nichols: U.S. Government and Defense Reform for a New Strategic Era*, Phase 2 Report (Washington, DC: Center for Strategic and International Studies, July 2005), 17.

20. Project on National Security Reform (PNSR), *Forging a New Shield* (Arlington, VA: Center for the Study of the Presidency, November 2008), vi–vii, downloadable in free e-Book or PDF format from http://www.scribd.com/doc/38667628/Forging -a-New-Shield-SSI-2008-National-Security-Strategy; and Bruce R. Pirnie, *Civilians and Soldiers: Achieving Better Coordination* (Santa Monica, CA: RAND, 1998), 14.

21. "The more ambitious post–Cold War peace operations, currently [as of this 1998 writing] styled 'complex contingency operations,' blur the traditional distinction between peace and war." Pirnie, *Civilians and Soldiers*, 10.

Chapter 2

Current Practices—Military

The first step toward analyzing regional-level US foreign policy and national security planning and implementation is to understand the organizations and mechanisms the United States currently employs in these processes. Numerous actors, including ambassadors, country-level representatives of various federal agencies, and regional military geographic combatant commands and their subordinate forces around the globe—as well as headquarters of both military and civilian agencies in Washington—must work together to plan and execute US foreign policy and ensure national security.

This book focuses on two primary actors, the Department of Defense (primarily the military) and the Department of State, including the US Agency for International Development (USAID). It also considers the role of the National Security Council. The US military has made several attempts to take the lead in improving interagency unity of effort at the regional level.

Military-Led Interagency Coordination Mechanisms

Since World War II, the military has developed three primary tools to drive interagency unity of effort from the military side—the political advisor, the joint interagency task force, and the joint interagency coordination group.

Political Advisors

Since 1952 the State Department has provided the military with political advisors, or POLADs (officially renamed foreign policy advisors in 2004, but the former term is still more commonly used), to directly advise senior military leaders on foreign policy issues.[1] As of January 2008, 26 POLAD positions were allocated to the four service chiefs in the Pentagon, six geographic combatant commands, four functional combatant commands, NATO headquarters and its key subordinate commands, as well as several subordinate US commands in combat zones. Congress funded 10 additional POLAD positions in 2009 in support of operations in Iraq and Afghanistan.[2]

The POLAD at the GCCs is a State Department FSO with ambassadorial rank assigned to provide foreign policy advice directly to the combatant commander. POLADs aid in assessing the diplomatic implications of military planning and strategy, serve as the principal source of counsel on international issues to the respective commander, provide the combatant commander with a State Department perspective, and serve as an information conduit between the combatant commander and the State Department (both the Bureau of Political-Military Affairs and the appropriate regional bureau). However, POLADs have no formal role as a coordinator between the State Department and the military and no authority to commit the State Department to any course of action. Indeed, the essence of the POLADs' effectiveness is their ability to function as personal and confidential advisors to the military commander. Any requirement for formal reporting back to the State Department could compromise the necessary relationship of personal trust and confidence between the POLAD and the commander.[3]

While POLADs have no formal role in civil-military coordination, they form relationships up and down the military chain of command, as well as with other military headquarters, embassies, international organizations, NGOs, and civilian entities, all of which can facilitate interagency unity of effort. According to Dr. John Finney and Amb. Alphonse La Porta, both of whom served as POLADs to senior military commanders, the POLAD "can help translate the local environment into operational ground truth and can facilitate the conduct of operations on the ground through negotiation, facilitating allied and indigenous contacts, and providing access to local actors and institutions."[4]

Joint Interagency Coordination Group

As the United States prepared for the global war on terrorism in response to the 11 September 2001 terrorist attacks, planners and policy makers in the Defense Department recognized the complex nature of the counterterrorism mission, and many came to believe a "whole of government" response using all elements of national power would be required. To facilitate this, the Joint Staff requested, and in February 2002 the Deputies Committee of the NSC approved, a joint interagency coordination group concept and directed the combatant commands to each establish a JIACG "to provide interagency advice and expertise to combatant commanders and their staffs, coordinate interagency counterterrorism plans and objectives, and integrate military, interagency, and host-nation efforts."[5] By the time the NSC and Joint Staff issued their guidance, all of the combatant commands had already established some form of counterterrorism office and for the most part renamed whatever structure they had already created as a JIACG for counterterrorism (JIACG/CT).[6]

Originally, the JIACG was limited to the counterterrorism mission and prohibited "from making policy, tasking non-DoD personnel, or altering lines of authority and coordination channels already in place."[7] However, in the ensuing years the JIACG concept has evolved beyond counterterrorism—both under the guidance of the now-defunct US Joint Forces Command (USJFCOM)[8] and as a result of unique conditions and initiatives at the combatant commands—so that JIACGs now also support "military engagement, security cooperation, and deterrence activities, as well as operations ranging from crisis response and limited contingency operations to, if necessary, major operations and campaigns."[9]

USJFCOM—the combatant command charged with military-wide joint doctrine, transformation, and organizational standardization until it was disestablished in August 2011—attempted to guide and standardize the development of the JIACG across the COCOMs.[10] Broadening beyond the initial counterterrorism mission, or any other specific mission, USJFCOM envisioned a "full spectrum" JIACG at each COCOM as a full-time interagency planning and advisory body for the commander. The JIACG would support peacetime theater engagement as well as the full spectrum of military operations, and JIACG members would act as informational liaisons with their respective departments and agencies in Washington. The JIACG may also provide interface with host nations, IGOs, and NGOs.[11] If combatant commanders employed joint military forces in an operation, JFCOM envisioned that they could either retain the JIACG at the COCOM headquarters or integrate selected members into the joint task force (JTF) established to conduct the operation.[12]

JFCOM codified its vision of the JIACG into doctrine in the two volumes of Joint Publication (JP) 3-08, *Interagency, Intergovernmental Organization, and Nongovernmental Organization Coordination during Joint Operations*.[13] Additionally, in March 2007, JFCOM issued the *Commander's Handbook for the Joint Interagency Coordination Group* to provide nondoctrinal "best practices," a "common, practical baseline for continuing the evolution of the JIACG," and "a bridge between the evolving JIACG and its migration into doctrine."[14] Per these documents, JFCOM envisioned a standard COCOM JIACG as a "separate staff directorate or element of approximately 12 personnel" led by a full-time civilian director and "consisting primarily of USG [US government] civilian personnel with extensive interagency experience."[15] The notional staffing includes three military personnel, three DOD civilians (including the director), two FSOs, and one representative each from the USAID and the Departments of Justice, Homeland Security, and Transportation. JFCOM's "standard model" for interagency coordination at the regional level is shown in figure 1.

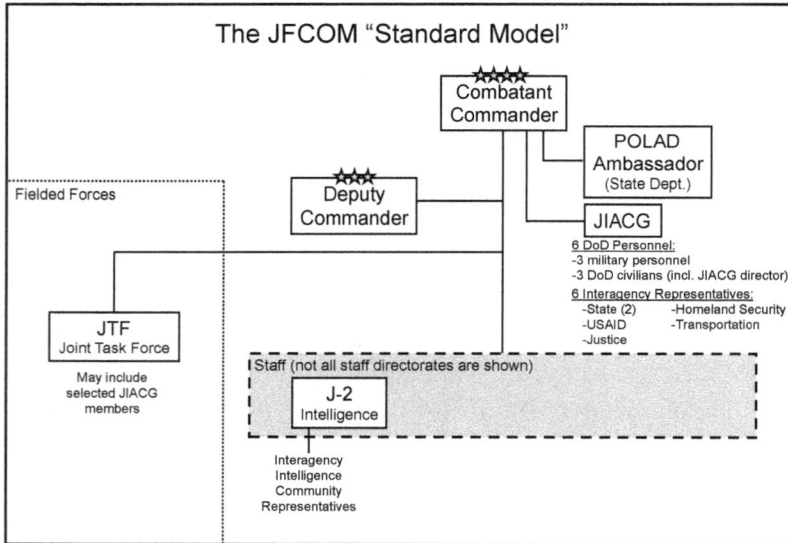

Figure 1. JFCOM standard model for interagency coordination

Essentially, in the absence of other mechanisms to facilitate interagency unity of effort at the regional level, the DOD attempted to establish its own organic capability by creating the JIACGs and empowering the combatant commanders to conduct interagency coordination. However, because the JIACG is located in one agency (the DOD) and has no presidential directive or legislative sanction, other agencies are under no obligation to participate. Indeed, the initial

JIACG concept was not well received by the other agencies and departments asked to participate, as many perceived a military-led JIACG as an erosion of their autonomy or authority.[16]

Because other executive branch agencies are so much smaller than the DOD, providing even one or two qualified individuals to each of the GCCs is a significant drain on their available personnel. Thus, many agencies proposed providing representatives to the JIACGs on an as-needed basis to develop a specific plan or to participate in an exercise or crisis rather than providing permanent representatives. William Olson, who served as both a deputy assistant secretary of state and a deputy assistant secretary of defense, says even if there is enough work to justify a full-time JIACG during a crisis, it is not clear that justification exists for the full-time use of limited personnel resources otherwise.[17] However, part-time JIACG staffing creates a lack of continuity and inhibits team building.

In December 2003, the DOD attempted to make it easier for other agencies to send personnel to the JIACGs by using DOD funds to pay for individuals from the State Department, Federal Bureau of Investigation (FBI), and Treasury to staff JIACGs at nine COCOMs. However, as Col Michael Bogdanos, USMCR, who served in US Central Command's (CENTCOM) JIACG, notes, "This decision overlooked the possible effect on the nonreimbursed agencies, [which] became less inclined to continue providing representatives for JIACGs after they learned they did not make the final cut."[18] Similarly, Bogdanos criticizes JFCOM's standard 12-person model for excluding other agencies such as Treasury, the FBI, the Drug Enforcement Administration (DEA), the CIA, and other organizations which played key roles during the time he served with CENTCOM's JIACG. He says each COCOM should be permitted to fund representatives from the agencies and departments best suited to its regional issues rather than following a one-size-fits-all model.[19]

The COCOM staff now has potentially two (or more) State Department representatives—the commander's POLAD and State's representative to the JIACG. The relationship between the JIACG and the POLAD is neither agreed upon nor well documented. As the JIACG concept was developed, POLADs reportedly believed they should not be a part of the JIACG because it would undermine their current role with the commander.[20] However, former POLADs Finney and La Porta disagree, saying POLADs should both serve their individual commanders and exercise some level of oversight over the JIACG "to provide a broad regional picture and to help in bridging U.S. agency, region, and multilateral interests," perhaps even dual-hatting the POLAD as the JIACG director.[21] Currently, the nature of the POLAD-JIACG relationship is left up to each individual COCOM.

In interviews conducted in 2003 with personnel from State, Defense, Justice, and Treasury, participants pointed out several pros and cons of the JIACG concept. On the positive side, JIACGs can provide civilian agencies with access to DOD resources, facilitate information sharing, remove institutional barriers, and provide the DOD with outside perspectives. One participant said the regional focus is good since "terrorists don't care about borders."[22] On the negative side, respondents perceive a lack of JIACG mission clarity. Some like a narrow focus on counterterrorism, while others believe the JIACG should have a larger scope. Many cited a lack of understanding of the JIACG's role on both the military and civilian sides. Participants also said the lack of continuity on JIACG staffs was a problem. Finally, they felt the JIACG was too DOD-centric, saying, "The military is driving the JIACG process too much. . . . JIACGs should not be beholden to DOD or regional [combatant commanders]."[23]

The issue remains open as to whether the JIACG is an effective solution for achieving interagency unity of effort at the regional level. The construct is military-centric and still has little input or commitment from other agencies.[24] Additionally, the JIACG construct expects to produce unity of effort but still does not provide any leader with unity of command. Olson concludes that "it is not clear that the JIACG concept or its reality can deliver" on the level of interagency unity of effort expected of it.[25]

Joint Interagency Task Force

In addition to the POLAD and the JIACG, a combatant commander may create a subordinate joint task force with enough interagency representation to be designated a joint interagency task force. Currently, two long-standing units are so designated—JIATF-West (JIATF-W) under US Pacific Command (PACOM) and JIATF-South (JIATF-S) under US Southern Command (SOUTHCOM). Both date back to 1989 and are focused on the counternarcotics mission. A third unit, JIATF-Iraq (JIATF-I) was established in 2008 to facilitate interagency unity of effort against threats to Iraq's stability but has since been disestablished.[26] NATO's International Security Assistance Force (ISAF) and US Forces–Afghanistan (USFOR-A) established three combined joint interagency task forces (CJIATF) to focus on the complex "nexus of insurgency, narcotics, corruption, and criminality" in Afghanistan—CJIATF-Nexus, CJIATF-435, and CJIATF-Shafafiyat.

In current US joint military doctrine, JIATFs are mentioned only in JP 3-07.4, *Joint Counterdrug Operations*; JP 3-05.1, *Joint Special Operations Task Force Operations*; and JP 3-40, *Combating Weapons of Mass Destruction*.[27] A 2007 JFCOM white paper, while acknowledging that the JIATF concept is "not fully developed in joint doctrine," defined the entity as "an interagency organization under a single military director that coordinates counterdrug operations at the operational and tactical level," seemingly limiting the JIATF construct to the counternarcotics mission, though the concept is at least mentioned in doctrine dealing with the counter-WMD (weapons of mass destruction) and special operations missions.[28] The white paper further notes that, unlike a JIACG, a JIATF "exercises tactical control over attached elements when executing a mission."[29]

Like the JIACG, the JIATF is codified in neither executive order nor legislation; a JIATF derives its authority through a memorandum of agreement signed by the head of each participating agency or department.[30] The JFCOM white paper notes that while agencies subordinate some of their assets under another agency's leadership, the JIATFs do not have true unity of command because "the different agencies still retain many of their authorities, responsibilities, and prerogatives." However, because many of the participants' field-level headquarters are collocated in the JIATF in something of an integrated command structure, the organization has the ability to cut across traditional agency stovepipes and facilitate rapid integrated action. The JFCOM white paper concludes that existing JIATFs took a long time to develop the level of trust needed to work collaboratively, so planners should not expect to form new ones rapidly for a crisis operation.[31]

Interagency Structures at the Geographic Combatant Commands

The US military has five geographic combatant commands with significant foreign policy responsibilities: US Central Command (CENTCOM), US Pacific Command (PACOM), US European Command (EUCOM), US Southern Command (SOUTHCOM), and US

Africa Command (AFRICOM).[32] This list begins with the most traditional war-fighting GCC and ends with one whose primary function is theater engagement. Each GCC has evolved a unique structure and set of tools to promote interagency unity of effort in the planning and execution of national security within its respective region.

US Central Command

CENTCOM's interagency entities at the unified command headquarters level include the commander's POLAD, a JIACG (now called the interagency action group or IAG), a target synchronization board (TSB), and three JIATFs in Afghanistan.[33] CENTCOM's structures to facilitate interagency unity of effort are shown in figure 2.

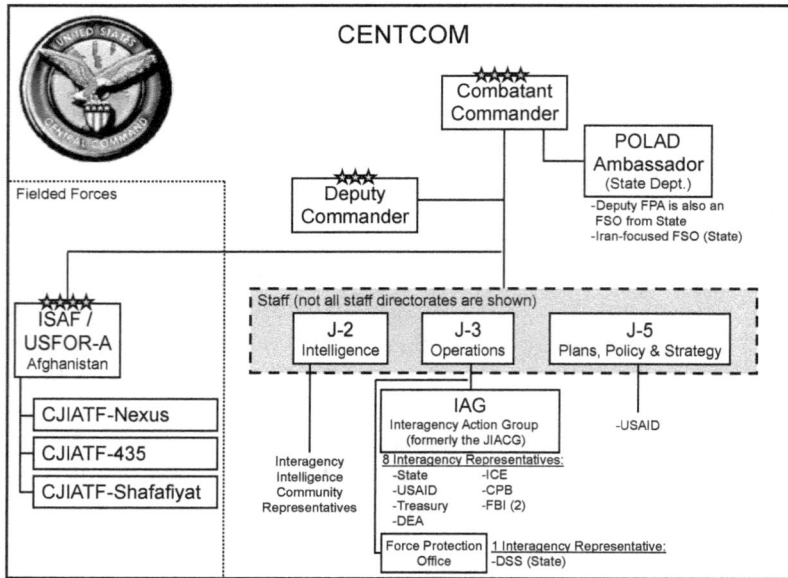

Figure 2. CENTCOM structures for interagency unity of effort

The ambassador serving as the POLAD, assisted by two deputies from the State Department and a military foreign area officer focused on Middle East peace, executes the traditional role as the primary foreign policy advisor to the commander.[34] Both the POLAD and the

State Department's liaison to the IAG are conduits for coordination and information sharing from CENTCOM to the State Department headquarters and to the US embassies in each country in CENT-COM's area of responsibility (AOR). Other elements of the staff, such as the military officers serving as security cooperation desk officers for each country in the AOR, also frequently conduct business directly with both the State Department headquarters and the US embassy in their assigned country.[35] At CENTCOM, there is no formal relationship between the POLAD's office and the IAG.

CENTCOM formed a JIACG in October 2001 specifically for operations in Afghanistan, initially as more of a counterterrorism task force and intelligence fusion center than a staff coordination element. (Given its mission, this organization should probably have been called a JIATF rather than a JIACG.) The unit deployed to Afghanistan in November 2001 with representation from the FBI, the CIA, the National Security Agency (NSA), the State Department's Diplomatic Security Service (DSS), the Customs Service, and New York's Joint Terrorism Task Force, among others—a total of 36 US military personnel and 57 non-DOD personnel, as well as several British and Australian special forces personnel—leaving a small detachment at CENTCOM headquarters in Tampa to facilitate communication from Afghanistan back to the various agencies in Washington.[36] In Afghanistan the unit functioned primarily as an intelligence-gathering fusion center and assisted in operating the main interrogation facility in Bagram. Bogdanos concludes that although the unit achieved several tactical successes in Afghanistan, it lacked the resources to assist in shaping theater- or national-level interagency strategy.[37]

Upon returning to the United States in April 2002, CENTCOM's JIACG transformed from a counterterrorism-specific task force to more of a "full-spectrum" coordinating group akin to the JFCOM model. By September 2002, the JIACG came under the supervision of CENTCOM's director of operations (J-3),[38] dual-hatted as the JIACG director, and CENTCOM established a JIACG force structure of 26 military positions.[39] Prior to establishment of a full-spectrum JIACG, CENTCOM's plans were usually in final form before being seen by other agencies. Bogdanos says that through the efforts of the full-spectrum JIACG, "all relevant agencies participated in the plan's actual development." While the JIACG representatives of the various agencies could not speak for or coordinate on behalf of their agencies, they were able to conduct "informal coordination with their parent agencies in advance of the plan's release, enabling them to advise CENTCOM of what that particular agency's official position would ultimately be." In addition, the JIACG "provided both interagency-trained liaison officers and task-organized teams" to CENTCOM's subordinate commands around the world. "This export of liaison officers and mini-JIACGs brought the same force-multiplying benefits to subordinate commands that [the] JIACG brought to CENTCOM."[40]

In March 2003, the JIACG again assumed a tactical focus. The majority of its personnel deployed to Iraq "to search for evidence [of] terrorist-financing networks and terrorist activity in the United States, to investigate United Nations (UN) Security Council Resolution violations, and to initiate criminal investigations of U.S. and foreign individuals who aided Iraq with its weapons of mass destruction programs."[41] Lt Col Terry Sopher, the first CENTCOM JIACG J-3 and later its deputy director, says that the JIACG was not as successful in Iraq as it had been in Afghanistan due to "leader turbulence and the resultant shifting of mission and focus, rotation of personnel," and lack of JIACG involvement in planning the invasion of Iraq, with the DOD citing operational security in its refusal to authorize the interagency representatives access to the developing plan.[42]

In July 2004, the JIACG again returned to CENTCOM headquarters and resumed its full-spectrum focus, providing interagency advice and facilitating coordination of CENTCOM operations and plans.[43] It reported to the CENTCOM deputy commander rather than to the J-3, to whom it had reported prior to departing for Iraq.[44] Today, CENTCOM's interagency action group (formerly the JIACG) once again reports to the J-3 and currently has several military billets and eight interagency billets: one each from the State Department, USAID, Treasury, DEA, Immigration and Customs Enforcement (ICE), and Customs and Border Protection (CBP), and two from the FBI.[45] Each agency retains operational control of its personnel, but the senior IAG leader at headquarters or in the field has tactical control. Since its establishment in 2001, the director and deputy director of the IAG have been military personnel.[46] Prior to the end of US military operations in Iraq in December 2011, the IAG had military liaison officers at the headquarters of the Multinational Force–Iraq (MNF-I), the FBI's Baghdad operations center, and the Iraq Threat Finance Cell (co-led by CENTCOM and the Treasury Department to disrupt the flow of money to both insurgents and terrorists in Iraq) in addition to the headquarters presence in Tampa. The IAG still maintains a liaison presence in Afghanistan at the US Embassy in Kabul.[47]

Besides the interagency personnel in the POLAD's office and the IAG, CENTCOM has a representative from the USAID working for the director of plans, policy, and strategy (J-5) and a State Department diplomatic security service officer in the J-3 force protection office. Filling the interagency billets continues to be a challenge, though most at CENTCOM are currently filled.[48]

In August 2004, its deputy commander decided CENTCOM needed a higher-level entity than the action-officer-level JIACG to facilitate interagency coordination, so he established an interagency executive steering committee, since renamed the Target Synchronization Board.[49] Today, the TSB operates out of the IAG, and the interagency personnel from the IAG sit on the board, together with representatives from other headquarters directorates and from CENTCOM's deployed task force in Afghanistan. The TSB meets approximately weekly and is chaired either by the IAG director or the J-3.[50]

CENTCOM has also established JIATFs in the field. In August 2008, it established a joint interagency task force in Baghdad, Iraq (JIATF-I). According to Robert Birkenes, an FSO who served as the USAID representative to JIATF-I, Amb. Ryan Crocker and Gen David Petraeus jointly created JIATF-I as an interagency planning team focused on threats to Iraq's stability from Iran and al-Qaeda. JIATF-I included representatives from the USAID, the State Department, the Department of Energy (DOE), and the Department of Homeland Security (DHS).[51]

JIATF-I participated in the development of a joint campaign plan (JCP) for Iraq, "the first interagency attempt to define all priorities, objectives and approaches to be taken by all U.S. agencies in Iraq." The JCP was jointly approved by Ambassador Crocker and Gen Ray Odierno in December 2008. Upon implementation of the JCP, JIATF-I identified nonmilitary means to assist in countering threats to Iraq from foreign terrorists and Iran and worked with both the embassy and MNF-I to track progress toward achieving the goals spelled out in the plan. Birkenes credits JIATF-I with creating and managing the whole-of-government strategy for Iraq as expressed in the JCP and with assisting in weakening violent extremists in Iraq, leading to a 40 percent decrease in weekly attacks against coalition forces after a year of operation.[52] The mission of the JIATF has since been subsumed by the US Embassy in Baghdad.[53]

In 2010 the ISAF and USFOR-A established three combined joint interagency task forces to focus on the complex "nexus of insurgency, narcotics, corruption, and criminality" in Afghanistan.[54] These include CJIATF-Nexus, CJIATF-435, and CJIATF-Shafafiyat. The addition of *combined* to the unit designation indicates these organizations are multinational as well as joint and interagency.

CJIATF-Nexus focuses on counternarcotics intelligence collection, campaign planning, and targeting. It analyzes key trafficking networks and assists with related anticorruption efforts by identifying corrupt Afghan powerbrokers. Established in early 2010, the unit reached full operational capability later that year. It provides intelligence analysis support to other US and NATO units, such as CJIATF-Shafafiyat, as well as to Afghan counternarcotics forces.[55]

CJIATF-435 focuses on detention operations and the criminal justice system. It evolved from JTF-435, established in September 2009, reaching initial operational capability as a CJIATF in January 2010 and full operational capability in July 2010. CJIATF-435 was responsible for US detention operations in Afghanistan until that function transferred to the Afghan government in March 2012. It currently works with that government to assist in strengthening its judicial system—including investigative and prosecutorial capabilities—with the goal of developing an Afghan-led, Afghan-owned judicial process.[56]

CJIATF-Shafafiyat (which means "transparency" in Dari) focuses on corruption. The unit was established in August 2010 and reached full operational capability in October 2010. It was formed to "foster a common understanding of the corruption problem in Afghanistan, plan and implement ISAF anti-corruption efforts, and integrate USFOR-A anti-corruption activities with those of key partners."[57]

Little information is available about these three CJIATFs beyond their missions and recent activities, such as interagency composition, organizational structure, and the nature of the memoranda of understanding that govern interagency contributions to these organizations. Also not clear is the command relationship between the ISAF/USFOR-A commander and the embassy coordinating director of rule of law and law enforcement.[58] Because of the lack of doctrinal guidance on JIATFs and the ongoing field-driven evolutions to US and coalition organizations in Afghanistan, some CENTCOM planners question whether all three of these are actually CJIATFs under a subordinate commander or actually elements of the USFOR-A, ISAF, or embassy staffs.[59]

US Pacific Command

The US Pacific Command has a POLAD and has had a JIACG since 2001 and a JIATF since 1989. Additionally, PACOM briefly experimented with establishing a second JIACG under crisis conditions. Today, the JIACG is part of the new J-9 Pacific Outreach Directorate, with the POLAD dual-hatted as the J-9 director.[60] PACOM's current structures to facilitate interagency unity of effort are shown in figure 3.

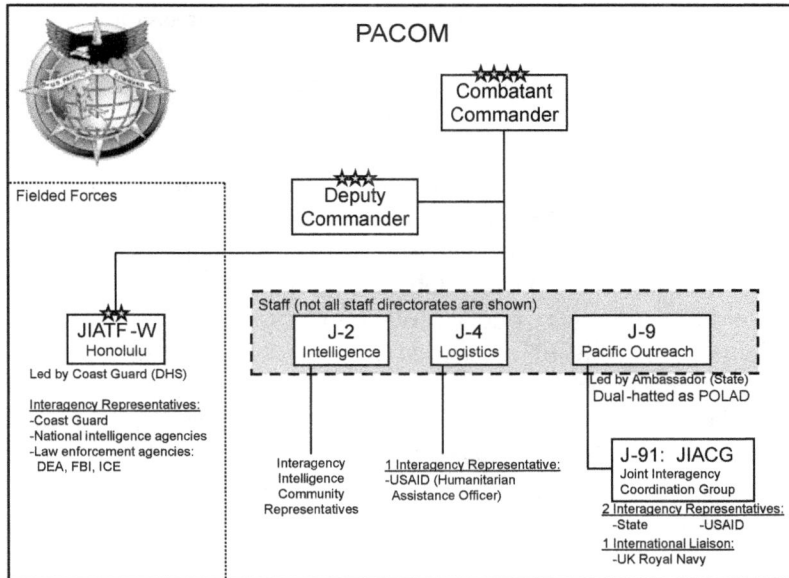

Figure 3. PACOM structures for interagency unity of effort

Prior to 9/11, PACOM's then-commander ADM Dennis Blair proposed the creation of a JIATF for counterterrorism (CT) in the Asia-Pacific region (JIATF-CTAP). By December 2001, this organization evolved into PACOM's JIACG for counterterrorism (JIACG/CT). Admiral Blair declared that the JIACG/CT would be the command's office of primary responsibility for the global war on terrorism and directed the organization to conduct planning for a whole-of-government CT campaign in the region.[61] According to retired ambassador Edward Marks, a contractor on PACOM's JIACG/CT, the organization began by focusing on tactical issues like actionable intelligence and measures to eliminate key terrorist actors but, by late 2002, expanded its focus to developing working relations with US embassies as well as bilateral and multilateral engagements with governments in the region. Marks characterized the JIACG/CT as a "tiger team" that pulled together disparate elements of the PACOM staff across J-code lanes and produced a CT program for PACOM that was "well coordinated if not integrated with the programs of the other members of the interagency community."[62]

For a time, the JIACG/CT placed liaison teams in key US embassies to facilitate communication between the JIACG at PACOM headquarters and the tactical operations of the ambassador and the interagency country team. After a year, the liaison teams were deemed unnecessary, as the defense attaché or military group commander already at the embassy could provide that function.[63]

The JIACG/CT was led by a military O-6 officer and initially staffed with more than 40 military personnel (both active and reserve), but PACOM had difficulty getting interagency participants. By the end of 2002, it had just three interagency personnel: a full-time analyst from the NSA, a retired FSO from State, and an officer from Treasury's Office of Foreign Assets Control (OFAC) on 60-day temporary duty assignment.[64] An FBI officer served between 2004 and 2005, and one USAID senior staff member served in 2005. From its inception until mid 2005, PACOM's JIACG/CT was the "most robust JIACG as measured by personnel and budget allocation among all of the combatant commands."[65] Over time, manning authorizations declined, and by midyear, the organization had just 12 authorized military billets, one DOD civilian billet, five DOD contractors, and three interagency representatives, though the agencies had difficulty filling the non-DOD billets.[66]

From its creation until mid 2005, the JIACG/CT was an advisory group reporting to the PACOM commander through the chief of staff, though the JIACG/CT personnel worked in the J-3 for administrative purposes.[67] However, in mid 2005 PACOM commander ADM William Fallon assessed that the JIACG/CT was not well integrated with the rest of the staff and transferred responsibility for CT operations to the J-3 along with most of the personnel, including most interagency representatives. The remaining, much smaller organization was named simply the JIACG and aligned under the J-5, where it remained for several years, working on maritime security, the counterterrorism fellowship program, and some funding management responsibilities.[68]

The JIACG received a substantial increase in importance and visibility when PACOM commander ADM Robert Willard elected in October 2009 to create a new J-9 Pacific Outreach Directorate, which became operational on 15 January 2010.[69] The J-9 is led by PACOM's POLAD (who also retains the traditional role as a direct foreign policy advisor to the commander) and includes the JIACG, as well as a public-private partnership division, a legislative affairs division, and PACOM's Washington liaison office. The mission of the new J-9 is to "orchestrate and enable enduring, collaborative partnerships between PACOM leadership/staff [and] key U.S. government, nongovernmental and international partners by facilitating introductions, information sharing, and collaboration in support of U.S. objectives" in the AOR.[70] The JIACG within this new J-9 has a representative from the State Department and one from the USAID, as well as a liaison from the Defense Threat Reduction Agency (DTRA), a Royal Navy officer acting as the UK advisor, five US military officers, and a DOD civilian. The military officers on the JIACG further broaden PACOM's interagency relationships by forming and maintaining relationships with Washington-based representatives from Commerce, Homeland Security, Treasury, and the Department of the Interior who are not assigned to PACOM. Beyond the JIACG and the POLAD's office, PACOM also has interagency intelligence representatives in the intelligence directorate (J-2) and a USAID humanitarian assistance advisor in the logistics directorate (J-4) who can advise its logisticians in response to humanitarian emergencies.[71]

After the December 2004 Asian tsunami, the PACOM commander established a second JIACG, called a full-spectrum JIACG, to focus on interagency coordination in response to the disaster, staffing it with 30 individuals from across the PACOM staff. The USAID detailed two experts from its Office of Foreign Disaster Assistance (OFDA), but after spending some time in the JIACG, they moved to the J-3's joint operations center, where they were better able to coordinate with Washington-based relief agencies and with the field, as well as provide their expert advice directly to the J-3. Because the disaster struck without warning and relief operations began immediately, there was no time for interagency operational planning. Furthermore, the initial PACOM response operation was never officially transferred to another agency, thus alleviating the need for a formal post-emergency transfer plan. While the relief operation is generally considered to have been a success, Ambassador Marks found little evidence that this JIACG contributed much, saying that despite its "full-spectrum" name, it was in effect an "ad hoc, short-term, single subject JIACG" with no interagency representation and largely redundant to other interagency coordination channels.[72]

The other significant interagency organization in PACOM is the Joint Interagency Task Force–West (JIATF-W), PACOM's executive agent for DOD support to counternarcotics initiatives in the region. JIATF-W provides interagency intelligence fusion, supports US law enforcement, and develops partner-nation counternarcotics capabilities with the goal of detecting, disrupting, and dismantling narcotics-related transnational threats in the region. JIATF-W was initially established in California in 1989 as Joint Task Force-5 (JTF-5). It was granted additional interagency authorities and renamed JIATF-W in 1994 and was collocated with PACOM headquarters in Hawaii in 2004. JIATF-W is led by a US Coast Guard rear admiral and consists of "approximately 82 uniformed and civilian members of all five military services as well as representatives from the national intelligence community and U.S. federal law enforcement agencies" including the DEA, FBI, and ICE.[73]

JIATF-W has used its interagency mix of capabilities to achieve US counternarcotics goals in the region by deploying intelligence analysts to US embassies to support law enforcement agencies, constructing interagency intelligence fusion centers for partner nations, developing infrastructure such as border patrol stations and customs checkpoints in four partner nations, and conducting counternarcotics training for six partner-nation militaries and law enforcement agencies.[74]

In pursuing its counternarcotics mission, JIATF-W is closely aligned with PACOM's counterterrorism, theater security cooperation, and maritime security missions. The synergy between counternarcotics and counterterrorism has been particularly helpful, because many of the capabilities needed to fight narcotics trafficking are also useful in fighting terrorism. In addition, many governments in the region have been much more open to initial cooperation with the United States in counternarcotics while reluctant to openly join in its global war on terrorism. The initial counternarcotics cooperation often opens the door to follow-on engagement to develop host nation capabilities for combatting local terrorist, insurgent, and criminal threats.[75]

US European Command

EUCOM entities for facilitating interagency unity of effort include the traditional POLAD and a JIACG, now called the J-9 Directorate of Interagency Partnering. In January 2010, EUCOM commander ADM James Stavridis dual-hatted the POLAD as the EUCOM civilian deputy (ECCD), creating a command structure with a military commander, a military deputy, and a civilian deputy—similar to structures previously established at SOUTHCOM and AFRICOM. The EUCOM commander is dual-hatted as NATO Supreme Allied Commander, Europe, and spends much time at NATO headquarters in Mons, Belgium, leaving day-to-day EUCOM operations in the hands of the Stuttgart, Germany–based military and civilian deputy commanders.[76] EUCOM's current structures to facilitate interagency unity of effort are shown in figure 4.

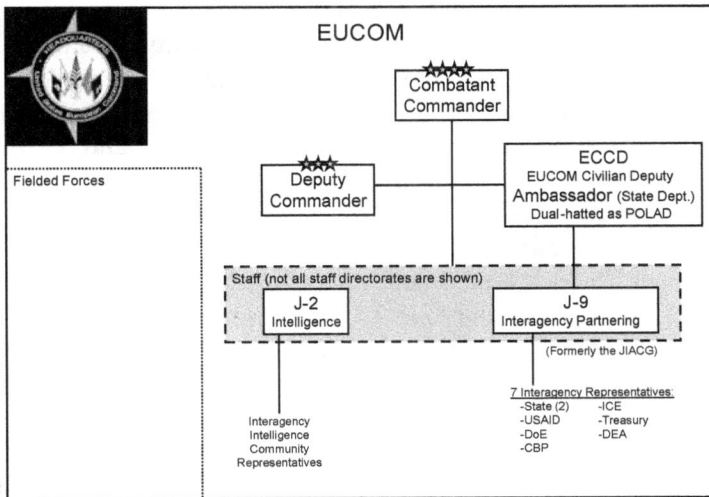

Figure 4. EUCOM structures for interagency unity of effort

EUCOM established a JIACG in October 2001 in response to NSC and Joint Chiefs of Staff (JCS) guidance. From 2001 to 2002, its focus was on interagency and international coordination of actions to facilitate US goals in the global war on terrorism in the region, such as overflight rights, maritime interdiction, and intelligence sharing.[77] EUCOM's JIACG started as a stand-alone staff element in the headquarters with a DOD civilian senior executive service (SES) director and an Army general officer deputy director who reported to the EUCOM commander through the chief of staff and deputy commander. As with other COCOMs, EUCOM staffed its JIACG with military billets from across the headquarters, but non-DOD interagency participation was more difficult to obtain. However, by July 2002, the JIACG had either representatives from or access to individuals from State, Commerce, Justice, Treasury, several intelligence agencies, and other specialized experts.[78]

In 2003 EUCOM broadened the JIACG's portfolio beyond counterterrorism to include participation in the full spectrum of plans and operations in the region, including security cooperation.[79] Along with this broadening of mission, the JIACG transitioned from a stand-alone staff reporting to the chief of staff to an element of the operations directorate (J-3). Under the new construct, the SES-level civilian director was eliminated, and the director became a brigadier general who also served as the deputy J-3. At this time, the JIACG consisted of 29 military personnel plus interagency representatives from the FBI, DEA, ICE, and Treasury's OFAC, while representatives from State, the DOE, DTRA, Defense Information Systems Agency (DISA), National Geospatial-Intelligence Agency (NGA), Coast Guard, and several intelligence agencies were present elsewhere in the EUCOM headquarters with linkages to the JIACG.[80] In addition to its presence in the J-3, the JIACG maintained full-time representation in EUCOM's standing joint force headquarters to both maintain situational awareness and provide interagency input to EUCOM's current operations.[81]

In 2007 the JIACG became the commander's interagency engagement group (CIEG) and moved from the J-3 to the commander's special staff, headed by an SES-level DOD civilian. The CIEG focused on developing relationships by hosting a series of conferences with interagency, international, and academic participants to provide EUCOM leadership and staff with a broad range of inputs on issues such as global supply chain management, money laundering, drug trafficking, Islamic identity in Europe, and challenges the command would likely face in 2020.[82]

In November 2009, under EUCOM's new commander, Admiral Stavridis, the CIEG became the J-9 partnering directorate. The directorate still has an SES-level DOD civilian director who reports to the State Department ambassador serving as the dual-hatted POLAD and EUCOM civilian deputy—the only staff directorate reporting directly to the ECCD.[83] While PACOM kept a JIACG division within its J-9 partnering directorate, EUCOM eliminated a separately named organization and spread the interagency coordination mission across its new J-9. The EUCOM J-9's mission is to "integrate the efforts of all [USG] agencies at the strategic, operational, and tactical levels," lead "the EUCOM effort to integrate interagency, academia, NGOs [international organizations], and private sector partners to better execute the EUCOM mission through a 'Whole of Society Approach,'" and advise the EUCOM commander "on objectives, support requirements, authorities, and limitations of other [USG] agencies."[84] The J-9, by mid 2010, had interagency representatives from State (2), ICE, USAID, and Treasury, and expected to acquire representatives from the DOE, the CBP, and the DEA.[85]

US Southern Command

It is particularly important to ensure that US foreign policy in SOUTHCOM's region of Latin America and the Caribbean does not have a military face and voice. Between 1898 and 1994, the US government successfully intervened at least 41 times to change governments there, and Latin Americans remember this.[86] According to a 2006 Senate Foreign Relations Committee report, "In Latin America . . . military and intelligence efforts are viewed with suspicion, making it difficult to pursue meaningful cooperation on a counterterrorism agenda," and "Latin American suspicions of American pressure and what is seen as an unspoken threat of military intervention run deep."[87]

Given this sensitivity and that US goals in Latin America and the Caribbean are less about preparing for military operations and more about building international partnerships—working with other US agencies as well as NGOs and IGOs—SOUTHCOM has developed structures to facilitate interagency unity of effort in the region.[88] These include a State Department ambassador dual-hatted as the POLAD and the civilian deputy to the SOUTHCOM commander; a JIACG, now called the J-9 partnering directorate; and a JIATF for counternarcotics operations hailed as the model both for JIATFs and for interagency cooperation in general. It also formed a headquarters command structure that until recently was built around partnership rather than a traditional J-code structure. SOUTHCOM structures to facilitate interagency unity of effort are shown in figure 5.

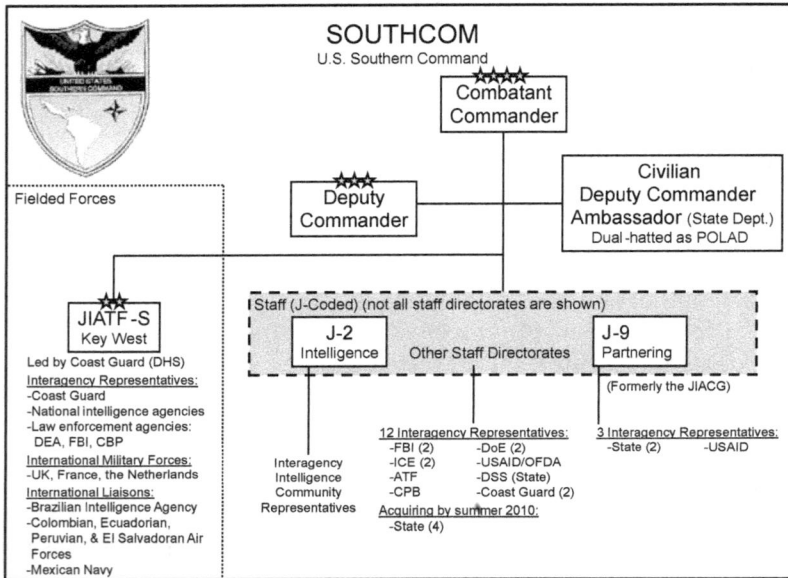

Figure 5. SOUTHCOM structures for interagency unity of effort

Looking first at the overall headquarters structure, former SOUTHCOM commander (and EUCOM commander as of June 2009), Admiral Stavridis said in 2008, "We are working to create an organization that can best adapt itself to working with the interagency, with our international partners and even with the private-public sector."[89] On 1 October 2008, SOUTHCOM transitioned to a structure with two deputies reporting to the four-star military commander—a three-star military deputy focused on military operations and an ambassadorial-rank FSO as the civilian deputy focused on civil-military activities. SOUTHCOM chose to do away with the traditional stand-alone POLAD, instead using this FSO as the civilian deputy and foreign policy advisor to the COCOM.

In October 2008, SOUTHCOM also replaced the traditional J-coded staff structure with a new six-directorate structure—three mission directorates to promote regional security, stability, and partnering, respectively, and three functional directorates to support the mission directorates.[90] However, in January 2010, new SOUTHCOM commander Gen Douglas Fraser transitioned back to the standard J-code structure. This change was largely a result of the January 2010 earthquake in Haiti. To assist SOUTHCOM in the response effort, hundreds of military officers from US Northern Command (NORTH-COM) and other staffs came to augment the SOUTHCOM staff and establish a joint task force. During this influx, SOUTHCOM found reverting to the standard structure greatly simplified staff coordination.[91]

SOUTHCOM formed a JIACG in 2003, initially staffed by a single lieutenant colonel in the J-9 transformation directorate, to "facilitate coordination, enhance information sharing, and integrate the planning efforts between [SOUTHCOM] and the interagency community." In 2004 JIACG duties passed to two contractors who periodically convened meetings of interagency personnel assigned to SOUTHCOM's JIATF-S or to their respective agencies' Miami field offices to collaborate on specific requirements dealing with counternarcotics, foreign internal defense for SOUTHCOM partner nations, and contingency planning for stabilization operations. By 2005 the JIACG expanded to include four military personnel and two or three DOD civilians, as well as the contractors. This larger DOD team worked with five part-time representatives (one each) from State, Treasury, the FBI, Customs and Border Protection's Office of Border Patrol, and the Bureau of Alcohol, Tobacco, Firearms, and Explosives. Moreover, the J-3 operations directorate sent liaison officers to the JIACG in the J-9 "to maintain staff interoperability." In 2006 SOUTH-COM commander ADM James Stavridis established a more robust, full-time JIACG, still within the J-9.[92] In the 2008 reorganization, the J-9 directorate became the new partnering directorate, and the JIACG changed its name to become the interagency coordination group under the integration division within the partnering directorate.[93]

In January 2010, when SOUTHCOM reverted to the J-code structure, the partnering directorate became the J-9. What started as the JIACG is now simply called the J-9 partnering directorate.[94] The J-9 has three interagency billets—two from the State Department and one from USAID. Twelve other interagency billets are spread across the staff, including two from the FBI, two from ICE, one from the ATF, one from CBP, two from the DOE, one from USAID's OFDA, one from the State Department's DSS, and two from the Coast Guard. Four additional FSOs from the State Department were projected to join SOUTHCOM in the summer of 2010.[95] The number of agencies represented in SOUTHCOM is larger than in any other GCC, in large part because many of the agencies have regional offices near the SOUTHCOM headquarters. In addition to maintaining contacts with Washington and with US embassy country teams, the interagency staff across the SOUTHCOM headquarters coordinates frequently with these regional offices, meeting monthly to discuss regional issues. Through the State Department representative, the J-9 has also established a dialogue with several NGOs.[96]

SOUTHCOM's Joint Interagency Task Force–South (JIATF-S) in Key West, Florida, was created in 1999 from the consolidation of two other counternarcotics task forces that the DOD established in 1989.[97] The JIATF's mission is to detect, monitor, and consign suspected narcotics trafficking targets to appropriate law enforcement agencies; promote regional security cooperation; and coordinate US country team and partner-nation counternarcotics initiatives.[98] Because the Posse Comitatus Act limits the use of the US military in federal law enforcement, military personnel and assets can detect and monitor counternarcotics targets; however, law enforcement agencies must execute any necessary actions. Because these agencies are represented in the JIATF, the transition from military monitoring to law enforcement action "happens with little or no disruption."[99]

JIATF-S has an integrated interagency structure, including a US Coast Guard admiral as its director, an officer from CBP as vice director, and participants from all US military branches, the DEA, FBI, Customs, Homeland Security, and elements of the US intelligence community. Interagency integration continues through the lower levels of the organization as well; while the directors for intelligence and operations are both military officers, the deputy for intelligence is from the DEA, and the deputy for operations is from CBP.[100] This integrated structure also includes a key element—all personnel assigned to the task force, regardless of their parent agency, are rated by their bosses on the task force rather than by someone from their parent agency, providing the all-important ability to reward personnel for their job at the task force rather than for loyalty to their agency or department.[101]

JIATF-S is also a multinational organization, with participants from countries both inside and outside SOUTHCOM's AOR working together both at the JIATF-S headquarters and in combined force packages across the region. The United Kingdom, France, and the Netherlands (all of which govern territories in the region) provide ships, aircraft, and liaison officers to the task force, and the commander of the Netherlands Forces Caribbean also commands a subordinate task group under JIATF-S. From within the AOR, JIATF-S has liaison personnel from the Argentinean air force, Brazilian intelligence agency, Colombian air force and navy, and Ecuadorian, El Salvadorian, and Peruvian air forces. While Mexico is not part of the SOUTHCOM AOR (it falls under NORTHCOM), the Mexican navy also has a liaison at JIATF-S. This robust liaison program not only facilitates operational cooperation but also improves information sharing across the region.[102]

Many have concluded that JIATF-S is the benchmark interagency organization to emulate. Dr. John Fishel, who has written extensively on civil-military relations, concludes that the JIATF-S model is an appropriate organizational construct "to coordinate the activity of many interagency players."[103] LCDR Tom Stuhlreyer, USCG, concludes that the organization makes best use of limited US resources across the interagency. He notes that JIATF-S narcotics seizure records were being broken at a time when fewer US military assets were available due to high operational requirements in Iraq, Afghanistan, and elsewhere in the global war on terrorism, demonstrating "the efficacy and force-multiplying aspect of the joint, interagency, and multi-national approach to operations at JIATF South."[104] The Government Accountabilty Office (GAO) credits SOUTHCOM with more success in interagency collaboration than other COCOMs, in part due to having JIATF-S in the command.[105] Indeed, SOUTHCOM approached its 2008 headquarters reorganization with the proven JIATF-S interagency model in mind.[106]

According to Fishel, "The real reason JIATF-S works is that it is structurally an organization that has unity of command. The Director is a commander with the authority to hire and fire, as well as to task, organize and direct actions."[107] However, because JIATFs are not codified in executive order or legislation, the authority remains largely voluntary. Stuhlreyer characterizes the JIATF as an interagency "coalition of the willing" and notes that while assigned military personnel are subject to normal military order and discipline, the interagency partners "are only obligated to remain invested in JIATF-South as long as the command assists them in achieving individual interagency goals."[108] However, because the counternarcotics mission of JIATF-S is a core mission of many of the interagency participants, these agencies are likely to continue to participate.

US Africa Command

On 30 September 2008, AFRICOM became the newest combatant command.[109] AFRICOM is unique among the military's combatant commands since it was created to focus on security cooperation and humanitarian issues more than war fighting and was envisioned from birth as an interagency entity. AFRICOM's first commander, GEN William E. "Kip" Ward, said the United States needed an integrated, interagency approach to Africa because of previous "lost opportunities to establish programs or partnerships [with African partner nations] because of misunderstandings or conflicts within the U.S. Government."[110]

Like SOUTHCOM and EUCOM, AFRICOM has a four-star military commander with a three-star deputy for military operations (DCMO) and an ambassadorial-rank FSO from State serving as the deputy for civil-military activities (DCMA). The DCMA supervises the coordination between the military and non-DOD agencies working on African issues; directs AFRICOM's civil-military plans and programs, outreach, and strategic communication effort; and leads the command's theater security cooperation policy development, resourcing, and assessment.[111] However, it has no authority over US ambassadors in Africa. Unlike SOUTHCOM and EUCOM, AFRICOM has a second senior FSO (below the rank of ambassador) serving as the commander's POLAD. AFRICOM chose to maintain two separate positions because that provides one FSO (the POLAD) to travel with the commander while the other (the DCMA) can either travel separately or remain at the headquarters to provide diplomatic expertise.[112] This additional FSO is certainly an asset to the combatant commander but may not be replicated across all of the GCCs because of the limited supply of senior FSOs. Additionally, AFRICOM has an individual from the USAID who serves as the commander's development advisor.

As did SOUTHCOM from 2008 to 2009, AFRICOM's focus on missions other than war fighting led the command to choose an organizational structure other than the traditional J-code staff. It organized around a set of "cross-functional directorates"; however, AFRICOM commander, Army general Carter F. Ham, returned to a traditional J-code structure. Similar to PACOM, EUCOM, and SOUTHCOM, AFRICOM's J-staff includes a J-9 outreach directorate focused on strategic communication and USG partnership and engagement with nations in Africa.[113] This directorate also manages AFRICOM's contacts with interagency, intergovernmental, nongovernmental, and multinational agencies relevant to the command's mission in Africa.[114] Unlike the other GCCs, AFRICOM has never had a JIACG; instead, it integrates interagency personnel across the staff. In 2008 AFRICOM was supposed to have approximately 42 interagency personnel.[115] As of December 2010, the command had four senior FSOs in key positions as well as more than 30 personnel from 13 USG departments and agencies serving in leadership, management, and staff positions. Some of the agencies represented include the Departments of State, Treasury, and Commerce; the USAID; and the US Coast Guard.[116] This is an increase from only 13 interagency personnel in October 2008.[117] Filling the billets has been challenging because even though AFRICOM reimburses the parent agencies for the salaries of the interagency personnel serving in the headquarters, many agencies simply do not have qualified personnel to spare.[118] AFRICOM's current structures to facilitate interagency unity of effort are shown in figure 6.

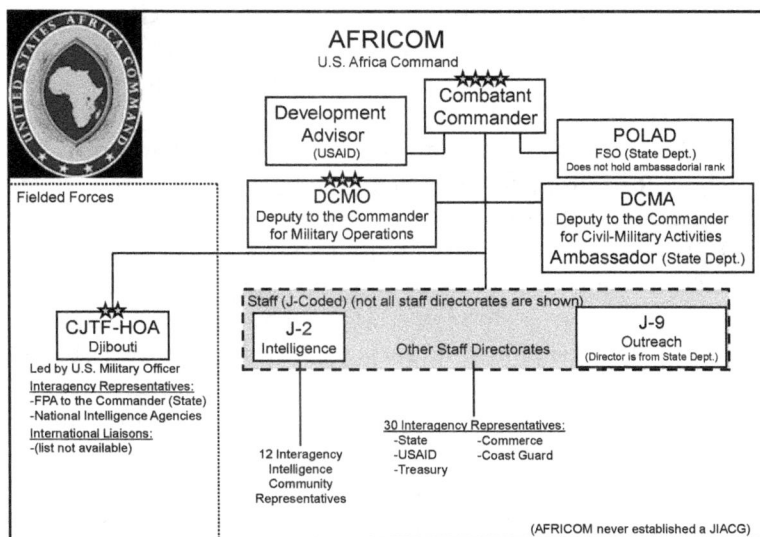

Figure 6. AFRICOM structures for interagency unity of effort

In addition to action officer–level positions, non-DOD agency personnel also hold leadership positions across the AFRICOM headquarters staff. The director of the J-9 outreach directorate is from State, the chief of the programs division under the directorate of strategy, plans, and programs is from the USAID, and the deputy director of resources is from Commerce. These interagency personnel rate their subordinates, both civilian and military, and have all the authorities of a military member in their position, with the exception that the interagency civilians cannot command US forces during military operations.[119] Many of the current interagency personnel, whether supervisors or not, are very senior in rank—equivalent to a general officer or member of the SES (because AFRICOM requested this senior-level representation). Some interagency representatives have thus become frustrated that they are buried too deeply in the staff and do not have authority commensurate with their rank. Over time, more of these billets may be converted to action officer–equivalent ranks (military majors and lieutenant colonels) to address this issue.[120]

In 2008 AFRICOM's DCMO, VADM Robert Moeller, and DCMA, Amb. Mary Yates, said AFRICOM would not create a JIACG, preferring to integrate interagency personnel throughout the command "where their impact can be the greatest."[121] Because the interagency personnel are dispersed across the headquarters, AFRICOM created the command collaborative forum (CCF) to bring together all of the interagency representatives at least once a month, together with the AFRICOM chief of staff and individuals from the operations and plans directorates. The CCF provides an opportunity for interagency personnel to coordinate with each other, provide and receive feedback, and ensure their voices are heard.[122]

AFRICOM does not have a joint interagency task force, but it has a combined joint task force in the Horn of Africa (CJTF-HOA), which "spends an enormous amount of time assisting in nonmilitary actions" while at the same time assisting local security forces in counterterrorism.[123] Established in October 2002 to counter violent extremism in East Africa, the task force is led by a two-star US military officer and includes personnel from all branches of the US military plus interagency civilians (a foreign policy advisor from the State Department and a few representatives from US intelligence agencies) and international liaisons from countries in the region. While the task force was established primarily as a direct-action counterterrorism organization, it has evolved today to focus on military-to-military counterterrorism training, as well as on international development operations such as building schools and clinics and conducting medical, dental, and veterinary civic action programs, all in coordination with the USAID and local US embassies.[124] CJTF-HOA has also assisted in several humanitarian operations, such as floods in Ethiopia and Kenya and a capsized passenger ferry in Djibouti. The organization aspires to be "a model for the integration of Defense, Diplomacy, and Development."[125] Given the successful track records of JIATF-W, JIATF-S, and JIATF-I in integrating interagency personnel into a subregional task force to conduct predominantly nonmilitary missions and that CJTF-HOA performs precisely such missions, it is a good candidate for reorganization as a JIATF. Nevertheless, AFRICOM says it gets all the interagency assistance it needs through direct liaison with the various embassy country teams and thus does not require an integrated civil-military command structure in the task force itself.[126]

Observers both in Africa and in the United States have criticized putting the military in charge of interagency engagement with Africa by establishing AFRICOM. For example, Edward Marks says AFRICOM, though well-intentioned, "will only exacerbate the problem of over-militarization of U.S. policy and programs."[127] Marks questions how military-to-military programs in Africa will be subordinated to larger US policy goals when the military is in charge. He says the United States "should be looking for a whole-of-government approach, not the tweaking of a military model designed primarily for warfighting."[128]

Summary of Current Structures at the GCCs

Since the JIACG concept was first introduced in 2001, interagency coordination structures have evolved differently in each of the geographic combatant commands. While JFCOM recommended a construct with an ambassadorial-rank POLAD reporting directly to the combatant commander and a JIACG consisting of six DOD and six non-DOD personnel, also reporting directly to the commander, none of the GCCs currently follow this model.

In CENTCOM the ambassadorial-rank POLAD reports directly to the commander, but the IAG is located in the J-3. Not counting the interagency intelligence community representatives in the J-2, CENTCOM has 13 non-DOD personnel assigned: three in the POLAD's office, eight in the IAG, one in the J-3's force protection office, and one in the J-5.

In PACOM the ambassadorial-rank POLAD has been dual-hatted as the director of the J-9 outreach directorate. The JIACG (which retains the JIACG name in PACOM) is now J-91, subordinate to the J-9, thus reporting to the POLAD/J-9 director rather than directly to the combatant commander. Excluding the interagency intelligence community representatives in the J-2, PACOM has four non-DOD personnel assigned to the staff: the POLAD/J-9 director, two representatives in the J-91 JIACG, and one representative in the J-4. In the field, PACOM has a sizeable contingent of non-DOD personnel, predominantly from law enforcement and intelligence, assigned to JIATF-W.

In EUCOM the ambassadorial-rank POLAD has been dual-hatted as the EUCOM civilian deputy commander. The JIACG is now called the J-9 interagency partnering directorate and is the only staff directorate that reports to the ECCD. Excluding the intelligence community representatives in the J-2, EUCOM has six interagency personnel assigned to the staff: the ECCD and five representatives in the J-9, with plans to increase the interagency representation to nine.

In SOUTHCOM, as in EUCOM, the ambassadorial-rank POLAD has been dual-hatted as the civilian deputy commander, and the JIACG is now called the J-9 partnering directorate. Excluding the intelligence community representatives in the J-2, SOUTHCOM has 16 non-DOD personnel assigned: the civilian deputy commander, three representatives in the J-9, and 12 representatives in other directorates on the SOUTHCOM staff. The command planned to have four additional representatives from the State Department by the summer of 2010, bringing the total number of non-DOD representatives on the staff to 20. In the field, SOUTHCOM has a sizeable contingent of non-DOD personnel—predominantly from law enforcement and intelligence—assigned to JIATF-S.

Finally, in AFRICOM, the POLAD reports directly to the commander but is a Foreign Service officer without ambassadorial rank. The ambassadorial-ranked FSO assigned to AFRICOM holds the position of deputy commander for civil-military activities. Unlike the other GCCs, AFRICOM has never had a JIACG, preferring to integrate non-DOD personnel across the staff. Not counting the intelligence community representatives, AFRICOM has about 32 non-DOD personnel assigned: the POLAD, the DCMA, and about 30 representatives assigned across the staff. In the field, AFRICOM has one representative from the State Department serving as the POLAD to the CJTF-HOA commander in Djibouti, and the CJTF also has representatives from the national intelligence agencies.

While the GCCs have made great strides in integrating non-DOD expertise and viewpoints into their staffs, planning processes, and operations, these constructs still fall far short of the ideal regional interagency construct. First, excepting the national intelligence community representatives with their very specialized functions, each GCC staff has only four to 32 representatives from non-DOD agencies serving on a staff of military officers, DOD civilians, and DOD contractors—numbering well over a thousand. Given these figures, the GCC staffs will always be principally military in outlook and processes. Second, while the organizational constructs have evolved, the non-DOD representatives still do not have any authority to coordinate on military plans or operations on behalf of their parent agencies, nor can they commit their agency's resources. Finally, while three of the five GCCs have elevated the ambassadorial-ranked FSO to the level of civilian deputy commander, they are still led by a four-star military officer. Thus, even when the organization intends to execute whole-of-government foreign policy, the top-level face of that policy—as seen by countries in the region—continues to be a military officer.

Notes

1. Howard J. T. Steers, "Bridging the Gaps: Political-Military Coordination at the Operational Level," research report (Newport, RI: Naval War College, 17 May 2001), 13.

2. John D. Finney and Alphonse F. La Porta, "Maximizing the Value of the Political Adviser Function," *Foreign Service Journal* 85, no. 10 (October 2008): 16. Dr. Finney has had an extensive career in political-military affairs at the Departments of State and Defense in Washington and abroad. Retired as a career diplomat, he serves as the POLAD to the chief of the National Guard Bureau. He served as the POLAD coordinator at State and as the POLAD to the chief of naval operations (CNO), USPACOM, and various other US and multinational commands. La Porta served 38 years in the Foreign Service, including as ambassador to Mongolia and POLAD to the commander of NATO's Allied Joint Force Command Naples.

3. Ibid., 18.

4. John D. Finney and Alphonse F. La Porta, "Integrating National Security Strategy at the Operational Level: The Role of the State Department Political Advisors," in *Affairs of State*, ed. Gabriel Marcella, 287–88.

5. COL Charles N. Cardinal, USA, CDR Timber P. Pagonas, USN, and Amb. Edward Marks, "The Global War on Terrorism: A Regional Approach to Coordination," *Joint Force Quarterly* 32 (Autumn 2002): 50. At the time of this article, Colonel

Cardinal was chief of staff of the 25th Infantry Division (the Army component to PACOM), Commander Pagonas was assigned as strategy, plans, and policy officer to the PACOM JIACG/CT, and Ambassador Marks was the State Department representative to the PACOM JIACG/CT. See also USJFCOM, *Commander's Handbook for the Joint Interagency Coordination Group* (Norfolk, VA: USJFCOM Joint Warfighting Center, 1 March 2007), III-1.

6. Edward Marks, "PACOM, JIACG, and the War on Terror," Camber Corporation on contract to the Joint Interagency Coordinating Group on Counterterrorism, PACOM, 18 August 2005, 7.

7. Col Matthew F. Bogdanos, USMC, "Joint Interagency Cooperation: The First Step," *Joint Force Quarterly* 37 (2nd Quarter 2005): 12.

8. The USJFCOM was a joint military functional combatant command that provided trained and ready forces to other combatant commanders and supported the development and integration of new joint, interagency, and multinational capabilities for the joint force.

9. USJFCOM, *Commander's Handbook*, III-2.

10. William J. Olson, "Interagency Coordination: The Normal Accident or the Essence of Indecision," in *Affairs of State*, ed. Gabriel Marcella, 222. Dr. Olson is a professor at the Near East and South Asia Center for Strategic Studies. He has served as both a deputy assistant secretary of state and a deputy assistant secretary of defense.

11. Neyla Arnas, Charles Barry, and Robert B. Oakley, *Harnessing the Interagency for Complex Operations* (Washington, DC: Center for Technology and National Security Policy, National Defense University, August 2005), 14; and Alan G. Whittaker, Frederick C. Smith, and Elizabeth McKune, "The National Security Policy Process: The National Security Council and Interagency System," in *Affairs of State*, ed. Gabriel Marcella, 152.

12. USJFCOM, *Commander's Handbook*, III-6.

13. Ibid., I-6. See also JP 3-08, *Interagency, Intergovernmental Organization, and Nongovernmental Organization Coordination during Joint Operations*, vol. 1, 17 March 2006.

14. USJFCOM, *Commander's Handbook*, i.

15. Ibid., vii, III-8.

16. LTC Terry R. Sopher, USANG, "Joint Interagency Coordination Groups (JIACGs): A Temporary Solution to a Long Term Requirement," Master of Strategic Studies Degree report (Carlisle Barracks, PA: Army War College, 3 May 2004), 4.

17. Olson, "Interagency Coordination," 244–45.

18. Bogdanos, "Joint Interagency Cooperation," 14.

19. Col Matthew F. Bogdanos, USMC, *Transforming Joint Interagency Coordination: The Missing Link between National Strategy and Operational Success*, Case Studies in National Security Transformation, no. 9 (Washington, DC: Center for Technology and National Security Policy, National Defense University, August 2007), 13. See also Bogdanos, "Joint Interagency Cooperation," 14.

20. Arnas, Barry, and Oakley, *Harnessing the Interagency*, 14.

21. Finney and La Porta, "Integrating National Security Strategy at the Operational Level," 294.

22. Marcy Stahl, *Joint Interagency Coordination Group (JIACG) Training and Education Survey Results* (Vienna, VA: Thought Link Inc., 15 January 2004), 15. In

2003, on behalf of JFCOM and the National Defense University, Thought Link Inc. conducted interviews with 26 USG officials—from State (12), Justice (5), Defense (6), and Treasury (3)—associated directly or indirectly with the JIACG concept to learn agency perceptions of the concept and to identify the training and education needs of JIACG participants. Nearly all of the interviewees were familiar with the concept. Two were active members of a JIACG, about half had some direct experience or interaction with JIACGs, and most of the rest had some experience with other interagency groups.

23. Ibid., 16.

24. Olson, "Interagency Coordination," 243–44.

25. Ibid., 247.

26. John T. Fishel, "The Interagency Arena at the Operational Level: The Cases Now Known as Stability Operations," in *Affairs of State*, ed. Gabriel Marcella, 427–28; and Robert M. Birkenes, "Interagency Cooperation: The JIATF in Iraq," *Foreign Service Journal* 86, no. 9 (September 2009): 29.

27. JP 3-07.4, *Joint Counterdrug Operations*, 13 June 2007; JP 3-05.1, *Joint Special Operations Task Force Operations*, 26 April 2007; and JP 3-40, *Combating Weapons of Mass Destruction*, 10 June 2009. JP 3-07.4 briefly describes JIATF-S and JIATF-W but gives no broader doctrinal applications of JIATFs. JP 3-05.1 describes the JTF as the operational focal point for interagency coordination and mentions it may be assigned a subordinate JIATF to assist with interagency coordination. JP 3-40 provides the brief statement above but then notes "JIATFs currently do not have authority to conduct WMD interdiction."

28. USJFCOM, "Provincial Reconstruction Teams," Joint Warfighting Center predoctrinal research white paper no. 07-01, 21 November 2007, 14.

29. JP 3-40, *Combating Weapons of Mass Destruction*, B-32–33.

30. Ibid.

31. USJFCOM, *Insights and Best Practices*, 14–15.

32. While US Northern Command (NORTHCOM) is also a GCC (its AOR includes Canada and Mexico), it is not examined in this study because of its overwhelming focus on domestic operations.

33. Brig Gen Robert H. Holmes, USAF, *Statement of Brigadier General Robert H. Holmes, Deputy Director of Operations, United States Central Command, before the House Armed Services Committee Subcommittee on Terrorism, Unconventional Threats and Capabilities on Irregular Warfare*, prepared statement, Washington, DC, 110th Cong., 2d sess., 26 February 2008, 2, http://www.dod.mil/dodgc/olc/docs/testHolmes080226.pdf.

34. LTC Fadi Petro, USA (CENTCOM special advisor to the commanding general for Middle East peace), interview by the author, 9 March 2010.

35. Holmes, *Statement*, 5.

36. Bogdanos, *Transforming Joint Interagency Coordination*, 4.

37. Bogdanos, "Joint Interagency Cooperation," 11.

38. The typical J-coded joint US military staff includes the following eight directorates: J-1, manpower and personnel; J-2, intelligence; J-3, operations; J-4, logistics; J-5, plans, policy, and strategy; J-6, communications; J-7, training, exercises, and engagement; and J-8, resources and assessments. Recently, some staffs have added a J-9 partnering directorate.

39. Bogdanos, "Joint Interagency Cooperation," 12; and Bogdanos, *Transforming Joint Interagency Coordination*, 7.

40. Bogdanos, "Joint Interagency Cooperation," 12–13.

41. Ibid., 14.

42. Sopher, "Joint Interagency Coordination Groups," 11.

43. Holmes, *Statement*, 4.

44. Bogdanos, "Joint Interagency Cooperation," 18.

45. James Bond (State Department representative to CENTCOM IAG), interview by the author, 11 March 2010.

46. Arnas, Barry, and Oakley, *Harnessing the Interagency*, 10–11.

47. Holmes, *Statement*, 4–5.

48. Bond, interview.

49. Bogdanos, "Joint Interagency Cooperation," 18; and Holmes, *Statement*, 4.

50. Bond, interview.

51. Birkenes, "Interagency Cooperation," 28.

52. Ibid., 29–32.

53. Bond, interview.

54. Department of State, Bureau of South and Central Asian Affairs, "U.S. Counternarcotics Strategy for Afghanistan," Dept. of State website, 24 March 2010, http://www.state.gov/p/sca/ci/af/2010/141491.htm.

55. Ibid.; DOD, "Report on Progress toward Security and Stability in Afghanistan," report to Congress in accordance with section 1230 of the National Defense Authorization Act for Fiscal Year 2008 (Public Law 110-181), as amended, November 2010, 62, 84; and Liana Sun Wyler and Kenneth Katzman, *Afghanistan: U.S. Rule of Law and Justice Sector Assistance* (Washington, DC: Congressional Research Service [CRS], 9 November 2010), 37.

56. DOD, "Report on Progress," 61; and Wyler and Katzman, *Afghanistan*, 33.

57. DOD, "Report on Progress," 10, 62.

58. Wyler and Katzman, *Afghanistan*, 22. The creation of a coordinating director of rule of law and law enforcement (CDROLLE) "represents the first time in which [rule of law] issues are the core element of a portfolio handled by a permanent, Ambassador-rank official at the U.S. Embassy in Kabul. Under the CDROLLE directorate are representatives from the State Department's International Narcotics and Law Enforcement Affairs Bureau (INL), DOD, DOJ [Dept. of Justice], FBI, DEA, Department of Homeland Security's Immigration and Customs Enforcement, and the U.S. Marshals Service."

59. USCENTCOM operational planners, interview by the author, January 2011.

60. LTC Phil DuPont, USA (PACOM deputy foreign policy advisor), and LCDR Rob Hawthorne, USN (PACOM/J-9), interviews by the author, 11 March 2010.

61. MAJ David S. Doyle, USA, "Interagency Cooperation for Irregular Warfare at the Combatant Command," monograph (Fort Leavenworth, KS: School of Advanced Military Studies, US Army Command and General Staff College, 14 April 2009), 37–38.

62. Marks, "PACOM, JIACG, and the War on Terror," 2–3, 9.

63. Ibid., 9.

64. Ibid., 8.

65. Doyle, "Interagency Cooperation for Irregular Warfare," 37–38.

66. Marks, "PACOM, JIACG, and the War on Terror," 8.

67. Doyle, "Interagency Cooperation for Irregular Warfare," 38.

68. Ibid., 12; and Hawthorne, interview.

69. John Crowley (State Department liaison to PACOM's JIACG), interview by the author, 15 March 2010.

70. "Pacific Outreach Directorate: PACOM J9," briefing to IAWG, 9 March 2010, provided to the author by MAJ Lance Okamura of PACOM's JIACG.

71. Hawthorne, interview; and Crowley, interview.

72. Marks, "PACOM, JIACG, and the War on Terror," 16.

73. USPACOM, "Joint Interagency Task Force–West," accessed 25 February 2010, http://www.pacom.mil/staff/JIATFWest/index.shtml. See also JP 3-07.4, *Joint Counterdrug Operations*, I-2; and Marks, "PACOM, JIACG, and the War on Terror," 17.

74. USPACOM, "Joint Interagency Task Force-West."

75. Marks, "PACOM, JIACG, and the War on Terror," 3.

76. Lt Col Carlene Perry, USAF (EUCOM/J-9), interview by the author, 15 March 2010.

77. COL Harry A. Tomlin, USA, *The Joint Interagency Coordination Group (JIACG): The United States European Command Experience and the Way Ahead* (Syracuse, NY: Maxwell School of Citizenship and Public Affairs, Syracuse University, 1 October 2003), 10, 17.

78. Ibid., 15–17.

79. Ibid., 11, 22.

80. Ibid., 18–20.

81. A standing joint force headquarters (SJFHQ) is a staff organization that provides a combatant commander with a full-time, trained command and control element that enhances the command's peacetime planning efforts, improves operational-level situational awareness, and stands ready to serve as the nucleus of or augment for a JTF headquarters during crisis operations (ibid., 21).

82. USEUCOM, "Biography of Mr. Michael G. Ritchie, Director of Interagency Partnering," http://www.eucom.mil/english/bio2.asp?bioid=DAF6183B-F421-4BDF -839B-94D68C3A38A0.

83. Perry, interview; and "United States European Command (EUCOM) Interagency Partnering Directorate, ECJ9," briefing, 12 March 2010, provided to the author by Mike Anderson, deputy director, EUCOM/J-9.

84. USEUCOM, "Biography"; and "United States European Command (EUCOM) Interagency Partnering Directorate, ECJ9."

85. Perry, interview.

86. Paul D. Taylor, "The Outlook for U.S. Foreign Policy in Latin American and the Caribbean: The Challenges of Transforming Goodwill into Effective Policy," in *American Foreign Policy: Regional Perspectives*, Proceedings of a Ruger Chair Workshop, 13–15 May 2009, ed. Richmond M. Lloyd (Newport, RI: Naval War College, 2009), 86.

87. Senate, *Embassies as Command Posts*, 12–13. When the discussion at a May 2009 workshop of foreign policy scholars and retired ambassadors turned to SOUTHCOM and US actions in Latin America, "the general consensus of the group was that the U.S. government would be best served by a military with a more reserved, secondary role in regional policy implementation—not the agency leading policy formulation and implementation." One panelist said that "because of the rela-

tive lack of interstate conflict the U.S. military should not be 'out front' in the region," though other participants said it was important for the US military to work with Latin American militaries as they continue to reshape themselves. Laurence L. McCabe, "Panel II: Western Hemisphere—Summary of Discussion," in *American Foreign Policy*, ed. Richmond M. Lloyd, 96–97.

88. SOUTHCOM has pioneered a number of exercises, conferences, modeling and simulation systems, and planning systems to coordinate its efforts with those of US ambassadors and their country teams in the region to promote interagency and international partnerships. For example, see William W. Mendel and Lt Col David G. Bradford, USAF, *Interagency Cooperation: A Regional Model for Overseas Operations*, McNair Paper 37 (Washington, DC: National Defense University, Institute for National Strategic Studies, March 1995), 41–42, 49, 64.

89. Donna Miles, "SOUTHCOM Transformation Promotes New Approach to Regional Challenges," American Forces Press Service, 28 August 2008, http://www .southcom.mil/AppsSC/news.php?storyId=1323.

90. Gabriel Marcella, "Understanding the Interagency Process: The Challenge of Adaptation," in *Affairs of State*, ed. Gabriel Marcella, 35–36; and Miles, "SOUTHCOM Transformation."

91. CAPT Kevin Hutcheson, USN (SOUTHCOM/J-9 deputy director for interagency integration), and Kirk Dahlgren (USAID senior development officer, SOUTHCOM/J-9), interviews by the author, 9–10 March 2010.

92. Doyle, "Interagency Cooperation for Irregular Warfare," 41–43.

93. Ibid., 12, 42.

94. Dahlgren, interview.

95. Ted Halstead (SOUTHCOM/J-9), interview by the author, 9 March 2009.

96. Doyle, "Interagency Cooperation for Irregular Warfare," 45.

97. Fishel, "Interagency Arena at the Operational Level," 427–28.

98. JP 3-07.4, *Joint Counterdrug Operations*, I-2.

99. Richard M. Yeatman, "JIATF-South: Blueprint for Success," *Joint Force Quarterly* 42 (3rd Quarter 2006): 27.

100. Fishel, "Interagency Arena at the Operational Level," 427–29; and Yeatman, "JIATF-South," 26.

101. Stahl, *Joint Interagency Coordination Group (JIACG) Training and Education Survey Results*, 43.

102. Fishel, "Interagency Arena at the Operational Level," 429; USJFCOM, *Insights and Best Practices: Interagency, Intergovernmental, and Nongovernmental Coordination*, 15; and LCDR Tom Stuhlreyer, USCG, "The JIATF Organization Model: Bringing the Interagency to Bear in Maritime Homeland Defense and Security," *Campaigning*, Spring 2007, 42–43.

103. Fishel, "Interagency Arena at the Operational Level," 439. See also Yeatman, "JIATF-South," 26.

104. Stuhlreyer, "JIATF Organization Model," 43.

105. GAO, *Interagency Collaboration: Key Issues for Congressional Oversight of National Security Strategies, Organizations, Workforce, and Information Sharing*, GAO-09-904SP (Washington, DC: GAO, September 2009), 26.

106. Miles, "SOUTHCOM Transformation."

107. Fishel, "Interagency Arena at the Operational Level," 429.

108. Stuhlreyer, "JIATF Organization Model," 42.

109. Robert T. Moeller and Mary C. Yates, "The Road to a New Unified Command," *Joint Force Quarterly* 51 (4th Quarter 2008): 68. At the time of this article, Vice Admiral Moeller was AFRICOM deputy for military operations and Ambassador Yates was AFRICOM deputy for civil-military activities.

110. GEN William E. Ward and Thomas P. Galvin, "U.S. Africa Command and the Principle of Active Security," *Joint Force Quarterly* 51 (4th Quarter 2008): 65. General Ward was the AFRICOM commander until March 2011.

111. Moeller and Yates, "Road to a New Unified Command," 71.

112. Col James Jacobson, USAF (AFRICOM deputy foreign policy advisor), interview by the author, 10 March 2010.

113. USAFRICOM, "Organizational Chart, Headquarters U.S. Africa Command," 8 December 2011, http://www.africom.mil/pdfFiles/AFRICOM%20Org%20 Chart.pdf.

114. Moeller and Yates, "Road to a New Unified Command," 70.

115. Maj Clifton D. Reed, USAF, "The Battle Within: DOD and Interagency Coordination for Regional Conflicts—AFRICOM and the Interagency Management System as Models," research report (Maxwell AFB, AL: Air Command and Staff College, April 2008), 3–5; and Moeller and Yates, "Road to a New Unified Command," 72.

116. Jacobson, interview; and USAFRICOM, "About United States Africa Command," accessed August 2011, http://www.africom.mil/AfricomFAQs.asp.

117. GAO, *Interagency Collaboration*, 32–33.

118. Reed, "Battle Within," 3–5; and Moeller and Yates, "Road to a New Unified Command," 72.

119. Moeller and Yates, "Road to a New Unified Command," 71.

120. Senior AFRICOM staffer, unattributed interview by the author, March 2010.

121. Moeller and Yates, "Road to a New Unified Command," 71.

122. Senior AFRICOM staffer, unattributed interview.

123. Isaac Kfir, "The Challenge That Is USAFRICOM," *Joint Force Quarterly* 49 (2nd Quarter 2008): 111.

124. Senior AFRICOM staffer, unattributed interview.

125. AFRICOM, "CJTF-HOA Factsheet," http://www.hoa.africom.mil/AboutCJTF -HOA.asp.

126. Senior AFRICOM staffer, unattributed interview.

127. Edward Marks, "Why USAFRICOM?," *Joint Force Quarterly* 52 (1st Quarter 2009): 148.

128. Ibid., 149. See also Robert Munson, "Do We Want to 'Kill People and Break Things' in Africa?," *Strategic Studies Quarterly* 2, no.1 (Spring 2008): 97–110.

Chapter 3

Current Practices—US Civilian Agencies

US government organizations outside the military have also been designed to facilitate interagency unity of effort, primarily in the Department of State (DOS) and the National Security Council. Although not directly involved in regional foreign policy planning and execution, several other USG interagency organizations contribute to the process.

State Department Structures for Civil-Military Coordination

The State Department is the lead foreign affairs agency for the United States. As such, it has the primary role for interagency coordination of the development and execution of US foreign policy.[1] Thus, we might expect the DOS to have robust capabilities to lead interagency foreign policy processes and to synchronize the efforts of the military and other agencies with overall US foreign policy goals.

The State Department is much smaller in terms of both personnel and budget than the Defense Department. While the military is organized in a three-level hierarchy—the strategic level in Washington, the operational level at the geographic combatant commands, and the tactical level of individual military units—the DOS is predominantly a two-tiered organization, with its strategic level in Washington and the tactical structure of the US embassies. The DOD has a workforce of approximately three million and an annual budget of about $660 billion, while State has fewer than 60,000 people, of whom only 6,400 are FSOs, and an annual budget of about $50 billion. At any given time, about two-thirds of FSOs are serving abroad.[2]

The DOS headquarters entities most relevant in examining civil-military unity of effort in regional US foreign policy are the undersecretary of state for political affairs (P) with its six regional bureaus, the Bureau of Political-Military Affairs (PM Bureau), the Bureau of Conflict and Stabilization Operations (CSO), and the USAID. These are highlighted in the organizational chart at figure 7.

United States
Department of State

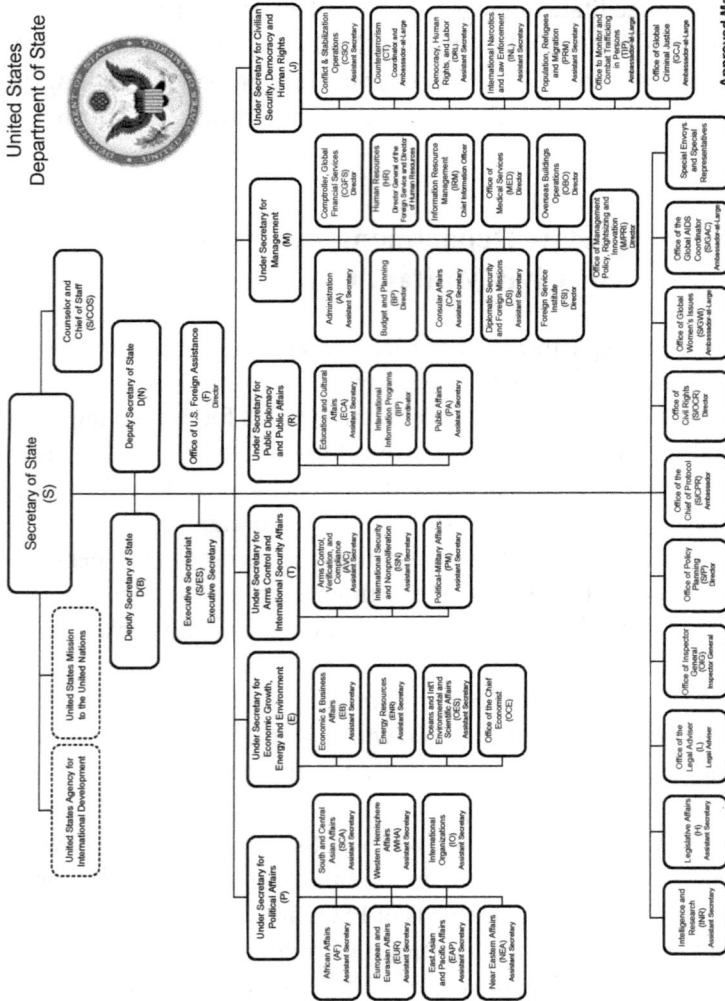

Secretary of State (S)

Counselor and Chief of Staff (S/COS)

Deputy Secretary of State (D)

Deputy Secretary of State (D/B)

Office of U.S. Foreign Assistance (F) Director

Executive Secretariat (S/ES) Executive Secretary

United States Agency for International Development

United States Mission to the United Nations

Under Secretary for Political Affairs (P)

- African Affairs (AF) Assistant Secretary
- European and Eurasian Affairs (EUR) Assistant Secretary
- East Asian and Pacific Affairs (EAP) Assistant Secretary
- Near Eastern Affairs (NEA) Assistant Secretary
- South and Central Asian Affairs (SCA) Assistant Secretary
- Western Hemisphere Affairs (WHA) Assistant Secretary
- International Organizations (IO) Assistant Secretary

Under Secretary for Economic Growth, Energy and Environment (E)

- Economic & Business Affairs (EB) Assistant Secretary
- Energy Resources (ENR) Assistant Secretary
- Oceans and Int'l Environmental and Scientific Affairs (OES) Assistant Secretary
- Office of the Chief Economist (OCE)

Under Secretary for Arms Control and International Security Affairs (T)

- Arms Control, Verification, and Compliance (AVC) Assistant Secretary
- International Security and Nonproliferation (ISN) Assistant Secretary
- Political-Military Affairs (PM) Assistant Secretary

Under Secretary for Public Diplomacy and Public Affairs (R)

- Education and Cultural Affairs (ECA) Assistant Secretary
- International Information Programs (IIP) Coordinator
- Public Affairs (PA) Assistant Secretary

Under Secretary for Management (M)

- Administration (A) Assistant Secretary
- Budget and Planning (BP) Director
- Consular Affairs (CA) Assistant Secretary
- Diplomatic Security and Foreign Missions (DS) Assistant Secretary
- Foreign Service Institute (FSI) Director
- Comptroller, Global Financial Services (CGFS) Director
- Human Resources (HR) Director General of the Foreign Service and Director of Human Resources
- Information Resource Management (IRM) Chief Information Officer
- Office of Medical Services (MED) Director
- Overseas Buildings Operations (OBO) Director
- Office of Management Policy, Rightsizing and Innovation (M/PRI) Director

Under Secretary for Civilian Security, Democracy and Human Rights (J)

- Conflict & Stabilization Operations (CSO) Assistant Secretary
- Counterterrorism (CT) Coordinator and Ambassador-at-Large
- Democracy, Human Rights, and Labor (DRL) Assistant Secretary
- International Narcotics and Law Enforcement (INL) Assistant Secretary
- Population, Refugees and Migration (PRM) Assistant Secretary
- Office to Monitor and Combat Trafficking in Persons (TIP) Ambassador-at-Large
- Office of Global Criminal Justice (GCJ) Ambassador-at-Large

- Intelligence and Research (INR) Assistant Secretary
- Legislative Affairs (H) Assistant Secretary
- Office of the Legal Adviser (L) Legal Adviser
- Office of Inspector General (OIG) Inspector General
- Office of Policy Planning (S/P) Director
- Office of the Chief of Protocol (S/CPR) Ambassador
- Office of Civil Rights (S/OCR) Director
- Office of Global Women's Issues (S/GWI) Ambassador-at-Large
- Office of the Global AIDS Coordinator (S/GAC) Ambassador-at-Large
- Special Envoys and Special Representatives

Approved May 2012

Figure 7. **Department of State organizational chart** (*Reprinted from* "Department Organization Chart," May 2012, US Department of State website, http://www.state.gov/r/pa/ei/rls/dos/99494.htm).

Undersecretary for Political Affairs—Regional Bureaus

The State Department has six regional bureaus—African Affairs (AF), East Asian and Pacific Affairs (EAP), European and Eurasian Affairs (EUR), Near Eastern Affairs (NEA), South and Central Asian Affairs (SCA), and Western Hemisphere Affairs (WHA)—each headed by an assistant secretary and all reporting to the undersecretary of state for political affairs.[3] A director is assigned to each country to "set policy guidelines, coordinate outside the bureau, and administer and implement the programs for his assigned country" as well as to communicate the direction of the regional assistant secretaries to US embassies around the world.[4]

The undersecretary for political affairs is the State Department's fourth-ranking official and a senior career diplomat. The undersecretary manages overall regional and bilateral policy issues and oversees the six regional bureaus as well as the Bureaus of International Organization Affairs (IO) and International Narcotics and Law Enforcement. IO conducts multilateral diplomacy with global intergovernmental and international organizations such as the UN.[5]

The regional bureaus are the DOS focal point for the development and implementation of US foreign policy strategies requiring interagency coordination.[6] The assistant secretaries who lead the six regional bureaus advise the undersecretary for political affairs and the secretary of state on regional issues and assist in supervising and coordinating all US government activities across the interagency community within their assigned regions.

The regional assistant secretaries are technically chartered to issue direction to US embassies in their region. However, the ambassadors leading these embassies are appointed by the president and generally deal directly with the secretary of state, bypassing the regional assistant secretary.[7] Thus, in a military analogy, the position of regional assistant secretary is much less like a GCC, who exercises command authority over the military elements in a specific AOR, and more like a director on the Joint Staff at the Pentagon, who advises the chairman of the JCS and develops policy and guidance for military forces but does not exercise any command authority over fielded forces.

Two of the many DOS functional bureaus are of particular relevance to military-diplomatic unity of effort for foreign policy: the long-standing Bureau of Political-Military Affairs and the newer

Office of the Coordinator of Reconstruction and Stabilization (S/CRS), established after the 2003 US invasion of Iraq.

Bureau of Political-Military Affairs

The PM Bureau—headed by an assistant secretary and staffed by nearly 300 FSOs, civil service officers, contractors, and uniformed military personnel—is State's lead for all operational military matters and its primary link with the DOD.[8] It manages diplomatic personnel support to military organizations, such as DOS personnel serving as POLADs to the COCOMs and other senior military leaders, as well as those serving on the Joint Staff and in the Office of the Secretary of Defense (OSD) as part of the State-DOD officer exchange program.[9]

Another of the bureau's functions is providing US foreign policy direction in several military-related areas, including defense strategy and policy, military operations, the overseas sale of military equipment by US companies, and security assistance to overseas partners. It also assists the military diplomatically in negotiating status-of-forces agreements, securing basing and overflight rights for US forces deploying overseas, coordinating foreign participation in US-led military coalitions, and facilitating the training and education of foreign military personnel and international peacekeepers.[10]

Bureau of Conflict and Stabilization Operations

Congress established the Office of the Coordinator of Reconstruction and Stabilization in August 2004 to "lead, coordinate and institutionalize U.S. government civilian capacity to prevent or prepare for post-conflict situations, and to help stabilize and reconstruct societies in transition from conflict."[11] In January 2012, the office became the Bureau of Conflict and Stabilization Operations (CSO).[12] Coordinating US civilian agencies, the US military, and multilateral organizations in developing and executing plans for a coordinated reconstruction and stabilization response is one of its taskings. Training and deploying US government civilians to reconstruction and stabilization operations either in partnership with the US military or as part of international peacekeeping missions is another.[13] At the time of transition, the bureau had a headquarters staff of about 170, plus a Civilian Response Corps (CRC) of approximately 900 active and standby volunteers from across the interagency trained and ready to deploy to the field.[14] In its first year of operation, CSO broadened the CRC by creating a network of experts from outside the federal government, including state and local officials as well as representatives from think tanks and nonprofit and international organizations.[15]

Key elements within the CSO staff include the Offices of Policy and Programs, Overseas Operations, Civilian Response Corps and Deployment Support, Partnerships, and Learning and Training. Policy and Programs provides early warning of unstable states that may require intervention. Overseas Operations develops contingency plans for such efforts and deploys and manages in-country response teams. Civilian Response Operations and Deployment Support develops, trains, equips, deploys, and coordinates the CRC for such operations. Partnerships coordinate preventative strategies with foreign partners, international organizations, NGOs, and the private sector.[16] Since its establishment in 2012, CSO has supported efforts in 15 countries, focusing on mitigating the effects of the Syrian crisis, the violent elections in Kenya, the high level of criminal violence in Honduras, and the large number of land mines in Burma (Myanmar).[17]

Initially, Congress was slow to provide adequate resources for S/CRS to fulfill its mandated mission.[18] Its first head, Amb. Carlos Pascual, resigned after only 14 months, expressing frustration over the lack of support.[19] Three years later, the situation began to improve. The Congressional Research Service reports that by August 2007, S/CRS had a staff of about 70—including 19 permanent DOS personnel, with others detailed from the USAID, the OSD, JFCOM, the Joint Staff, the Army Corps of Engineers, the CIA, and Treasury.[20] According to Amb. John Herbst, the S/CRS coordinator then, "It took until early 2007 for the federal government to reach an agreement on an operational plan for S/CRS, and then it took 18 months to receive the initial funding to put these plans into effect." S/CRS received a direct appropriation for the first time in 2009—a total of $140 million for reconstruction and stabilization personnel and support costs, providing the resources to establish its current headquarters staff and CRC.[21]

Staffing the CRC was a slow process because Congress did not make direct funding available to establish, train, and equip it until fiscal year 2009. By August 2007, CRC-A had 11 trained volunteers while CRC-S had about 300. By 2008 the CRC-A increased to 33 personnel.[22] By the end of 2009, it had reached 78 members while the CRC-S expanded to 554 members, with congressional funding available to increase the active corps to 250 members and the standby corps to 2,000.[23] During 2009, 177 CRC personnel deployed to 17 reconstruction and stabilization activities in Africa, Latin America, and Central and East Asia.[24]

On 16 April 2010, the State Department announced that the active corps had reached 100 and the standby corps 800 members.[25]

US Agency for International Development

The USAID is the lead agency in providing humanitarian assistance and supporting development and democracy around the world. While nominally an independent agency following the 1999 reorganization of US foreign affairs agencies, it receives general direction and overall foreign policy guidance from the secretary of state, and the USAID administrator holds a rank equivalent to a deputy secretary of state.[26]

Development is a key piece of US overseas capabilities in peacetime as well as in disaster or postconflict reconstruction and stabilization operations. The DOS often speaks of better coordinating the "three Ds"—diplomacy, development, and defense. Secretary of State Hillary Clinton said in January 2010, "Development must become an equal pillar of our foreign policy, alongside defense and diplomacy, led by a robust and reinvigorated [USAID]."[27]

However, the USAID's resources and capacity to provide personnel to interagency coordination cells or to assist other agencies in planning and operations is limited. The agency's staff in Washington plus its more than 100 offices around the world consists of only about 1,100 FSOs, another 1,100 civil service employees, and an additional 5,000 foreign nationals serving with USAID overseas offices. Because it is so small, the USAID often relies on contractors, NGOs, and international organizations to carry out even its core responsibilities.[28] Retired ambassador David Litt said, "USAID's cadre of Foreign Service Officers is so miniscule that the agency no longer has the organic expertise in health, education, and agriculture that it once enjoyed. It now relies on the private sector to fill that need without adequate policy and programmatic supervision."[29] Recognizing this, Secretary Clinton noted in January 2010, "For too long, we've relied on contractors . . . and we have diminished our own . . . institutional capacities. This must change. . . . USAID and the State Department must have the staff, the expertise, and the resources to design, implement, and evaluate our programs."[30] The secretary also remarked that the USAID must be able to coordinate development activities across Washington and in the field, a capability it currently lacks, saying,

> You have all the other agencies who are providing assistance of some sort or another. It's not coordinated at the country level and it is certainly not coordinated at the national level or the international level. . . .

> We . . . have to have better coordination on the whole-of-government front. I have been in countries where I've asked to see everybody doing any development, and the ambassador nicely invites people that are on a list given to him or her. He or she has never met the people, has no idea who they are or what they do, and even more, the people themselves have never met each other.[31]

The USAID has three offices under its Bureau of Democracy, Conflict, and Humanitarian Assistance particularly relevant to civil-military coordination: Foreign Disaster Assistance, Transition Initiatives (OTI), and Military Affairs (OMA). Its organizational structure is shown in figure 8.

Since 1964 the Office of Foreign Disaster Assistance has been charged with both providing and coordinating the USG interagency provision of humanitarian assistance to natural disasters and emergencies abroad, with a focus on immediate needs such as saving lives, reducing suffering, and mitigating the economic and social impacts of disasters. The OFDA has approximately 250 permanent staff and consultants, quite large for a USAID organization. When an interagency response involves the military, such as the 2004 Asian tsunami or the 2010 Haitian earthquake, the OFDA may send a liaison officer to either the relevant GCC headquarters or to the military field command to coordinate disaster response activities.[32]

The USAID created the Office of Transition Initiatives in 1994 "to support U.S. foreign policy objectives by helping local partners advance peace and democracy in priority countries in crisis."[33] The OTI typically works in 10–12 countries each year and focuses on short-term (two to three years) assistance in areas such as postconflict reconciliation, restarting local economies, and developing independent local media. The OTI is small, with a staff of fewer than 50 personnel and an annual budget of about $50 million (less than 0.5 percent of the USAID budget), though it also receives funds from other sources such as supplemental appropriations for contingency operations and DOD Section 1207 funds. The OTI's largest total funding to date was $226 million in fiscal year 2004. With the limited number of full-time staff, the OTI hires numerous contractors to round out its necessary personnel pool.[34] James Stephenson, head of the USAID's Iraq mission in 2006, said synergy between OTI personnel and the military in postconflict operations is critical but has been difficult to achieve because providing the right USAID experts in the conflict zone is complicated by the small pool available.[35]

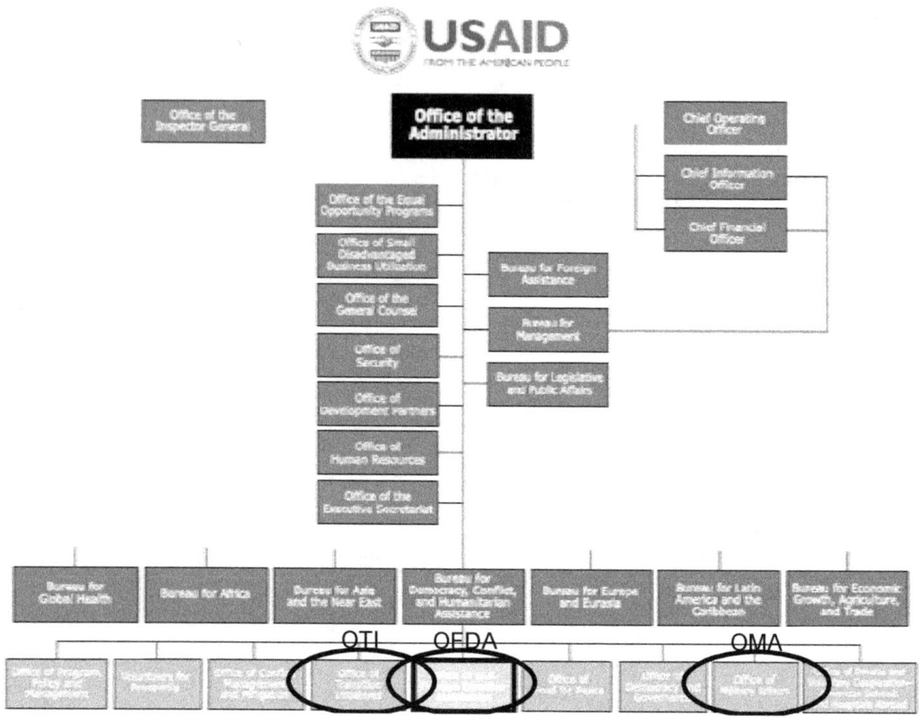

Figure 8. USAID organizational chart. (*Reprinted from Office of U.S. Foreign Disaster Assistance, Annual Report for Fiscal Year 2008* [Washington, DC: USAID, 2009], 17, http://pdf.usaid.gov/pdf_docs/PDACM965.pdf.)

In 2005 the USAID established the Office of Military Affairs to improve coordination with the military for developing doctrine as well as for planning and executing joint endeavors. These include conducting humanitarian relief after natural disasters, strengthening fragile states such as Afghanistan, supporting key underdeveloped states such as Pakistan, and addressing strategic issues such as the global war on terrorism. Speaking shortly after the OMA's establishment, USAID assistant administrator for the Bureau of Democracy, Conflict, and Humanitarian Assistance, Michael Hess, said, "Since post-conflict reconstruction is a pillar of the U.S. national security strategy, it is imperative for USAID to have an operational link with the military on how to better coordinate strategic development goals."[36] The OMA has a staff of just 16 personnel, including advisors posted with the geographic combatant commands.[37]

US Embassies

In most countries where the United States has diplomatic relations, it maintains an embassy headed by an ambassador and staffed with DOS personnel, as well as those from many other US agencies, together comprising the embassy "country team." Dr. Gabriel Marcella characterizes the country team as "a miniature replica of the Washington interagency."[38] Today, personnel from approximately 45 USG agencies serve at one or more embassies abroad, and they often outnumber the DOS personnel there. According to Amb. Louis Nigro, "State employees make up just over one-third of the staff at U.S. Government posts worldwide."[39]

In this environment, interagency coordination and unity of effort can be difficult for the ambassador to achieve. The Center for the Study of the Presidency's Project on National Security Reform (PNSR) research team observes that "representatives from different agencies often pursue their organizational interests at the expense of a broader, integrated approach,"[40] and former secretary of state Condoleezza Rice testified to Congress that it has "become an almost impossible task of coordinating massive numbers of agencies on the ground."[41]

In an attempt to achieve interagency unity of effort, all US ambassadors since the Kennedy administration receive a letter of appointment from the president making them the president's personal emissary and charging them "to exercise full responsibility for the direction, coordination, and supervision of all executive branch officers in (name of country), except for personnel under the command of a U.S. area military commander."[42] However, many observers contend that the authority given to ambassadors there is ambiguous. The PNSR study team further identifies that other agencies often view them as DOS rather than as presidential representatives and that the letter of appointment does not clearly establish their authority over the interagency country team. Consequently, other agencies sometimes perceive ambassadors as attempting to assert authority they do not have.[43]

In civil-military coordination, the letter gives ambassadors authority over US military personnel in country except those under COCOM control. Dr. John Fishel, who has written extensively on civil-military relations, says this exception applies only when "major U.S. military operations are being conducted in the country" and does not apply to security assistance or military exercises.[44] Nevertheless, GCCs have not always interpreted the authority this way and have sometimes claimed authority over peacetime military activities in the host nation. Marcella suggests that this ambiguity requires the ambassador and COCOM (or their bosses—the secretaries of state and defense) to work together to agree on specific issues of control over US military personnel in country.[45]

US Regional Missions

While US embassies and their ambassadors serve bilateral relations between the United States and a single foreign state, the United States has a few regional missions that conduct multilateral diplomatic relations with certain regional entities. Currently, there are diplomatic missions to the European Union (EU), the Organization for Security and Cooperation in Europe (OSCE), the Organization of American States, the African Union, and the Association of Southeast Asian Nations. The United States has maintained diplomatic relations with the EU and its forerunners since 1953, with a permanent US mission in Brussels, Belgium, since 1961. An ambassador leads this US mission to the EU, which also includes representatives from the Departments of State, Agriculture, Commerce, Homeland Security, Treasury, Justice, and Defense, as well as USAID and the Office of the US Trade Representative.[46] The United States also has missions to NATO in Brussels and to the OSCE in Vienna, both led by ambassadors. The mission to NATO includes personnel from the Departments of Defense and State, and the mission to the OSCE has a team of more than

30 staffers from State, the JCS, and the joint congressional/executive branch Commission on Security Cooperation in Europe.[47]

Because the OAS is headquartered in Washington, DC, the US mission to the OAS is also located there. It is headed by an ambassador and supported by representatives drawn largely from the State Department's Bureau of Western Hemisphere Affairs.[48] The US mission to the African Union is in Addis Ababa, Ethiopia. It is headed by an ambassador and includes representatives from State, USAID, and the DOD, including military officers serving as liaisons from AFRICOM and CJTF-HOA.[49] The United States recently established a permanent mission to the ASEAN in Jakarta, Indonesia. On 25 January 2010, the United States announced the arrival of the first officer to the mission, acting as the resident representative of the US ambassador for ASEAN affairs, and the first ambassador to the ASEAN, David L. Carden, was appointed in April 2011.[50]

The National Security Council

Established by the National Security Act of 1947, the NSC provides the president with a national, strategic-level forum for interagency coordination of foreign policy and national security issues. Although the NSC is a national-level strategic body, its policy committees sometimes fill a staffing gap between policies at the strategic level and execution in the field because most executive branch agencies lack regional-level staff organizations.

The four statutory members of the NSC are the president, vice president, secretary of state, and secretary of defense; the two statutory advisors are the chairman of the JCS and the director of national intelligence. President Obama added the secretary of energy as a statutory member of his NSC and the secretary of the treasury, attorney general, secretary of homeland security, US representative to the UN, White House chief of staff, and the national security advisor as additional members. Still others attend if the agenda includes issues related to the economy, homeland security, counterterrorism, or science and technology.[51] The cabinet secretaries meeting without the president are referred to as the Principals Committee (PC) and a gathering of their deputy secretaries as the Deputies Committee (DC).

Below the PC and DC in President Obama's NSC are the interagency policy committees (IPC), each chaired by an undersecretary or assistant secretary from an executive-branch agency, which manage "the development and implementation of national security policies by multiple agencies of the United States Government." The IPCs are "the main day-to-day fora for interagency coordination of national security policy" that could be aligned by mission or function or by geographic area and provide policy analysis for the DC and PC. The IPCs replaced Pres. George W. Bush's policy coordination committees (PCC).[52] However, the IPC approach can fail to produce optimal, coordinated policies because each IPC representative comes from a home agency or department and is generally inclined to protect that agency's turf or equities at the expense of broader interagency unity of effort.[53] Alternatively, the requirement to achieve interagency consensus at the IPC can lead to a sluggish policy formulation process and to satisficing decision-making processes.

The president appoints a national security advisor, who is not subject to congressional confirmation, to support the work of the NSC and coordinate the activities of the national security staff (NSS). The national security advisor and the NSS work directly for the president; the cabinet principals on the NSC have no authority over the national security advisor or NSS.[54] The NSS does both the daily and long-term integration and coordination of national security and foreign policy across the US government. The NSS is frequently pulled in two different directions. On the one hand, it is asked to be an interagency coordinating body, while on the other hand, it has sometimes been called on by the president to take policy control over an issue or to direct and/or monitor policy execution in a given area.[55] The Tower Commission's report on the 1986 Iran-Contra scandal strongly cautioned that the NSS and national security advisor should not be engaged in operations or the implementation of policy.[56]

While it would seem that the NSC and NSS should be an ideal structure to ensure interagency coordination at the strategic level, many say the NSC often fails to coordinate in practice. For example, former CENTCOM commander Gen Anthony Zinni, USMC, wrote, "In Washington, there is no one place, agency, or force that directs interagency cooperation. The only such cooperation is on an ad hoc, person-to-person or group-to-group basis. So if you have a problem like putting Iraq back together after Saddam . . . there's nowhere to start."[57] After interviewing former JCS chairman Gen Peter Pace, USMC, American Forces Press Service journalist Jim Garamone stated, "It's after the president makes a decision that the process slows up. Each department or agency takes its share of the mission and goes back into its 'stovepipe' to do the work." Pace stated that "there is no one below the president ensuring the agencies work together."[58]

Other Interagency Structures

While the National Security Council is in theory the only necessary body for interagency foreign policy and national security coordination in Washington, highly visible failures have led to the creation of other interagency entities—from new federal agencies, to mission-oriented interagency centers, to mission-focused special envoys. However, Secretary of the Air Force Michael Donley cautions that these "new organizations and activities are being created piecemeal, so far without discussion of the broader interagency framework in which they operate."[59] While these organizations largely function at the national, strategic level in Washington, a brief description of why and how they were created and how they are structured is in order.

Department of Homeland Security

The Department of Homeland Security was established after 9/11 in response to the perceived failings among many executive-branch agencies with roles in homeland security. The creation of the DHS brought together the domestic security activities of more than 40 separate agencies under one head. Initially established by executive order on 8 October 2001 as the Office of Homeland Security, it was formally established into law as a new federal department on 25 November 2002.[60]

Office of the Director of National Intelligence

Similarly, the Office of the Director of National Intelligence (ODNI) was formed as a result of the 9/11 Commission's identification of failures of separate US intelligence agencies to coordinate terrorist threat information. Per the commission's findings and recommendations, Congress passed the Intelligence Reform and Terrorism Prevention Act of 2004 stating that "interagency coordination of intelligence should be and is a significant and complex function unto itself and should be separated from management of the CIA or any other particular agency."[61]

National Centers

National centers have been established for counterintelligence, critical infrastructure protection, and counterterrorism. These interagency entities are located and funded in a specified lead agency and staffed by personnel detailed from other agencies. They have been created by executive order, though two were subsequently codified in legislation.[62]

The National Counterintelligence Center was established in 1994 by executive order in response to the CIA and FBI's failure to discover long-time spy Aldrich Ames. It was staffed by senior counterintelligence and other specialists from across the national security and intelligence communities to improve interagency counterintelligence activities. In 2002 Congress codified the organization into law, aligning it under the new ODNI and renaming it the Office of the National Counterintelligence Executive.[63]

In response to a 1997 report from the President's Council on Infrastructure Protection, executive order established the National Infrastructure Protection Center at the FBI in 1998. Interagency staffing comes from the FBI, the intelligence community, Defense, Transportation, and Energy, as well as a public-private partnership with private corporations that own much of the US critical national infrastructure.[64]

Initially formed by the president in January 2003 as the Terrorist Threat Integration Center, it was reestablished as the National Counterterrorism Center (NCTC) by executive order in August 2004 and codified into law in December 2004. Aligned under the ODNI, the NCTC combines counterterrorist elements from the intelligence, homeland security, law enforcement, and defense communities. The NCTC fuses and analyzes all-source intelligence on terrorism, maintains a shared database and systems for interagency counterterrorist information sharing, and functions as the operational planner and coordinator for interagency counterterrorism operations across the USG, assigning operational responsibilities to lead agencies.[65]

The Project on National Security Reform study team assessed in September 2009 that the NCTC "represents one of the most mature interagency planning models in the U.S. government today." However, because the NCTC lacks formal authority over participating departments and agencies, bureaucratic resistance creates barriers to the development of true whole-of-government strategic and operational counterterrorism plans, so "unity of effort remains an elusive goal." The participating agencies have their own "deeply institutionalized" counterterrorism policies and processes and thus often avoid following an integrated strategy that runs counter to their established norms. This dichotomy leads individuals to try "to achieve their individual objectives using their existing authorities, rather than attempting to develop partnerships and cooperative arrangements with other departments in a harmonized and integrated approach."[66]

Presidential Special Representatives

President Obama, like many presidents before him, has delegated responsibility for interagency coordination and implementation of several foreign policy matters to special envoys or special representatives who report either to the president, the national security advisor, or the secretary of state. They focus on issues such as nuclear nonproliferation or global partnerships as well as specific unstable regions of the world. The 2009 PNSR study on interagency reform characterizes these special representatives as "an established, if often unsatisfactory approach" because their "abilities to coordinate policy and strategy vary widely" and because they are ad hoc additions to the system.[67]

Recently, some envoys have constructed interagency support staffs drawn from the departments and agencies relevant to their missions. Such staffing action may help produce better interagency coordination because an agency whose representatives help develop envoys' policies may be more willing to support them. This would not only produce a more coordinated policy but also lessen the president's involvement in direct dispute resolution.[68] While the special envoy to Sudan is a good example of what this approach can accomplish, it also illustrates some of the drawbacks of the envoy system in general. Former special envoy Scott Gration built an interagency support staff that arguably contributed to recent US successes in brokering settlements to the crises in Sudan after many years. However, limitations remain that are similar to those of the Interagency Policy Committee model at the NSC. First, although Special Envoy Gration officially reported to the secretary of state, he also could report directly to the president and thus overburden him with crisis management at the expense of strategic leadership. Second, the special envoy had no formal authority to compel interagency collaboration. Third, special envoys have only limited control over funds or resources outside the lead agency.[69]

Summary of Nonmilitary Interagency Structures

The civilian side of the US government has several organizations and structures playing key roles in interagency unity of effort for planning and implementing foreign policy at the regional level. However, none of the current structures provides all of the organizational attributes needed to produce the desired unity of effort.

Regional bureaus at the State Department provide some strategic-level interagency policy coordination in Washington, but they are much less effective at the operational level. The assistant secretaries who head these regional bureaus are staff officers who provide support to the undersecretary of state for political affairs and the secretary of state. The bureaus are not structured like the military's GCCs in that these secretaries do not have the authority to compel interagency unity of effort at the regional level.

The State Department's Bureau of Conflict and Stabilization Operations has established a good model for interagency unity of effort for planning and execution, but this model is limited to reconstruction and stabilization operations. Also, because CSO only recently received sufficient funding from Congress and has not yet been fully used in a real-world operation, there is little track record to judge whether the construct and concepts will produce the desired level of interagency unity of effort, even in its assigned mission area.

State's Bureau of Political-Military Affairs and the US Agency for International Development both provide critical capabilities to the US civil-military national security and foreign policy team, but neither plays a leading role in coordinating interagency planning and execution. While the USG needs these offices on the team, it should not look to them to take a leading role in an improved interagency structure.

At US embassies around the world, each ambassador has *de jure* authority over all US interagency actors in the country, including the military (except during "major military operations"), which should produce a high degree of interagency unity of effort at the country level. However, the ambassador does not always have *de facto* control, as the military GCC or civilian agencies in Washington sometimes work directly with their agency's counterparts in the country rather than through the ambassador. Even when an ambassador achieves a high degree of control over US activities in his or her assigned country, no mechanism exists to ensure unity of effort with other US ambassadors in the region.

US regional missions conduct multilateral diplomacy, unifying civil-military engagement with a handful of regional IGOs such as NATO, the EU, the AU, and the ASEAN. However these regional US missions are in no way regional headquarters like the military's GCCs. The staff at each regional US mission is much smaller than a GCC staff, and the ambassador at each mission is focused only on engagement with the specified IGO and has no regional synchronization role or authority over other US ambassadors in the region.

In Washington, the National Security Council and its supporting national security staff provide a strategic-level, interagency, policy-coordinating body that has occasionally been tasked to synchronize and monitor policy execution—sometimes with negative results. Even when the results are positive, placing too much execution responsibility in the NSS risks overburdening the White House and distracting from the NSC's primary role in strategic policy formulation and coordination.

Congress created both the Department of Homeland Security and Office of the Director of National Intelligence to unify homeland security and intelligence organizations in response to perceived coordination failures associated with the 9/11 attacks. In many ways, the formation of these two organizations mirrors the DOD reorganization that the 1986 Goldwater-Nichols Act mandated, which created today's successful US joint military team. Some interagency reform advocates believe similar legislation may be required to achieve interagency unity of effort for regional-level foreign policy planning and execution.[70]

The national centers for counterintelligence, infrastructure protection, and counterterrorism represent recent attempts to improve interagency unity of effort in a specific mission area. Two of them (counterintelligence and counterterrorism) are codified in law, making them effectively permanent and providing a better chance of sufficient, continuous funding. These centers have generated successes in their mission areas that probably would not have occurred if each participating agency had been working separately, but these constructs still do not provide their directors with a level of authority commensurate with assigned responsibilities. Thus, while the centers provide some lessons for interagency reform, they still fall short of providing the authority required to execute interagency responsibilities.

Finally, the president has assigned mission-specific interagency coordination and implementation for some issues to special envoys. In some cases, these envoys have assembled interagency staffs to assist in their missions and to provide a point of entry to the various agencies required. While these envoys can achieve successes with sufficient backing from the president and/or key cabinet secretaries, they have no formal legal authority to compel interagency unity of effort. Absent such formal authority, these ad hoc constructs risk overburdening the White House or the cabinet secretary assigned to support their activities.

None of the currently available civilian structures appears able to produce the desired level of interagency unity of effort for the planning and execution of US foreign policy at the regional level.

Notes

1. Alan G. Whittaker, Frederick C. Smith, and Elizabeth McKune, "The National Security Policy Process: The National Security Council and Interagency System," in *Affairs of State*, ed. Gabriel Marcella, 137.

2. Louis J. Nigro Jr., "The Department of State and Strategic Integration: How Reinforcing State as an Institution Will Improve America's Engagement with the World in the 21st Century," in *Affairs of State*, ed. Gabriel Marcella, 258–59; USJFCOM, *Insights and Best Practices: Interagency, Intergovernmental, and Nongovernmental Coordination (A Joint Force Operational Perspective)*, Focus Paper no. 3 (Norfolk, VA: USJFCOM Joint Warfighting Center, July 2007), 2, http://jko.cmil.org/file/109/view; Secretary of State Hillary Rodham Clinton, "President's Proposed Budget Request for Fiscal Year 2011 for the Department of State and Foreign Operations," Testimony before the Senate Appropriations Subcommittee on State, Foreign Operations, and Related Programs, Washington, DC, 24 February 2010; and White House Office of Management and Budget, "The U.S. Department of Defense 2010 Budget," fact sheet, 1, http://www.whitehouse.gov/omb/assets/fy2010_factsheets/fy10_defense.pdf.

3. DOS, "Department Organization Chart," DOS website, May 2012, http://www.state.gov.

4. MAJ Mark L. Curry, USA, "The Interagency Process in Regional Foreign Policy," monograph (Fort Leavenworth, KS: School of Advanced Military Studies, US Army Command and General Staff College, 5 May 1994), 6–7.

5. DOS, "Under Secretary for Political Affairs," DOS website, http://www.state.gov/p/; and DOS, "Bureau of International Organization Affairs," DOS website, http://www.state.gov/p/io/other/133723.htm.

6. USJFCOM, *Commander's Handbook for the Joint Interagency Coordination Group* (Norfolk, VA: USJFCOM Joint Warfighting Center, Joint Innovation and Experimentation Directorate, 1 March 2007), IV-5.

7. Ibid., 9, 17.

8. Andrew J. Shapiro, assistant secretary of state for political-military affairs, "Political-Military Affairs: Smart Power Starts Here" (keynote address, ComDef 2009, Washington, DC, 9 September 2009).

9. Nigro, "Department of State and Strategic Integration," 279–80; and John D. Finney and Alphonse F. La Porta, "Integrating National Security Strategy at the Operational Level: The Role of the State Department Political Advisors," in *Affairs of State*, ed. Gabriel Marcella, 281–82.

10. Office of the Federal Register, National Archives and Records Administration, *The United States Government Manual 2009/2010* (Washington, DC: Government Printing Office, 2009), 297–98, http://www.gpoaccess.gov/gmanual/index.html.

11. Whittaker, Smith, and McKune, "National Security Policy Process," 141.

12. DOS, Office of the Spokesperson, "U.S. Department of State Launches Bureau of Conflict and Stabilization Operations," fact sheet, 22 November 2011; and DOS, Bureau of Conflict and Stabilization Operations, "CSO: One-Year Progress Report," 8 March 2013, DOS website, http://www.state.gov/j/cso/releases/other/2013/206410.htm.

13. Kennon H. Nakamura and Susan B. Epstein, *Diplomacy for the 21st Century: Transformational Diplomacy*, CRS Report for Congress (Washington, DC: CRS, 23 August 2007), 9; and Nigro, "Department of State and Strategic Integration," 266.

14. DOS, Office of the Coordinator for Reconstruction and Stabilization, "Staff List—Current as of April 5, 2010," http://www.crs.state.gov/index.cfm?fuseaction=public.display&shortcut=4X3I; and DOS, Office of the Spokesman, "Civilian Response Corps Reaches 100 Active Members," 16 April 2010.

15. DOS, "CSO."

16. Ibid.

17. DOS, "What We Do," DOS website, http://www.state.gov/j/cso/what/indes.htm.

18. Gabriel Marcella, "Understanding the Interagency Process: The Challenge of Adaptation," in *Affairs of State*, ed. Gabriel Marcella, 27.

19. Nora Bensahel and Anne M. Moisan, "Repairing the Interagency Process," *Joint Force Quarterly* 44 (1st Quarter 2007): 107.

20. Nakamura and Epstein, *Diplomacy for the 21st Century*, 8–9.

21. S/CRS, *2009 Year in Review: Smart Power in Action* (Washington, DC: DOS, 1 March 2010), 5–7.

22. Nakamura and Epstein, *Diplomacy for the 21st Century*, 9.

23. DOS, *2009 Year in Review*, 6, 8.

24. Ibid., 6, 14–15.

25. DOS, "Civilian Response Corps Reaches 100 Active Members."

26. The White House, Office of the Press Secretary, "Foreign Affairs Reorganization," fact sheet, 30 December 1998, http://www.fas.org/news/usa/1998/12/98123003_tlt.html.

27. Secretary of State Hillary Rodham Clinton, "Remarks on Development in the 21st Century," Peterson Institute for International Economics, Washington, DC, 6 January 2010.

28. Nigro, "Department of State and Strategic Integration," 276.

29. David C. Litt, "New Directions for U.S. Foreign Policy in the Greater Middle East," in *American Foreign Policy*, ed. Richmond M. Lloyd, 175.

30. Clinton, "Remarks on Development in the 21st Century."

31. Ibid.

32. Ibid.

33. USAID, Office of Transition Initiatives, *15 Years: 1994–2009* (Washington, DC: USAID, 2009), 1, http://www.globalcorps.com/sitedocs/oti15yearreport.pdf.

34. Ibid., 2, 6–7, 14; and USAID, "Transition Initiatives," http://www.usaid.gov/our_work/cross-cutting_programs/transition_initiatives/. In §1207 of the FY 2006 National Defense Authorization Act, Congress authorized the DOD to transfer up to $100 million per year to the secretary of state for "reconstruction, security, or stabilization assistance to a foreign country." This assistance can be in the form of either services or funds. Congress then reauthorized this authority in §1210 of the FY 2008 Defense Authorization Act. These funds have hence been informally referred to as "Section 1207 funds."

35. James Stephenson, "Military-Civilian Cooperation: A Field Perspective," *Foreign Service Journal*, March 2006, 60–62.

36. Todd Bullock, "USAID Announces New Office of Military Affairs," DOS International Information Programs, 24 October 2005. See also Thomas E. Johnson Jr., "Working It Out with the Military: The View from Kabul," *Foreign Service Journal* 84, no. 6 (June 2007): 18.

37. Bullock, "USAID Announces New Office of Military Affairs"; and USAID, "USAID-DoD Relations," 19 October 2005, 2, 5–6, http://www1.usaid.gov/about_usaid/acvfa/usaid_dod_relations.pdf.

38. Marcella, "Understanding the Interagency Process," 32–33.

39. Nigro, "Department of State and Strategic Integration," 260–61.

40. PNSR, *Forging a New Shield*, 40.

41. Condoleezza Rice, quoted in ibid.

42. Marcella, "Understanding the Interagency Process," 33.

43. PNSR, *Forging a New Shield*, 242; and PNSR, *Turning Ideas into Action* (Arlington: Center for the Study of the Presidency, September 2009), 29.

44. John T. Fishel, "The Interagency Arena at the Operational Level: The Cases Now Known as Stability Operations," in *Affairs of State*, ed. Gabriel Marcella, 422.

45. Marcella, "Understanding the Interagency Process," 33.

46. DOS, US Mission to the EU, "About the Mission," USEU website, http://useu.usmission.gov/root/about-the-mission.html.

47. DOS, US Mission to the OSCE, "The U.S. Mission to the OSCE," OSCE website, http://osce.usmission.gov/infoosce.html.

48. DOS, US Mission to the OAS, "Introduction" and "United States Delegation," http://www.usoas.usmission.gov.

49. DOS, US Mission to the AU, "About Us," http://www.usau.usmission.gov/about-us.html; and "Key Officers," http://www.usau.usmission.gov/key-officers.html.

50. ASEAN Secretariat, "US to Open Mission to ASEAN in Jakarta," press release, Phuket, Thailand, 22 July 2009; Embassy of the United States of America, Bangkok, "United States Moves on New Mission to ASEAN," press release, Bangkok,

Thailand, 25 January 2010, Bangkok; and DOS, "U.S.-ASEAN Cooperation," http://www.state.gov/r/pa/prs/ps/2011/07/168943.htm.

51. The White House, Presidential Policy Directive 1 (PDD-1), *Organization of the National Security Council System*, 13 February 2009, 2.

52. Ibid., 4–5.

53. PNSR, *Turning Ideas into Action*, 116.

54. Whittaker, Smith, and McKune, "National Security Policy Process," 117.

55. Marcella, "Understanding the Interagency Process," 15. See also Christopher L. Naler, "Are We Ready for an Interagency Combatant Command?," *Joint Force Quarterly* 41 (2nd Quarter 2006): 27.

56. Whittaker, Smith, and McKune, "National Security Policy Process," 113.

57. Chris Strohm, "Former Commander Calls for New Military-Civilian Planning Organization," *Government Executive.com*, 7 December 2004, http://www.govexec.com/defense/2004/12/former-commander-calls-for-new-military-civilian-planning-organization/18156/; and Naler, "Are We Ready for an Interagency Combatant Command?," 27.

58. Jim Garamone, "Discussion Needed to Change Interagency Process, Pace Says," American Forces Press Service, 17 September 2004.

59. Michael Donley, *Rethinking the Interagency System*, Occasional Paper no. 05-01 (McLean, VA: Hicks & Associates, March 2005), 5. Donley was the secretary of the Air Force until June 2013. His 30 years of government service include positions on the professional staff of the Senate Armed Services Committee, five years on the National Security Council staff, and positions in both the Department of the Air Force and the OSD. While on the NSC staff, Donley coordinated White House policy on the 1986 Goldwater-Nichols DOD Reorganization Act and both conceived and organized the President's Blue Ribbon Commission on Defense Management. While serving as a senior fellow at the Institute for Defense Analyses, he consulted to the Commission on Roles and Missions of the Armed Forces and participated in two studies on the organization of the Joint Staff and the Office of the Chairman of the Joint Chiefs of Staff. USAF, "Biography, Michael B. Donley," http://www.af.mil/information/bios/bio_print.asp?bioID=11336&page=1.

60. DHS History Office, *Brief Documentary History of the Department of Homeland Security: 2001–2008* (Washington, DC: DHS, 2009), 3, 7.

61. Donley, *Rethinking the Interagency System*, pt. 1, 9.

62. Ibid., 3.

63. Ibid.; and Office of the National Counterintelligence Executive, "About the NCIX," http://www.ncix.gov/about/index.html.

64. Donley, *Rethinking the Interagency System*, pt. 1, 3–4; and *Free Encyclopedia of Ecommerce*, "National Infrastructure Protection Center (NIPC)," http://ecommerce.hostip.info/pages/770/National-Infrastructure-Protection-Center-NIPC.html.

65. Donley, *Rethinking the Interagency System*, pt. 1, 4.

66. PNSR, *Turning Ideas into Action*, 110. In April 2009, NCTC director Michael Leiter asked the PNSR to conduct a comprehensive analysis of the NCTC's Directorate of Strategic Operational Planning and offer recommendations "for removing barriers to enhanced mission effectiveness."

67. Ibid., 54.

68. Ibid., 53–54.

69. Ibid., 115–16.

70. For example, see Murdock and Flournoy, *Beyond Goldwater-Nichols*; and Lt Col Edward W. Loxterkamp, USAF, Lt Col Michael F. Welch, USAF, and CDR Richard M. Gomez, USN, *The Interagency Process: The Need for New Legislation* (Norfolk, VA: Joint Forces Staff College, 27 September 2003).

Chapter 4

The Need for Improvement

The United States conducts a broad range of activities overseas requiring coordinated actions of multiple agencies. These include peacetime security cooperation, counterterrorism cooperation, humanitarian relief operations in the wake of a disaster, complex reconstruction and stabilization operations, and combat and COIN operations. Reviewing each type of mission will help illustrate both the successes and challenges the United States has experienced in executing these complex interagency operations.

Security Cooperation

Security cooperation is a term used to describe programs conducted between the United States and partner nations—either bilaterally or on a regional basis—to shape the future security environment in ways favorable to US interests. Security cooperation activities promote partner nation military interoperability with US forces, build and strengthen defense partnerships, foster more capable and professional militaries in friendly countries, enhance US influence with the partner nation, and provide access for US forces in or through the partner nation when required. The OSD identifies security cooperation objectives; the OSD staff, Joint Staff, service staffs, and GCCs develop regional and country-specific security cooperation plans; and the GCCs, their service components, and the security cooperation offices (SCO) at each embassy take the lead in executing the program, with support from the State Department's Political-Military Bureau and the interagency US embassy country teams.[1]

In addition to security cooperation objectives that the secretary of defense has identified, the GCCs may execute additional peacetime theater engagement activities under the heading of "Phase Zero" or "shaping" activities. The term refers to the first of six phases of a military operation, which include Phase 0: Shape; Phase I: Deter; Phase II: Seize the Initiative; Phase III: Dominance; Phase IV: Stabilization; and Phase V: Enabling Civil Authority.[2] The word *shaping* has come to mean almost any activity that might prepare the United States for a future contingency operation, leading to concerns that the military is conducting activities that overlap with DOS diplomatic and US-AID developmental goals and programs.[3] Programs under the heading of Phase Zero activities should in theory be limited to those specifically spelled out in approved operational plans and should be coordinated with the State Department at both the Washington and embassy levels, but for reasons of operational security, this is not always done.[4]

In the early years of the security cooperation program, coordination between State and Defense was limited. The DOD's security cooperation plans were not shared until the chairman of the JCS and the secretary of defense had reviewed and approved them, offering no opportunity for unity of effort in development of these plans.[5] The GCCs have improved the security cooperation planning process in recent years by developing mechanisms such as POLADs and JIACGs to get earlier interagency input.

The funding for security cooperation activities traditionally comes from two sources: *US Code* Title 10, which funds military activities, and *US Code* Title 22, which funds programs controlled by the State Department but administered by the DOD's Defense Security Cooperation Agency (DSCA). Title 22 encompasses a broad range of activities, including foreign military sales (FMS), foreign military financing (FMF), international military education and training (IMET), and the global peace operations initiative (GPOI).[6] The GAO says the proportion of foreign assistance that the State Department funded and DOD executed increased from 7 percent of official development assistance in 2001 to an estimated 20 percent in 2006.[7]

Some, such as Albert Zaccor at the Atlantic Council of the United States, caution that security cooperation objectives and programs should be strictly limited to "specific enumerated defense and security objectives and assistance to foreign establishments playing a role in national security or defense" to avoid the temptation to define security cooperation so broadly that it becomes "a surrogate for foreign policy."[8] Similarly, Thomas E. Johnson Jr., an FSO who served as a USAID program officer in Kabul, says that "the military's 'mission creep' into the Foreign Service lanes seems to be happening without sufficient thought, planning or coordination."[9] For example, the Commander's Emergency Response Program (CERP), "intended to enable commanders to 'respond to humanitarian relief and reconstruction within their areas of responsibility by carrying out programs that will immediately assist the . . . population'" is instead often used for long-term projects, which Johnson says impedes the USAID's ability to maximize unity of effort in developmental assistance.[10]

Beginning in fiscal year 2006, Congress provided an additional source of security cooperation funding directly to the DOD called "Section 1206 funding" (named after §1206 of the 2006 National Defense Authorization Act), giving Defense both the funding and authority to train and equip foreign police forces and militaries at the direction of the president and requiring only that it coordinate with State in the implementation of these programs.[11] In 2009 the GAO reported that the DOD and DOS "had developed a coordinated process for jointly reviewing and selecting project proposals," noting that while coordination between the GCCs and US embassies "did not occur consistently" in 2007, "officials reported better coordination in the formulation of fiscal year 2007 proposals."[12] In 2006 Section 1206 funding was $200 million and grew to $400 million by 2012.[13] The result is that the DOD provides a greater proportion of US foreign assistance than does the DOS, increasingly putting a military "face" on the aid that countries receive.[14] Additionally, Congress created three country-specific Title 10 security cooperation funds—the Afghanistan Security Forces Fund (ASFF), the Iraq Security Forces Fund (ISFF), and the Pakistan Counterinsurgency Fund (PCF)—to build the capabilities of security forces in these three countries. At $11.6 billion in fiscal year 2011, the ASFF was one of the largest appropriations in the DOD.

A 2006 Senate Foreign Relations Committee report finds that the added funding for military involvement in theater engagement has led to increased US military presence in embassies and elsewhere in partner countries. Thus, not only must an already overburdened embassy handle the associated personnel support requirements, but also lines of authority between State and Defense may become blurred and hamper interagency unity of effort at the country level. At the same time, DOS funding and personnel were cut for several years, creating capability gaps that a well-funded DOD stepped in to fill.[15] Further, some host countries have expressed concern over the expanded role of the US military in addressing nonmilitary problems such as building schools and drilling water wells. Ethiopia, for example, ordered a US military civil affairs team that had been conducting just such development projects out of the country to prevent any perception that the US military was taking sides in regional disputes, possibly leading to cross-border hostilities.[16] Testimony on the creation of AFRICOM during congressional hearings in the summer of 2007 echoed many of the same concerns.[17]

While there are concerns the military is taking the lead role in security-related engagements, current organizational structures focus the State Department on bilateral relationships, while the military's GCCs lead the DOD to take a more theater-level perspective. The DOD argues this regional-level perspective is often key to ensuring interagency unity of effort and coordination with other US partners working toward compatible goals in the host countries throughout the region. For example, RADM Hamlin Tallent, then serving as EUCOM's director of operations, testified to Congress in 2005 that "EUCOM's [security cooperation] strategy is derived from *regional* priority and policy themes stated in the Secretary of Defense's Security Cooperation Guidance. EUCOM has taken a *regional* approach that links individual country objectives to *broader theater goals*" (emphasis added).[18]

Examples of regional initiatives conducted by EUCOM include the Africa Clearinghouse,[19] which "brought thirteen African countries together with NATO, the United Nations, and the European Union," and the Southeast Europe Clearinghouse, which "is open to all NATO, European Union, and partner countries (Russia and Ukraine specifically) that have engagement programs in Southeastern Europe" (the former Yugoslavia). Another is the South Caucasus Clearinghouse, which "focuses on defense reform, energy security, maritime security, disaster response, peacekeeping, and training and education" and provides "a forum for EUCOM, our European partners, and international organizations like NATO and the Organization for Security and Cooperation in Europe to coordinate security cooperation programs with Armenia, Azerbaijan, and Georgia."[20] EUCOM runs all of these clearinghouse activities from its headquarters in Stuttgart, Germany. Citing the Africa Clearinghouse, Rear Admiral Tallent testified that EUCOM created it because "we were finding . . . when we were down in Africa [that the United States and its European allies] were fumbling around over each other. We would go in and train a group in Ghana, let us say, only to find out the French had trained them the year before, the same group, so we were duplicating efforts. It was just insane." As part of the Trans-Sahara Counter Terrorism Initiative in late 2004 or early 2005, EUCOM brought together the chiefs of defense from the African countries in the region, which, according to Tallent, "was the first time they had ever met each other."[21]

Counterterrorism Engagement

Another key security engagement between the United States and partner nations is in counterterrorism, particularly after 9/11. US counterterrorist engagements involve many interagency players— State, Defense, USAID, law enforcement and intelligence, Commerce, Treasury, and others. In 2005 Rep. Edward Royce (R-CA), chair of the House International Relations Subcommittee on International Terrorism and Nonproliferation, stated,

> While [military] train and equip programming is important, combating terrorism requires many tools, including development assistance and diplomacy. The potential implications of security assistance include its impact on the rule of law and on human rights, and these need to be constantly considered. . . . A good public relations campaign must be waged, too. When we are sending troops into countries, even just to train, it is critical that we couple it with a very good explanation, an explanation that will resonate with the locals, of what we are doing and why we are doing it.[22]

One example of a US interagency regional program is the Trans-Sahara Counterterrorism Partnership. The State Department's Bureau of African Affairs is the USG program lead, and other key players include the USAID, the DOD, and other elements of the DOS. However, interagency unity of effort remains a challenge. In a 2008 study, the GAO concluded that these agencies "had not developed a comprehensive, integrated strategy for the program's implementation." It noted that "the State Department, USAID, and DOD had developed separate plans related to their respective program activities that reflect some interagency collaboration. . . . [but that] these plans did not incorporate all of the desirable characteristics" for interagency unity of effort.[23]

The GAO also found that "roles and responsibilities—particularly between the DOS and the DOD—were unclear with regard to authority over DOD personnel temporarily assigned to conduct certain program activities in African countries." For example, in 2007 the DOD suspended most of its counterterrorist activities in Niger after the US ambassador limited the number of personnel who could enter the country. Although the DOD was highly critical of the ruling, the ambassador was considering the larger diplomatic issue of the country's fragile political environment, as well as the small US embassy's inability to support the large DOD contingent.[24]

The GAO also found interagency coordination between State and the US law enforcement community was lacking, remarking that "the State Department office responsible for coordinating law enforcement agencies' role in combating terrorism had not developed or implemented an overarching plan to use the combined capabilities of U.S. law enforcement agencies to assist foreign nations to identify, disrupt, and prosecute terrorists." It further noted that "the national strategies related to this effort lacked clearly defined roles and responsibilities."[25] The GAO reported that in one unnamed country "lack of clear roles and responsibilities led two law enforcement agencies, which were unknowingly working with different foreign law enforcement agencies, to move in on the same subject. According to foreign and US law enforcement officials, such actions may have compromised other investigations." The agency also noted, "Because the national strategies related to this effort did not clarify specific roles, among other issues, law enforcement agencies were not being fully used abroad to protect US citizens and interests from future terrorist attacks."[26]

The DOS office in Washington responsible for ensuring interagency coordination in developing, coordinating, and implementing US counterterrorism policy is the coordinator for counterterrorism. William Pope, then acting coordinator for counterterrorism, told Congress in March 2005, "In Washington, the Secretary of State, with assistance from my office, must continue to coordinate overseas counterterrorism assistance. In our missions overseas, the more nuanced work of ensuring collaboration among various members of the country team is and must remain the responsibility of the Chief of Mission."[27]

However, the necessary coordination is often not occurring. EUCOM's Tallent told Congress at the same March 2005 hearing that whole-of-government cooperation on counterterrorism is "one of the greatest challenges we have. . . . A sanctuary that we offer [terrorists] is our inability to work in an interagency approach in the time required to get the job done." He pointed out challenges to effective civil-military unity of effort in counterterrorism engagement, saying the "State Department does not have the same mechanisms and doctrine for planning that we have. . . . There are some culture problems.

There are some tool/equipment problems. There are procedural problems. All of this together is stifling our ability, I think, to do very quick interagency agreed-upon plans in this fight on terrorism."[28]

Response to Disaster or Humanitarian Crisis

With deterrence of the Soviet Union no longer the US military's primary raison d'être after the Cold War, evolving to other missions caused an increased use of military assets in response to foreign disasters or humanitarian crises. Over time, the US military has developed institutional expertise in humanitarian relief, and many of its exercises—such as PACOM's bilateral Cobra Gold with the Thai military—have humanitarian relief components. In 1995 the military began leading interagency exercises and discussions to create a standing US concept for response to such events, but no consistent model has yet been developed.[29]

Media reports on recent US responses to disasters or humanitarian crises tend to focus on the military component, despite the fact that the USAID's Office of Foreign Disaster Assistance is the lead agency for such events. Because the military is frequently the first US responder on the scene, with vastly more personnel and equipment than any other agency, it is often the most visible part of the response.

The 26 December 2004 Asian tsunami provides a good example of current interagency semicoordinated response to humanitarian crises. This tsunami stretched across South Asia and the coast of Africa and required "the largest humanitarian relief and recovery operation the world has ever seen in the wake of a natural disaster." The US response began within hours; however, the US government lacked a coherent, formalized, interagency approach, so the USAID, the State Department, the military, and other federal agencies each began responding individually using its own procedures.[30]

The military response was led by PACOM, which quickly put its joint operations center (JOC) on 24/7 operations and established a joint task force it called Combined Support Force (CSF) 536 to conduct military humanitarian response operations. While *combined* in a unit designation generally refers to a coalition military operation, CSF 536 never exercised operational control over non-US military forces responding in the region, though much of the international military effort relied on the robust command, control, and communications capabilities it provided. CSF 536 in turn established subordinate combined support groups (CSG) for each country where significant military forces responded to support the ambassador and US country team in that country. At the peak of the operation, over 17,000 US military personnel, 17 ships, and more than 170 aircraft were involved.[31]

Because many disasters substantially disrupt local transportation and communication infrastructure, one of the most urgent tasks of the relief effort is to restore these services. The CSGs executed search and rescue operations, transported and distributed relief supplies, provided emergency transportation, and contributed to the overall assessment of the disaster. Military involvement ends relatively early—once logistics and transportation infrastructures begin to recover, and local governments, NGOs, and other nonmilitary agencies reach increasing capability—but other agencies may be engaged for many months or even years.[32]

The USAID also responded quickly to the disaster. Its OFDA sent disaster assistance response teams (DART) to the affected countries, together with "culturally proficient experts" to act as liaisons with the host government and local population. Their first mission was to assess the impact so that relief assistance could be tailored for each country's needs and the ability of the local infrastructure to accept aid. Because of the vastness of the affected area, the OFDA trained US special operations forces and Marine units to augment the DARTs. It also sent a two-person team to PACOM to act as a liaison between PACOM, OFDA headquarters in Washington, and the DARTs in the field.[33]

In each affected country, the US ambassador acted as overall coordinator of US efforts. Many of the embassies had a disaster contingency plan in place for their country, which gave the State Department a starting place. Once the disaster occurred, the embassies developed disaster relief coordination mechanisms with the host government, other diplomatic missions in the country, local NGO and international organization representatives, and the US military. They also established status of forces agreements with the local governments, enabled smooth communication between the United States and the host nation, and facilitated the flow of US relief supplies through customs. Each embassy played a leading role in tailoring the US response to local requirements and the method by which the local government would accept foreign assistance.[34]

The State Department, the USAID, and PACOM formed an ad hoc cooperative arrangement to coordinate interagency policy in Washington, but it was assessed to be less effective than the regional-level coordination. At the regional level, PACOM provided interagency coordination by establishing a JIACG specifically for the disaster response. The two-person liaison team sent by the OFDA initially worked in this JIACG but soon moved to the PACOM JOC, where they were in a much better position to provide situational awareness to the military and fulfill their liaison role with Washington and the OFDA teams in the field. The disaster response JIACG experiment was not successful, as the emergency relief phase was largely over before it could get organized. However, the OFDA liaison team was very successful in fostering a high degree of mutual confidence among US interagency participants, thus leading to extensive cooperation in response operations.[35]

Despite the complications, the US response to the 2004 tsunami disaster is generally considered a success. The interagency coordination process worked well at the country level in the various embassies, the regional military response was effective, and the USAID's OFDA played its key role, though coordination of these efforts across the region was ad hoc. For single-country disasters, this may be good enough, but disasters that affect several countries benefit from a regionally coordinated response. While there is no formal interagency doctrine, process, or organization above the embassy level for US disaster response operations, PACOM's long experience in humanitarian relief planning, exercises, and operations—many times in concert with local partner countries and other US agencies—in this case provided a starting point for the ad hoc regional interagency response to the disaster.[36]

Complex Contingency Operations

While it might seem that combat operations belong uniquely to the Defense Department, all US actions since the Korean War have involved combat that is either relatively brief followed by a much longer period of interagency stabilization and reconstruction or that is episodic and conducted in parallel with a variety of interagency COIN operations. Such activities are often termed *complex contingency operations*. Five case studies—the 1964–73 Vietnam War, the

1989–90 regime change operation in Panama, the 1994–95 regime change operation in Haiti, the 2003–11 operations in Iraq, and the ongoing operations in Afghanistan—illustrate the complexity of achieving interagency unity of effort in such actions. All but the first occurred after the Goldwater-Nichols Act brought the military services together in a joint team, and thus provide the best examples of how the current civil-military system works during conflict operations. The Vietnam case is included because of lessons offered by the unique civil-military structure devised to facilitate unity of effort in that COIN operation.

Vietnam (1964–73)

Initially, US involvement in Vietnam occurred entirely within individual agency (as well as individual military service) "stovepipes." The military focused at first on providing advisors and training to the South Vietnamese military and later on direct military operations. Meanwhile, US civilian agencies—including the State Department, CIA, USAID, Department of Agriculture, and US Information Service—each separately pursued its own agendas, which grew to include many programs we would today call "reconstruction and stabilization," as well as COIN activities such as "pacification." Each agency operated separately in Washington, at the military headquarters and embassy in Saigon, and at the provincial level across South Vietnam. Though the US ambassador in Saigon was nominally in charge of civilian agencies operating in South Vietnam, he did not have the span of control to effectively supervise and coordinate all the activities with their separate agency budgets, lines of authority, and divergent institutional cultures. While the commander of the US Military Assistance Command–Vietnam (MACV) met regularly with the ambassador, coordination between military and civilian efforts was frequently lacking, and neither the MACV commander nor the ambassador had full authority over US efforts in the country.[37]

As US involvement continued to expand, programs grew in size and complexity, and the initially poor interagency coordination worsened. In 1967 the president, secretary of defense, and JCS created the office of Civil Operations and Revolutionary (later "Rural") Development Support (CORDS) to establish unity of command.[38] Civil development efforts previously supervised by the US Embassy in Saigon were integrated under MACV, placing both military operations and civilian development activities under the MACV commander, subject to the overall authority of the US ambassador (though in practice the MACV commander reported to PACOM, and disputes with the embassy were often elevated to Washington, diminishing the ambassador's de facto authority over MACV).[39] The civilian director of CORDS held ambassadorial rank equivalent to a four-star general and exercised control over all interagency assets involved in the counterinsurgency effort. In a significant organization innovation, the CORDS director was dual-hatted as a deputy to the MACV commander, ranking this civilian third in the US military chain of command in Vietnam, behind the MACV commander and military deputy.[40] The MACV-CORDS construct is shown in figure 9.

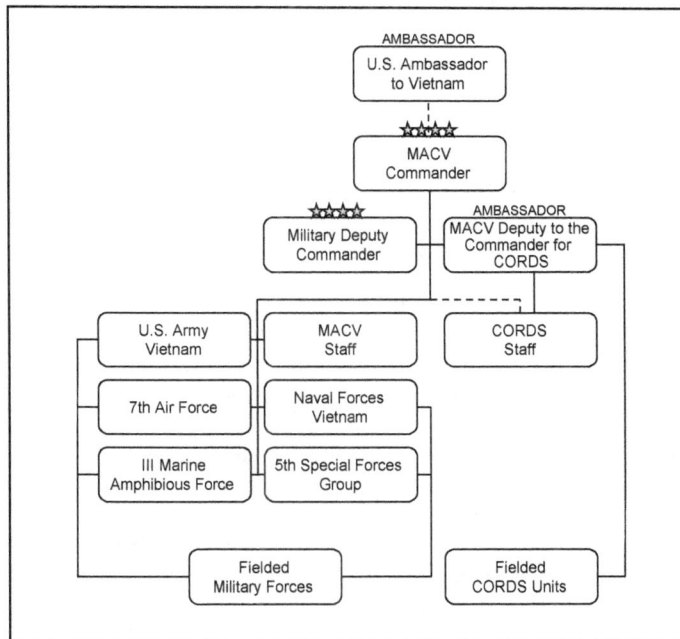

Figure 9. MACV-CORDS organizational structure. (Robert S. Pope, "Interagency Task Forces: The Right Tools for the Job," *Strategic Studies Quarterly* 5, no. 2 (Summer 2011): 116.)

This construct represents the first time a US ambassador operated in the chain of command under a general officer. It not only brought together the civilian COIN operations under a single leader but also integrated civilian and military COIN efforts. Additionally, the CORDS director's position in the military chain of command gave the civilian COIN leader regular access to the military commander and provided the civilian COIN effort access to military personnel, logistics, equipment, and funding. From the headquarters down through the provinces and hamlets, the CORDS structure was an integrated civil-military organization.[41] Richard Stewart, chief historian of the US Army Center for Military History, writes:

> Military personnel were . . . put in charge of civilians [and] civilians were . . . put in charge of military personnel to create a truly mixed, interagency team based on skills and abilities, not agency loyalty. . . . When a senior civilian was assigned to a key . . . position, almost invariably he had a military assistant reporting to him and the reverse was true when a military officer was in the principal slot. This blending of military and civilian authority included the use of the power of personnel evaluation or rating authority.[42]

While the creation of the integrated civil-military COIN organization vastly improved interagency unity of effort, developing and maintaining the organization faced significant bureaucratic hurdles. While the military was generally supportive of the CORDS construct, civilian agencies were less so.[43] Stewart notes that

> presidential leadership proved vital in overcoming the single greatest obstacle to mission success—the reluctance of Washington officials and senior leaders in the field to relinquish control over field operations. The State Department . . . resisted the idea that any of its development or pacification assets should fall under a military chain of command, even one headed by a civilian. Even after several broad hints from the [Johnson] administration, a presidential intervention was needed to change their minds.[44]

Once CORDS was established, its director had to continually fight Washington-based bureaucratic attempts to reduce its funding, shrink its structure, limit its scope, and keep additional programs from coming under its control.[45] This bureaucratic resistance to formal interagency command structures is probably the reason we have not seen more structures like CORDS in the decades after Vietnam. While it produced unity of effort through unity of command and solved the problem of resource asymmetries between military and civilian agencies by providing the latter access to military resources, the civilian agencies were never comfortable with the arrangement.[46]

Panama: Operations Just Cause and Promote Liberty (1989–90)

The 1989–90 US regime-change operation against Panamanian leader Manuel Noriega illustrates a lack of unity of effort, particularly in planning for postconflict operations. Beginning in 1987, SOUTHCOM developed two contingency plans for Panama: a combat plan (Operation Just Cause) and a postconflict reconstruction and stabilization plan (Operation Promote Liberty). These plans underwent extensive revision and military analysis in 1988 and 1989, but they were not coordinated with other US agencies.[47] According to a study by the Defense Science Board, the SOUTHCOM commander focused on the combat plan, while the postconflict plan received little attention from senior military officers in either SOUTHCOM or Washington.[48]

Postconflict operations primarily involve activities such as law enforcement, reestablishment of civil government, and other important reconstruction and stabilization tasks largely outside the military's core competencies. Yet for reasons of operational security, SOUTHCOM prohibited military planners from discussing the Promote Liberty postconflict plan with the US Embassy in Panama, even though they envisioned that the embassy would take the lead role in postconflict operations. Planners assumed that the US military would run operations in Panama for 30 days after removing Noriega and then turn that function over to the embassy.[49] However, as tensions between the United States and Panama increased prior to the invasion, the State Department reduced the embassy staff "to a single chargé d'affaires and a couple of clerks," but due to the lack of planner-level coordination, the military did not know this.[50] Strangely, when the secretary of state was informed of the postconflict timeline three days prior to the invasion, he did not object.[51]

Immediately after the 20 December 1989 invasion, civil authority in Panama collapsed, and looting and civil disorder were rampant. On the day of the invasion, the SOUTHCOM commander placed a civil-military operations task force under the control of the chargé d'affaires to try to get the country team operational again but with little immediate effect.[52]

In January 1990, two meetings involving 18 USG agencies were held to build the civilian interagency contribution to postconflict operations in Panama, but they failed to produce an effective plan or significant contributions from these agencies because they "resented being called in after the fact to solve what they saw as a self-induced 'military' mess."[53] The new US ambassador to Panama arrived in country two weeks after the initial assault with few resources and no effective interagency plan for stabilizing the country. On 17 January 1990, SOUTHCOM established a military support group (MSG) to act as part of the country team. The MSG's charter was to conduct stabilization and reconstruction activities including restoring public services, establishing internationally recognized standards of justice, and ensuring democracy.[54]

In February 1990, two months after the invasion, SOUTHCOM tasked the MSG to produce a coordinated interagency postconflict plan. The plan underwent two rounds of coordination with all appropriate agencies and was executed under embassy control as the first coordinated interagency plan for Panama since planning began in 1987. While there was now an approved interagency plan, only the military had the resources in place in Panama to execute it. Executing the plan did not truly become an interagency effort until six months after the invasion, and it took a full year after the invasion before the USAID began to fulfill its role. The delay was partially caused by Congress, which approved only half of the funds requested, and partly by the timing of other international events, such as the fall of the Berlin Wall, which distracted US foreign policy actors. As a result, many of the planned infrastructure, financial, and agricultural reforms never occurred, leading to the new Panamanian government's loss of faith in US commitments.[55]

There are several lessons learned from this operation. The military must not allow operational security concerns to exclude other key elements of the interagency from the planning process, particularly postconflict planning. By the same token, the rest of the interagency—which in this case was aware an operation was coming, if not its details—must not disengage and let the military do all of the planning. Finally, coordinated planning must start far enough before the operation to allow all interagency players time to get tactical plans, teams, and resources together, or the military will be alone in the country.

Haiti: Operation Uphold Democracy (1994–95)

The lessons learned from the Panama conflict seemingly went unheeded as the interagency embarked on the 1994–95 regime-change operation in Haiti to restore the elected president and government to power after a military coup. The GCC responsible for Haiti (US

Atlantic Command at the time) began planning in October 1993 for a military intervention in Haiti. Similar to Panama, the plan included a forced entry phase followed by postconflict operations. Also like the 1989–90 Panama operation, the military planners at the GCC excluded other agencies, claiming security concerns. Limited strategic-level interagency coordination took place in Washington, but operational-level planners were unaware of these agreements. The first comprehensive interagency coordination at the operational level occurred in September 1994, just a week prior to execution of Operation Uphold Democracy.[56]

A last-minute diplomatic effort eliminated the need to conduct the forcible entry operation, but once the United States reinstalled Haitian president Jean-Bertrand Aristide, civil order collapsed and the Haitian military began conducting violent actions against civilians. Despite the lessons learned from Panama just five years earlier, neither the US military nor civilian agencies had considered the dissolution of the Haitian security forces and the collapse of civil order. The US military was again surprised that civilian agencies were not immediately ready with state-building programs to strengthen the Haitian government and restore civilian law enforcement, so emergency restoration of essential services again fell to the military, the only US actors on the scene. Development planners on the civilian side were upset that the military did not wish to accept responsibility for the state-building efforts—responsibility assigned during strategic interagency discussions in Washington but not communicated to the operational military planners at the combatant command.[57] Despite increased planning by key civilian agencies such as the USAID and Department of Justice, civilian agencies were slow to build the resources necessary to conduct their agreed-upon development operations and often expected more support from the military than it had planned to provide.[58]

While more strategic-level coordination was done for Haiti than for the previous operation in Panama, interagency planning did not occur at the operational level, and the United States once again embarked on a complicated postconflict operation without an integrated plan. Once the process began, the military wanted very little to do with postconflict operations, but civilian agencies were again slow to arrive with the necessary capabilities. Little had changed in the interagency culture in the years since Panama.

Afghanistan: Operation Enduring Freedom (2001–Present)

Operation Enduring Freedom (OEF), the US-led invasion of Afghanistan after the 9/11 attacks, provides an example of what happens, at least initially, to interagency unity of effort when the United States has almost no time to plan operations—combat or postcombat. It also reveals additional challenges of bringing together the US interagency with a larger alliance structure, in this case the NATO International Security Assistance Force. Finally, more than 10 years of US operations in Afghanistan have provided an opportunity for a slow evolution of thinking about the need for more effective, formal coordination of the civil-military COIN campaign.

As OEF commenced in October 2001, initial coordination occurred only between the military and the intelligence community (primarily the CIA) for the rapid planning and execution of operations with minimum use of US forces against al-Qaeda and the Taliban-led government of Afghanistan. Once the Taliban regime was toppled and US forces were on the ground in Afghanistan, initial coordination between the military and the development and diplomatic communities was largely nonexistent as well.

On the diplomatic front, establishment of an international coalition for operations in Afghanistan was hampered by the different, uncoordinated approaches of Defense and State. State's diplomats set out to build the broadest coalition possible and develop the greatest possible international support and legitimacy for the operation, while DOD planners were interested only in militarily effective partners rather than in symbolic contributions. Failure to coordinate meant potential international partners received different messages based on whether they were talking to Defense or State, leading to frustration and reluctance of some nations to participate in stabilization efforts.[59]

On the development front, military planners at CENTCOM were concerned about an immediate crisis, the possibility of famine. They established a coalition joint civil-military operations task force (CJCMOTF)—collocated with the US military headquarters in Afghanistan and with a liaison cell at CENTCOM headquarters in Tampa—to coordinate between the military and humanitarian aid organizations. The CJCMOTF established a humanitarian affairs working group that included coalition military partners, the OFDA, an NGO umbrella organization called InterAction, and the UN. The CJCMOTF also established several humanitarian liaison cells in

Afghan cities to conduct tactical-level liaison with USAID and NGO representatives. While this effort provided some field-level coordination between the military and development communities, there was no effective strategic- or operational-level coordination between CENTCOM headquarters in Florida and USAID headquarters in Washington.[60]

The reestablishment in 2002 of a US embassy in Kabul with the first postinvasion ambassador to Afghanistan created an opportunity for increased civil-military coordination and unity of effort. However, this opportunity was largely wasted as the embassy pursued developmental efforts and the reestablishment of the Afghan government while the US military, under Army lieutenant generals Dan McNeill and John Vines, focused on the counterterrorist mission. General Vines was emphatic that the military mission was counterterrorism and not COIN or nation-building, going so far as to prohibit those under his command from using the word *counterinsurgency* to describe their efforts.[61]

US civil-military coordination in Afghanistan greatly improved in 2003–05 under the next US team in the country, Amb. Zalmay Khalilzad and LTG David Barno, US Army. General Barno believed in the importance of civil-military coordination to achieving US goals, so he moved his living quarters to the embassy compound in Kabul, established an office next to Khalilzad's, and attended daily country team meetings. He also provided the ambassador with five military planners to work with embassy personnel to form an interagency planning group and produce a coordinated US strategy for Afghanistan. The resulting strategy shifted the focus from counterterrorism to COIN and nation-building, creating two regional headquarters to direct all coalition actions in each region and successfully conduct elections, reduce violence, and begin reconstruction.[62]

However, the Khalilzad/Barno civil-military coordination was personality driven and was in no way formalized or directed by either legislation or presidential executive order. When they were replaced in 2005 by Amb. Ronald Neumann and LTG Karl Eikenberry, US Army, the civil-military cooperation effectively ended. General Eikenberry returned the military's focus to counterterrorist kill-or-capture operations, increasing civilian casualties and consequently creating a steep decline in Afghan popular support for the United States.[63] Political scientist and Afghanistan expert Seth Jones concludes that this "effectively shatter[ed] the military-civilian coordination

Khalilzad and Barno had painstakingly fashioned during their tenure together,"[64] and Senator John McCain said that "between late 2003 and early 2004, we were moving on the right path in Afghanistan, [but] rather than building on these gains . . . we squandered them. Beginning in 2004, our integrated civil-military command structure was disassembled and replaced by a balkanized and dysfunctional arrangement."[65]

In 2007 the Neumann/Eikenberry team was replaced by Amb. William Wood (2007–09) and GEN Dan McNeill, USA (2007–08), followed by GEN David McKiernan, USA (2008–09). During this period, civil-military relations continued largely as they had under Neumann and Eikenberry, with the military primarily focused on kinetic counterterrorism operations and training the Afghan National Army, while civilian agencies worked independently on diplomatic and developmental goals. In early 2009, late in General McKiernan's tour, the United States began moving once again toward more civil-military coordination with the creation of the Executive Working Group (EWG), which each month brings together the in-country principals from State, the USAID, and the DOD to discuss civilian and military plans and operations and attempt to synchronize interagency efforts. The high-level EWG is supported by a working-level interagency staff called the Integrated Civilian Military Action Group (ICMAG), staffed by DOS personnel from S/CRS, USAID personnel, and US military personnel from the Regional Command East and ISAF.[66]

Many have been critical of the ad hoc nature of US civil-military coordination in Afghanistan. An April 2008 report from the House Armed Services Committee said, "Rather than depending exclusively on personalities for success, the right interagency structures and processes need to be in place and working."[67] A former senior military commander in Afghanistan said in early 2009 that the most serious challenge the United States faces there is "not the Taliban. It's not governance. It's not security. . . . It's the utter failure in the unity of effort department."[68] In April 2009, Secretary of Defense Robert Gates expressed his lack of satisfaction with General McKiernan's civil-military coordination efforts, saying the NATO ISAF commander needed to focus on "cooperation between civil and military efforts."[69]

The US leadership in Afghanistan changed again, with now-retired lieutenant general Karl Eikenberry becoming ambassador on 29 April 2009 and US Army general Stanley McChrystal becoming the NATO ISAF and USFOR-A commander on 15 June 2009. Under direction from Washington, the new team quickly set out to develop an integrated civil-military plan. They assembled a planning team led by the S/CRS and including other US civilian agencies as well as both USFOR-A and ISAF. On 10 August 2009, they released the *United States Government Integrated Civilian-Military Campaign Plan for Support to Afghanistan* under both of their signatures.[70]

Under the new plan, the United States created an integrated civil-military decision-making structure at all levels in Afghanistan. Several interagency groups work at the national level in Kabul. The Principals Group, consisting of the ambassador and the commanding general of ISAF and USFOR-A, is responsible for final coordination and decision making. The EWG, with interagency members from the embassy, USFOR-A, and US forces from ISAF, is a deputies-level body to make policy and decisions. A national-level working group for each "transformative effect" in the campaign plan monitors and assesses progress toward each desired effect. The Pol-Mil section of the embassy provides planning and assessment support for the EWG and national-level working groups. Also, embassy civilians have reorganized along functional rather than agency lines.[71]

In the field, the USG created civilian lead positions at the regional commands, at each subregional brigade task force, and for each province. These civilian leads coordinate the activities of all US civilians in Afghanistan at their level and subordinate levels who operate under the ambassador's authority. They also serve as the civilian counterpart to the military commander at that organizational level. This dual role as the leader of US interagency civilians and counterpart to the US military commander is intended to produce civil-military unity of effort at each level. Each region has also established a Regional Integrated Team consisting of the regional commander, the US special operations forces commander for that region, the civilian lead, and representatives from US agencies operating in the region. Each regional command also has a civil-military fusion cell responsible for maintaining a common operating picture of the region. Similar civil-military entities operate at the subregional, provincial, and district levels.[72] These structures have remained relatively consistent under subsequent USFOR-A/ISAF commanders GEN David Petraeus, USA (4 July 2010–18 July 2011), and Gen John R. Allen, USMC (18 July 2011–10 February 2013), and Amb. Ryan Crocker (25 July 2011–present). In addition, General Petraeus established the three previously described CJIATFs focused on interagency counternarcotics and rule-of-law issues. The past and current US organizational structures in Afghanistan are shown in figure 10.

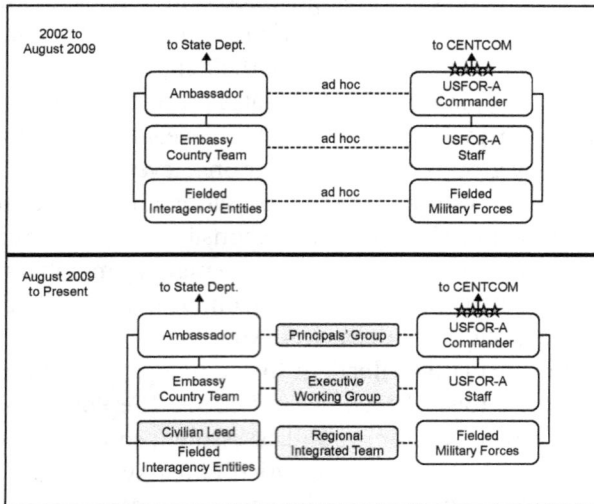

Figure 10. Past and current US organizational structure in Afghanistan
(Pope, "Interagency Task Forces," 127.)

While this parallel civilian-military organizational structure is the closest civil-military coordination the United States has produced in more than 10 years of operations in Afghanistan, it still falls short of the truly integrated CORDS structure employed in Vietnam. Dr. Christopher Lamb, acting director of the National Defense University's Institute for National Strategic Studies, and Dr. Martin Cinnamond, who worked in a number of UN positions in Afghanistan in 2007 and 2008, call the new structure "insufficient," saying, "It calls for parallel chains of command with coordination at every level. Historically, however, the way to ensure civil-military cooperation is to formally integrate the military and civilian chains of command."[73]

Iraq: Operations Iraqi Freedom and New Dawn (2003–11)

Unlike OEF, the United States controlled the timing of the Iraq invasion and should have had plenty of time to develop a coordinated postconflict plan. However, politics between the DOD and other US agencies (and lack of presidential orders to do so) prevented this. Planning for postconflict operations should have begun as early as 1998 when Congress passed the Iraq Liberation Act declaring that "it should be the policy of the United States to support efforts to remove the regime headed by Saddam Hussein from power."[74] CENTCOM began planning for military operations long before this, while the State Department began postconflict planning in October 2001 and the USAID in September 2002.

The postconflict plan actually implemented, however, came from the Pentagon. The DOD laid some groundwork shortly after the 9/11 terrorist attacks but did not start planning for postconflict operations until just two months before the start of OIF, when Pres. George W. Bush assigned it the lead for postwar planning and execution in Iraq.[75] On 20 January 2003, the DOD created the Office of Reconstruction and Humanitarian Assistance (ORHA) and named retired Army lieutenant general Jay Garner as its head. Garner and his staff— initially three or four people, increasing to nearly 200 by mid-March—developed the postwar plan. Several sources indicate that senior DOD leaders deliberately rejected interagency planning and coordination and prohibited the ORHA from incorporating the State Department's postwar plan or even hiring personnel who had been part of the DOS planning process.[76]

Garner and the interagency ORHA team arrived in Baghdad on 20 April 2003 and began implementing their postconflict reconstruction and stabilization plan. Organizationally, the ORHA was subordinate to CENTCOM's combined forces land component commander (CFLCC), so the military forces in Iraq and the interagency postconflict team were in the same chain of command. However, almost immediately after the ORHA arrived in Baghdad, Washington determined that its postwar plan was inadequate for the situation on the ground. The organization and its leader were quickly replaced with a more robust interagency organization led by a diplomat rather than a retired general.

On 12 May 2003, President Bush appointed Amb. L. Paul Bremer III as a presidential envoy to lead the new interagency effort in Iraq, the Coalition Provisional Authority (CPA), which both led the reconstruction and stabilization operation and acted as the occupation government until the United States returned sovereignty to Iraq in 2004. While many observers at the time saw the replacement of a retired general with an ambassador as an indication that influence over the occupation was shifting from the DOD to State, the CPA continued to fall under the DOD.[77] However, instead of reporting to CENT-COM forces in Iraq, the CPA bypassed both the military commander on the ground and CENTCOM headquarters in Tampa, reporting directly to the secretary of defense. Office of Management and Budget (OMB) director Mitch Daniels told Congress this change meant that CENTCOM now supported the CPA's reconstruction efforts rather than the ORHA working in support of CENTCOM's efforts.[78]

In practice, the CPA and the military operated in a largely uncoordinated dual reporting chain, eliminating the unity of command that had briefly existed when the ORHA had been subordinate to CENT-COM's CFLCC. Further complicating matters, because Bremer was a presidential envoy, he had lines of communication to the president, vice president, secretary of state, and national security advisor.[79] Since the CPA and the military reported separately to the secretary of defense, they often proceeded with different goals and assumptions. Lt Gen Ricardo Sanchez, USA, focused on COIN operations and the hunt for Saddam Hussein rather than on stabilization and reconstruction, and the CPA focused on stabilization and reconstruction, often lacking access to military resources required to get the job done.[80] During the year the CPA was in Iraq, Ambassador Bremer and General Sanchez "met often but never established procedures for anything more than ad hoc policy coordination."[81] The lack of coordination caused delays in security and logistics, which meant the CPA lacked a significant presence outside Baghdad for many months during the critical early phase of the occupation. Military commanders across Iraq were left to fill the void by developing their own policies on governance and other civilian matters in their areas of operation, making the CPA's job even more difficult because it had to reconcile these various systems established and promises made into a single coherent policy.

Interagency coordination was also problematic below the level of senior military and DOS leadership in Baghdad. Foreign Service officer James Stephenson, who headed the USAID's Iraq mission, reflects,

> During the first year of post-conflict operations, military-civilian coordination in civil affairs at the policy level was virtually nonexistent. U.S. forces had [adequate funds]. Accordingly, commanders had less incentive to approach executing agencies for assistance. Although [USAID] reached out to the civil affairs commander at [Combined Joint Task Force-7 (CJTF-7), later Multinational Force-Iraq (MNF-I)], and he to us, meaningful cooperation was ad hoc and generally occurred only at the operational level.[82]

Even when the military in the field did attempt better coordination with civilian agencies, the CPA sometimes did not respond. For example, MG Peter Chiarelli, commanding general of the Army's 1st Cavalry Division, with responsibility for Baghdad, wanted a close working relationship with the USAID. Stephenson and Chiarelli met with Ambassador Bremer to gain the necessary funding, but while Bremer "enthusiastically supported" their plans, the CPA took no action to provide the necessary funding for a coordinated military-USAID program in Baghdad.[83]

On 28 June 2004, the United States transferred sovereignty back to the Iraqi government. At that time, the CPA was disbanded and replaced with a US embassy and interagency country team led by Amb. John Negroponte, who took over leadership for civilian-run stabilization and reconstruction operations in Iraq. At this point, the embassy led the interagency effort and reported to the State Department, while military operations, now under GEN George Casey, USA, continued to report to the DOD through CENTCOM. Ambassador Negroponte's and General Casey's offices were collocated, and they attempted to coordinate their actions and those of their staffs, but they continued to report to separate cabinet secretaries with neither subordinate to the other.[84] Therefore, Washington politics sometimes intruded, as in March 2005 when Defense Secretary Donald Rumsfeld became furious because General Casey shared his strategy to accelerate the training of Iraqi army and police with Ambassador Negroponte and the embassy staff in Baghdad, who shared it with State Department officials in Washington before Rumsfeld received it for his approval through DOD channels.[85]

In the summer of 2005, General Casey tasked a colonel on his staff to produce a study grading the Iraq war effort to date. The report said the military commander in Iraq needed control of all aspects of the COIN campaign, including economic and political development, and recommended a model similar to the CORDS structure used in Vietnam in which the civilian in charge of development was dual-hatted as a deputy to the military commander. General Casey shared the suggestion with CENTCOM commander GEN John Abizaid, USA, and Secretary Rumsfeld but decided not to pursue it, saying, "I made the judgment that it was going to take an awful lot of energy to get it done and the likelihood of success was low."[86] At that time, the State Department was proposing to deploy a few hundred FSOs to provincial reconstruction teams to conduct development work in each of

Iraq's 18 provinces. Casey decided this was a reasonable first step, and his goal was to get the DOS to do more rather than take control of the economic and development aspects of the counterinsurgency.[87] From 2005 through the end of Operation New Dawn (OND) in 2011, the United States maintained essentially the same parallel structure in Iraq, with the military commander reporting to the DOD through CENTCOM and the ambassador leading the interagency country team and reporting to the secretary of state, while the commander and ambassador coordinated in an ad hoc manner.

OIF and OND demonstrate that even with adequate time for interagency planning, the lack of a formal, mandated process allows bureaucratic politics to prevent unity of effort, or even rudimentary coordination, during the planning phase. During 10 years of postconflict operations, the United States has maintained separate civilian and military chains of command, hampering unity of effort. Air Force Secretary Michael Donley concluded,

> The status of interagency decision makers (such as Ambassador Bremer in Iraq) complicates the authority of senior departmental and agency officials in Washington and the reporting chain of departmental personnel operating in the field. For example, when the U.S. creates an organization such as the Coalition Provisional Authority (CPA), originally established under DOD but ultimately composed of officials from across the U.S. government, are the key decision makers in the agency reporting to the President, to the head of a "lead department," or to their own agency head? To what extent can the head of such an agency coordinate and direct the use of all U.S. resources? This problem is especially important for the State Department, in which the U.S. ambassador is supposed to be the President's senior representative in a given country; and for DOD, which has a well-defined military chain of command which does not include ambassadors.[88]

In a 2009 study, the GAO assessed that "multiple U.S. agencies—including the State Department, USAID, and DOD—led separate efforts to improve the capacity of Iraq's ministries to govern, without overarching direction from a lead entity to integrate their efforts." It concluded that "the lack of an overarching strategy contributed to U.S. efforts not meeting their goal of key Iraqi ministries having the capacity to effectively govern and assume increasing responsibilities for operating, maintaining, and further investing in reconstruction projects."[89]

As these peacetime theater engagement, humanitarian relief, and wartime cases demonstrate, the United States can generally claim success in its interagency foreign endeavors, but it is often costly in resources, time, and foreign goodwill as the various elements of the interagency fail to work together in a synchronized manner.

Notes

1. USJFCOM, *Commander's Handbook for the Joint Interagency Coordination Group*, IV-9; RADM Hamlin Tallent, EUCOM director of operations, quoted in US House of Representatives, *Eliminating Terrorist Sanctuaries: The Role of Security Assistance—Hearing before the Subcommittee on International Terrorism and Nonproliferation of the Committee on International Relations*, 109th Cong., 1st sess., 10 March 2005, serial no. 109-19, 19; and COL Thomas M. Rhatican, USAR, "Redefining Security Cooperation: New Limits on Phase Zero and 'Shaping,' " strategy research project (Carlisle Barracks, PA: Army War College, 15 March 2008), 7.

2. JP 3-0, *Doctrine for Joint Operations*, 17 September 2006 (incorporating chg. 1, 13 February 2008), IV-26.

3. Rhatican, "Redefining Security Cooperation," 5–6.

4. Ibid., 17–18.

5. Ibid., 6.

6. Ibid., 7.

7. GAO, *Interagency Collaboration*, 24–25.

8. Albert Zaccor, *Security Cooperation and Non-State Threats: A Call for an Integrated Strategy*, occasional paper (Washington, DC: Atlantic Council of the United States, August 2005), 7. See also Rhatican, "Redefining Security Cooperation," i.

9. Thomas E. Johnson Jr., "Working It Out with the Military: The View from Kabul," *Foreign Service Journal* 84, no. 6 (June 2007): 15.

10. Ibid.

11. Senate, *Embassies as Command Posts*, 7.

12. GAO, *Interagency Collaboration*, 28.

13. Nina M. Serafino, *Section 1206 of the National Defense Authorization Act for FY2006: A Fact Sheet on Department of Defense Authority to Train and Equip Foreign Military Forces*, CRS Report RS22855 (Washington, DC: CRS, 28 September 2009).

14. LTC Thomas P. Galvin, USA, takes the other side of the security cooperation debate, arguing that the military needs *more* authority and *more* focus on this area. He notes, "Unity of effort suffers due to a number of factors . . . including budgetary restrictions, lack of interagency transparency, mismatched authorities and responsibilities, slow responsiveness, and outmoded legislation." Additionally, he criticizes the military "cultural mindset that relegates [security cooperation] . . . to secondary status behind traditional military [activities]." He contends that while the DOD has given security cooperation and Phase Zero responsibilities to the COCOMs, they lack the necessary authority because the State Department "controls most of the resources under Title 22 through the Foreign Assistance Act." Galvin says another problem is the lack of a "peer regional authority" to the COCOM at State "to discuss and solve regional disputes." Yet another problem is congressional legislation that "interferes" with security cooperation planning and execution. He praises §1206 funding and recommends that Congress continue to expand this funding line for security cooperation activities. LTC Thomas P. Galvin, USA, "Extending the Phase Zero Campaign Mindset: Ensuring Unity of Effort," *Joint Force Quarterly* 45 (2nd Quarter 2007): 46–50.

15. Rhatican, "Redefining Security Cooperation," 12.

16. Ibid., 12–13; and Senate, *Embassies as Command Posts*.

17. Rhatican, "Redefining Security Cooperation," 13–14.

18. House, *Eliminating Terrorist Sanctuaries*, 20.

19. EUCOM was assigned responsibility for most of the countries in Africa prior to the establishment of AFRICOM in 2008.

20. House, *Eliminating Terrorist Sanctuaries*, 21.

21. Ibid., 24, 30.

22. Ibid., 2.

23. GAO, *Interagency Collaboration*, 13–14.

24. Ibid., 14.

25. Ibid.

26. Ibid.

27. House, *Eliminating Terrorist Sanctuaries*, 13.

28. Ibid., 32–33.

29. Gary W. Anderson, " 'Interagency Overseas': Responding to the 2004 Indian Ocean Tsunami," in *Mismanaging Mayhem: How Washington Responds to Crisis*, ed. James Jay Carafano and Richard Weitz (Westport, CT: Praeger Security International, 2008), 194, 203.

30. Ibid., 193–94, 202.

31. Ibid., 195–96, 202.

32. Ibid., 195, 197–98, 202.

33. Ibid., 195, 204.

34. Ibid., 196, 198, 203.

35. Ibid., 195, 203.

36. Ibid., 194–95, 200.

37. Richard W. Stewart, "Winning Hearts and Minds: The Vietnam Experience," in *Mismanaging Mayhem*, ed. James Jay Carafano and Richard Weitz, 90. Stewart is the chief historian of the US Army Center of Military History.

38. Ibid.; and MAJ Ross M. Coffey, USA, "Improving Interagency Integration at the Operational Level: CORDS—A Model for the Advanced Civilian Team," monograph (Fort Leavenworth, KS: School of Advanced Military Studies, US Army Command and General Staff College, 25 May 2006), 24.

39. MG George S. Eckhardt, USA, *Vietnam Studies: Command and Control, 1950–1969* (Washington, DC: Department of the Army, 1991), 27, 29, 48, 69.

40. Coffey, "Improving Interagency Integration at the Operational Level," 19, 24.

41. Ibid., 24, 26; and Stewart, "Winning Hearts and Minds," 90–91.

42. Stewart, "Winning Hearts and Minds," 94.

43. Coffey, "Improving Interagency Integration at the Operational Level," 28–29.

44. Stewart, "Winning Hearts and Minds," 105–6.

45. Ibid., 106.

46. Coffey, "Improving Interagency Integration at the Operational Level," 4. See also John T. Fishel, "The Interagency Arena at the Operational Level: The Cases Now Known as Stability Operations," in *Affairs of State*, ed. Gabriel Marcella, 420–21.

47. Curry, "Interagency Process in Regional Foreign Policy," 23.

48. Office of the Under Secretary of Defense for Acquisition, Technology, and Logistics (OSD/ATL), *Defense Science Board 2004 Summer Study on Transition to and from Hostilities: Supporting Papers* (Washington, DC: OSD, January 2005), 11.

49. Curry, "Interagency Process in Regional Foreign Policy," 23.

50. OSD/ATL, *Defense Science Board 2004 Summer Study: Supporting Papers*, 12–13.

51. Curry, "Interagency Process in Regional Foreign Policy," 24.

52. Ibid., 27–28.

53. Ibid., 28.

54. Ibid., 24–25, 28.

55. Ibid., 28–29, 31–32.

56. Maj Stephen A. Clark, USAF, "Interagency Coordination: Strengthening the Link between Operational Art and the Desired End State," research report (Newport, RI: Naval War College, 8 February 1999), 10–11.

57. Ibid., 12–13.

58. Lt Col Ted T. Uchida, USAF, "Reforming the Interagency Process," Air Force Fellows research report (Maxwell AFB, AL: Air Force Fellows, May 2005), 33. Colonel Uchida was a 2004–05 Air Force Fellow at the Ridgeway Center for International Security Studies and Graduate School of Public and International Affairs, University of Pittsburgh.

59. Bensahel and Moisan, "Repairing the Interagency Process," 106.

60. Patrick N. Kelleher, "Crossing Boundaries: Interagency Cooperation and the Military," *Joint Force Quarterly* 32 (Autumn 2002): 108.

61. Seth Jones, *In the Graveyard of Empires: America's War in Afghanistan* (New York: W. W. Norton, 2009), 142.

62. Ibid., 139; and USJFCOM, *Insights and Best Practices: Interagency, Intergovernmental, and Nongovernmental Coordination: A Joint Force Operational Perspective*, Focus Paper no. 3 (Norfolk, VA: Joint Warfighting Center, July 2007), 13, http://jko.cmil.org/file/109/view.

63. Christopher J. Lamb and Martin Cinnamond, "Unified Effort: Key to Special Operations and Irregular Warfare in Afghanistan," *Joint Force Quarterly* 56 (1st Quarter 2010): 44.

64. Jones, *In the Graveyard of Empires*, 150.

65. Lamb and Cinnamond, "Unified Effort," 43–44.

66. Joshua W. Welle, "Civil-Military Integration in Afghanistan: Creating Unity of Command," *Joint Force Quarterly* 56 (1st Quarter 2010): 56. LT Joshua Welle, USN, was a civil-military planner for ISAF Regional Command South from November 2008 to August 2009.

67. House Armed Services Committee, Oversight and Investigations Subcommittee, *Agency Stovepipes vs. Strategic Agility: Lessons We Need to Learn from Provincial Reconstruction Teams in Iraq and Afghanistan*, Committee print 8 (Washington, DC: Government Printing Office, 2008), 32.

68. Greg Bruno, "Afghanistan's National Security Forces," Council on Foreign Relations Backgrounder, 16 April 2009, http://www.cfr.org/publication/19122/afghanistans_national_security_forces.html?breadcrumb=%2Fpublication%2Fby_type%2Fbackgrounder#2.

69. Secretary of Defense Robert M. Gates at a 13 April 2009 NATO Summit, quoted in Lamb and Cinnamond, "Unified Effort," 41.

70. Beth Cole and Emily Hsu, "Guiding Principles for Stability and Reconstruction: Introducing a New Roadmap for Peace," *Military Review* 90, no. 1 (January/February 2010): 15.

71. Karl W. Eikenberry and GEN Stanley McChrystal, USA, *United States Government Integrated Civilian-Military Campaign Plan for Support to Afghanistan* (Kabul,

Afghanistan: Embassy of the United States of America and US Forces Afghanistan, 10 August 2009), 29–30, ii.

72. Ibid., 28-30.

73. Lamb and Cinnamond, "Unified Effort," 50.

74. James Fallows, "Blind into Baghdad," *Atlantic Monthly* 293, no. 1 (January/February 2004): 54.

75. Maj Robert S. Pope, USAF, "Interagency Planning and Coordination for Stabilization and Reconstruction Operations," research report (Maxwell AFB, AL: Air Command and Staff College, April 2004), 8–9; and Johanna McGeary, "Looking beyond Saddam," *Time* 161, no. 10 (10 March 2003): 26–33. See also George Packer, "War after the War: Letter from Baghdad," *New Yorker*, 24 November 2003, 59–85, http://www.newyorker.com/fact/content/?031124fa_fact1.

76. Amb. Barbara K. Bodine, interview by the author, 9 February 2004. Ambassador Bodine served as the senior State Department member of the ORHA from January to May 2003. She stated,

> One reason for not much on planning for OHRA is there wasn't any . . . there was no planning, to be blunt. The issue is more complicated and depressing than that, however. There was a significant amount of planning—18 months or 2 years, $5 million dollars. It was chaired by State—the Project for the Future of Iraq—and managed by a gentleman named Tom Warrick. It was interagency, private sector, think tanks, NGOs, etc. It exhaustively examined what needed to be done, how to do it, etc. It involved 250 Iraqis—none with political ambitions. Problem is, OSD wanted nothing to do with it. So, it isn't that we didn't have a plan; it is we ignored the plan, and the planners.

See also Fallows, "Blind into Baghdad," 72; and David Rieff, "Blueprint for a Mess," *New York Times Magazine*, 2 November 2003, http://www.nytimes.com/2003/11/02/magazine/blueprint-for-a-mess.html?pagewanted=all&src=pm.

77. For example, see Andrew F. Tully, "Iraq: New U.S. Plan Seeks to Expedite Reconstruction," *Radio Free Europe/Radio Liberty*, 8 October 2003.

78. Mitchell E. Daniels Jr., director, US Office of Management and Budget (OMB), "Report to Congress Pursuant to Section 1506 of the Emergency Wartime Supplemental Appropriations Act, 2003 (Public Law 108-11)" (Washington, DC: OMB, 2 June 2003), 2.

79. See Amb. L. Paul Bremer III, *My Year in Iraq: The Struggle to Build a Future of Hope* (New York: Threshold Editions, 2006).

80. Ibid., 150.

81. Bensahel and Moisan, "Repairing the Interagency Process," 106.

82. Stephenson, "Military-Civilian Cooperation," 56.

83. Ibid., 56, 58.

84. Arnas, Barry, and Oakley, *Harnessing the Interagency*, 19; and Fishel, "Interagency Arena at the Operational Level," 431–33.

85. David Cloud and Greg Jaffe, *The Fourth Star: Four Generals and the Epic Struggle for the Future of the United States Army* (New York: Crown Publishers, 2009), 190–91.

86. Ibid., 201–4.

87. Ibid.

88. Michael Donley, *Rethinking the Interagency System*, pt. 2, Occasional Paper no. 05-02 (McLean, VA: Hicks & Associates, May 2005), 3.

89. GAO, *Interagency Collaboration*, 1–2.

Chapter 5

Options for Improvement

Since the passage of the Goldwater-Nichols DOD Reorganization Act of 1986, more than 100 major studies, books, articles, and professional military education (PME) student papers have addressed the topic of improving interagency unity of effort.[1] Many of these studies, particularly in the earlier years, focused on interagency problems and solutions at the strategic level in Washington. Following the 11 September 2001 terrorist attacks, much of the attention shifted to the counterterrorism mission. The US invasion of Iraq on 19 March 2003 and subsequent collapse of order refocused research and the resulting literature on stabilization and reconstruction operations and COIN warfare.

Among the most significant prior studies are the DOD-chartered 2001 Hart/Rudman Commission Phase III report, the 2004 Defense Science Board summer study by another DOD-chartered panel of specialists, *The 9/11 Commission Report* in 2004 from a congressionally mandated bipartisan panel, the 2005 *Beyond Goldwater-Nichols* Phase 2 report from the Center for Strategic and International Studies (CSIS) think tank,[2] the 2007 State Department in 2025 Working Group study, and the 2008 *Forging a New Shield* and 2009 *Turning Ideas into Action* reports from the Project on National Security Reform produced as a requirement of the 2008 National Defense Authorization Act that mandated a study of the interagency national security system by an independent, bipartisan organization. However, relatively few studies have looked at whole-of-government unity of effort at the operational level of foreign policy planning and execution across the spectrum of conflict.

At each of the organizational levels considered in this study—the regional level for steady-state operations and the subregional or country level during crisis operations—the reform proposals can be divided into four basic models: (1) an integrated interagency organization, (2) an organization led by the State Department, (3) an organization led by the military, or (4) a parallel structure with no single leader or organization in charge. We will examine these four potential reform models, first for regional steady-state operations and then for subregional crisis operations, with examples from the literature.

Reform Options at the Regional Level

Interagency coordination of foreign policy and national security planning and execution at the regional level is currently dominated by the military's geographic combatant commands. Because the US government does not have a strong regional-level structure or process for interagency coordination and unity of effort, the military has stepped into the breach and developed a series of mechanisms, including JIACGs, POLADs, and even combatant commands with organizational structures designed more for noncombat interagency operations than for military combat. However, the military-driven structures are all "coalitions of the willing," since the DOD has no authority to compel interagency participation in planning or to direct the actions of other agencies during mission execution.

A Regional Integrated Interagency Organization

The first reform model envisions creating a new organization in each region with responsibility and authority to coordinate interagency planning and lead interagency execution. In some versions, the geographic combatant command would be subordinate to the new interagency organization, while in others, the GCC is absorbed into the new organization. The most prominent proponents of this reform option include the CSIS Beyond Goldwater-Nichols study team and the PNSR, as well as many books, journal articles, and PME student papers. A review of the literature finds no proposals of this type prior to 2005, indicating that the challenges of the increasingly complex mission in Iraq likely inspired many of these authors.

Proponents have identified several advantages of this model. First, having members of a collocated staff working together on a daily basis is expected to lead to improved regional interagency coordination in both planning and execution. Second, shifting responsibility for regional interagency coordination to an organization outside of Washington would allow leaders there to focus on strategic and global issues. Third, the creation of regional interagency organizations would enhance the development of localized expertise across the participating agencies. Fourth, an organization with directive authority over all US embassies in the region would provide a mechanism to coordinate each embassy's country-level plans and operations. Finally, a regional interagency organization would address the power imbalance which is currently overwhelmingly tilted toward the military.

This model also has some disadvantages. First and foremost, if the leader of this organization does not come from the State Department, that agency's role could be further diluted, reinforcing perceptions around the world that it is not really in charge of US foreign policy. Second, many issues cross regional boundaries, requiring regional organizations to coordinate horizontally with one another as well as vertically with respective national headquarters and US actors at the country level. Finally, Washington would have to guard against the tendency of these regional organizations to become powerful fiefdoms operating independently of national-level direction.

The first proposals of a true interagency organization at the regional level are found in a pair of 2005 Naval War College papers. LT Peter Halvorsen, USN, recommends creating unified interagency staffs at the regional level that include all relevant executive branch agencies, either augmenting or replacing the GCCs.[3] The commander of this organization could be a military officer or a skilled professional from any department or agency, subject to Senate confirmation. These commanders would have directive authority over all US activities in their region. The regional commands could be structured along traditional military J-staff lines (renaming them I-staffs for interagency), or they could organize functionally, with components for military, intelligence, diplomacy, humanitarian assistance, and so forth.[4] Similarly, Maj J. D. York, USMC, proposed the creation of regional interagency directors (RID) with authority and responsibility for directing and coordinating all interagency activities at the regional level. These regional directors would have command authority over the agencies assigned to them and would also have authority over the US ambassadors or multilateral IGOs in the region. The RIDs would require Senate confirmation and would report directly to the president.[5]

In April 2005, the US Marine Corps Center for Emerging Threats and Opportunities (CETO) proposed a less ambitious regional interagency model. Rather than creating full regional commands, it recommended smaller crisis management groups (CMG), which would be standing interagency bodies to integrate civil-military planning and execution of major contingency operations, making them more like a JIACG under independent control, rather than subordinate to the GCC.[6]

The CSIS Beyond Goldwater-Nichols study team, in its July 2005 report, recommended emulating the success of the military's GCCs across the interagency to better integrate day-to-day policy execution regionally. Rather than establish an interagency entity in each region, the team proposed tasking existing regional senior directors on the National Security Staff to lead interagency coordination for their region—both at the strategic level in Washington and at the regional levels—by convening regular summits of senior US officials who hold policy execution responsibility for that region. They also recommended in the longer term establishing interagency organizations, called "regional security councils," to bring together senior representatives of all agencies executing US policy in the region to facilitate day-to-day unity of effort.[7]

In late 2005, Jeffrey Gardner further fleshed out the interagency organization proposal by recommending creation of a regional interest bureau (RIB) to fully integrate the planning and activities of all US agencies operating in the region. A presidential envoy (as described in chap. 3) would lead each RIB and have the "full authority of the President" to "direct the efforts of all executive agencies in the region." In this construct, agency headquarters would make policy and serve as force providers while personnel from each agency, including the geographic combatant commander and staff, would work together at the RIBs to implement these policies, much as the military services currently provide trained and ready forces to the combatant commanders.[8] Gardner's construct is shown in figure 11.

Also in late 2005, Mitchell Thompson, an instructor at the Defense Intelligence Agency's Joint Military Attaché School and experienced Middle East foreign area officer and advisor to CPA administrator L. Paul Bremer, proposed transforming the military's combatant commands into truly interagency regional organizations with the responsibility and authority to conduct the full spectrum of US foreign policy and national security operations in their regions. Each transformed organization would be led by a senior civilian with a long and distinguished career in executive branch agencies involved in foreign policy and national security. This leader would be nominated by the president and report to the national security advisor. Each would have a four-star military deputy, functionally aligned directors from across the interagency, and an interagency staff, as well as assigned military forces. While Thompson says the civilian director of this organization would carry the rank of ambassador, that individual would report directly to the president through the national security advisor rather than through the State Department, thus placing the NSC rather than State in charge of US activities abroad. Thompson envisions this as essentially the CORDS model elevated to the regional command level and reversed to put the senior civilian rather than the military commander in overall command.[9]

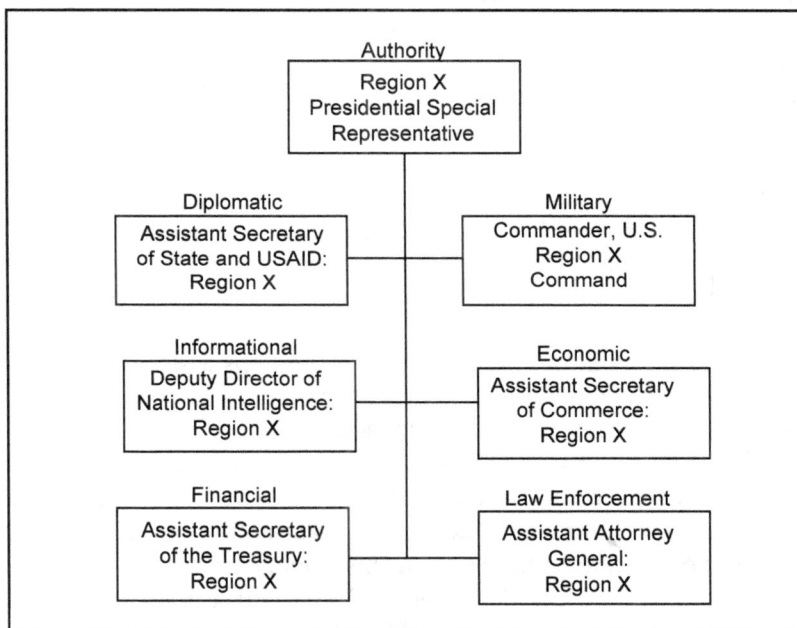

Figure 11. Regional interagency model—the regional interests bureau. (*Adapted from* Jeffrey V. Gardner, "Fight the 'Away Game' as a Team: Organizing for Regional Interagency Policy Implementation," *American Intelligence Journal* [Autumn/Winter 2005]: 57.)

Dr. James Carafano of the Heritage Foundation proposes in a 2008 essay disbanding the GCCs in some regions and replacing them with standing regional interagency structures he calls "joint interagency groups." Carafano describes these new regional structures as the expansion of the successful JIATF concept to the level of the regional operational headquarters. These organizations could be led by either a military officer or a civilian, based on the predominant US goals and missions in each region (which could send an alarming and probably unintended signal to countries in regions that find themselves hosting an interagency group with a US military leader in charge). Carafano does not describe the nonmilitary components that would presumably be present on the staff, but he does say the organization would have a military staff "tasked with planning military engagements, warfighting, and post-conflict operations" and that could be detached from the joint interagency group to form the nucleus of a JTF in the event of military operations in the region.[10] Carafano does not specify how this new regional interagency organization would relate to US ambassadors in the region or to the NSC and the cabinet departments and agencies in Washington.[11]

That same year, NSA analyst Dennis R. J. Penn recommended establishing new interagency organizations in each region to eliminate "all vestiges of militarized foreign policy" and produce unity of effort across three equal pillars of US engagement—diplomacy, development, and defense. These new organizations would be separate from the GCCs and would be led by "a forward-deployed National Security Council–level representative," meaning that this leader would probably hold the rank of undersecretary or perhaps assistant secretary and would report to Washington via the national security advisor and the NSS rather than to a cabinet agency.[12]

The PNSR's 2008 and 2009 studies also considered how to improve interagency coordination at the regional level. The team studied several models and ultimately recommended establishing regional issue teams in each region. These issue teams would be composed of senior representatives at the undersecretary or assistant secretary level from across the interagency. They would replace the regional interagency policy committees at the NSC and would report to higher-level interagency teams there, while US ambassadors and country teams in the region would report to the regional issue team, defining a clear interagency chain of authority from the president through the regional level to the country level.[13]

The PNSR considered but rejected a much more robust regional interagency organization they called an "integrated regional center" (IRC), which deserves brief mention here. Each IRC would preferably be collocated with the corresponding geographic combatant command and would act as the interagency headquarters for planning and executing US national security policy in the region. Each would be staffed by personnel from across the interagency possessing regional expertise and would be organized according to US goals in the region. The PNSR believes each IRC would need a staff of 500–1,000 people, and it would be led by a presidentially appointed and Senate-confirmed director, who could come from any national security–related agency or even from outside of government (i.e., a political appointee rather than a government professional, as is the case with about one-third of US ambassadors and many cabinet secretaries, undersecretaries, and assistant secretaries).[14] The director would have both the responsibility and the authority to execute US foreign policy, including directive authority over US ambassadors accredited to countries or multinational organizations in the region.[15] The regional director would have some authority over the GCC during peacetime, providing direction on security cooperation activities, but would not have authority over US military forces conducting combat operations (though the IRC and GCC would maintain a coordinating relationship during combat operations). The regional director would provide direction for US forces conducting postconflict operations as part of a larger interagency effort.[16]

Rather than adding another layer of bureaucracy, the IRCs would replace the regional interagency policy committees at the NSC. Regional policy would be delegated to the IRCs in each region, freeing Washington to concentrate on global issues and long-range strategy.[17] The NSC would establish broad guidance and goals, set strategic direction, provide national security strategy and policy, develop budget guidance, identify cross-regional issues, and deconflict IRC requests for departmental resources and support, while the IRCs would translate national security policy into interagency plans and oversee the execution of those plans.[18] Under this proposed system, cabinet secretaries would retain the ability to influence and challenge policies via the NSC process, but once an issue was assigned to an IRC rather than to a lead cabinet agency, the IRC would have the authority to refine policy and direct execution using assigned personnel and resources from across the interagency.[19]

A recent version of this type of reform model comes from a 2009 *Joint Force Quarterly* article by Army brigadier general Jeffrey Buchanan, Navy captain Maxie Davis, and Air Force colonel Lee Wight.[20] They recommended disbanding the GCCs and creating standing interagency organizations in each region which would report to the president through the NSC and would have responsibility for all aspects of US foreign policy in their respective regions. Each regional organization, which they call a "joint interagency command" (JIACOM), would be led by a civilian, possibly with a four-star military deputy, and would be staffed with representatives of all agencies executing aspects of US foreign policy in the region, including the military. The JIACOM director would have true directive authority for all regional US activities, including the military and the ambassadors and their country teams. Like the GCCs, the JIACOMs would have joint military forces assigned based on US requirements in the region.[21] Operational-level activities would be conducted by establishing subordinate JIATFs, making the operational activities both joint and interagency and providing command authority over all assigned interagency forces from the tactical level, through the JIATF commander, to the JIACOM director, to the president through the NSC.

State Leads at the Regional Level

The second regional-level interagency reform model puts the State Department in charge. Versions of this model vary from relatively modest proposals focused on strengthening the authority of the assistant secretaries of state in the regional bureaus to robust interagency organizations, as described in the previous section but headed by a State Department representative and reporting to the secretary of state rather than directly to the president or an element of the NSC. The major difference, then, between this and the previous interagency model, is that it clearly places the State Department in charge of regional foreign policy. The most prominent proponent of this reform option is the 2007 State Department–chartered "State Department in 2025" working group, though its proposal is relatively modest.[22] MAJ Brett Sylvia's 2006 Army School of Advanced Military Studies (SAMS) paper, "The Interagency Process in Regional Foreign Policy," provides the best description of the robust option, while MAJ Mark Curry's 1994 SAMS paper provides a third variant of this model.

In 1994 Curry proposed putting the State Department's regional bureaus in charge of all noncombat interagency operations in their region. His proposal would strengthen their ability to direct interagency activities by moving the regional assistant secretary and a small staff from Washington, possibly collocated with the geographic combatant commanders, while the regional deputy assistant secretaries and the country directors remained in Washington to focus on policy formulation.[23] It is not clear from Curry's description whether the assistant secretary would have additional authority to direct the actions of other agencies in the region. Absent that authority, this model is more likely to place the assistant secretary of state in a de facto subordinate role to the combatant commander and much larger GCC staff, while a lower-ranked deputy assistant secretary remaining in Washington would have even less authority in leading interagency coordination there.

Sylvia's 2006 proposal would establish regional interagency consulates (more appropriately called regional interagency missions), led by a State Department civilian of ambassadorial rank with a military deputy dual-hatted as the geographic combatant commander and a robust interagency staff organized along functional lines with divisions headed by assistant secretaries from relevant agencies. [24] The regional ambassador would report to the secretary of state but like country-level ambassadors would also be the president's personal representative in the region, reporting directly to the president as required. The military deputy would report to both the regional ambassador and through traditional military channels to the secretary of defense. While the State Department would be the lead agency for this organization, unresolved interagency disagreements could be elevated to the NSC for adjudication. Because the combatant commander would work for the regional ambassador, the ambassador would have access to military personnel, logistical, and communications resources to execute other US activities in the region.[25] This structure effectively creates an embassy-style country team at the regional level with a diplomat from the State Department directing all efforts. It is similar to the regional interagency structures described in the previous section in most ways, but in this model the State Department is clearly in charge, reinforcing its statutory lead role in foreign policy and making the organization more attractive to partners who would prefer to deal with a diplomat. Sylvia's proposed structure is shown in figure 12.

The "State Department in 2025" working group recommended a more modest proposal in 2007, with the State Department as the lead agency only for regional interagency planning. To increase State's regional presence and capabilities, they recommended that each State Department regional bureau establish a new deputy assistant secretary to represent it in the region and lead all regional planning efforts, staffing that position with a senior career diplomat with prior ambassadorial experience. Outside the planning arena, however, this individual would be subordinate to the geographic combatant commander, becoming the commander's POLAD and senior civilian deputy. Indeed, aside from the leading role in interagency planning, this is effectively a military-led model and is similar to current structures in AFRICOM, EUCOM, and SOUTHCOM, where the command's civilian deputy to the commander comes from the State Department and oversees the JIACG's role in interagency coordination.[26]

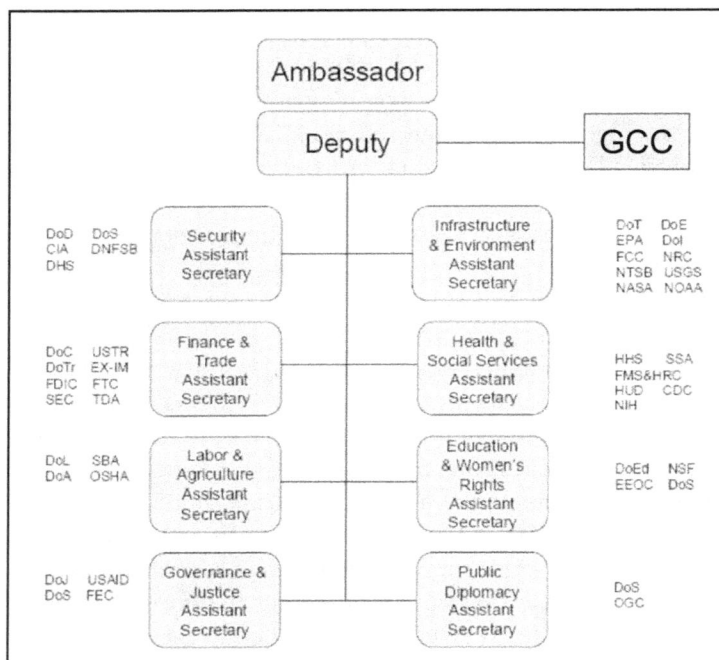

Figure 12. Regional state-led model—the regional interagency mission. (*Adapted from* Maj Brett G. Sylvia, USA, "Empowering Interagency Capabilities: A Regional Approach," monograph [Fort Leavenworth, KS: School of Advanced Military Studies, US Army Command and General Staff College, 25 May 2006], 55.)

Military Leads at the Regional Level

The third model designates the Department of Defense as the lead agency for regional interagency unity of effort and puts the military's GCCs in charge. Some versions of this model argue that the current JIACG construct either fills the bill or can do so with only minor tweaks, while more ambitious models would significantly increase the interagency representation at the GCC headquarters, all while maintaining a flag-rank military officer in charge and reporting through military channels to the secretary of defense. Significantly, all those who have proposed that the military should lead the interagency at the regional level have been either military officers or researchers at military schools. They argue that the combatant command is the only effective organization present in the region and has already taken great steps since 2001 to facilitate interagency coordination, so the United States should continue to build on this record of success. However, this model does nothing to alleviate concerns that the military plays too large a role in US foreign policy.

In a 1997 paper from the Center for Strategic Leadership at the Army War College, COL Michael Pasquarett and LTC James Kievit, USA, retired, proposed creating a set of interagency planning teams at each geographic combatant command. These operational planning groups (OPG) would focus on a specific mission and employ a core of planners from a wide variety of US government agencies, NGOs, and coalition partners, which would vary in size as the intensity or scope of the operation required. Depending on the mission, either a military flag officer or an ambassador could lead an OPG. In some cases, the planning group could become the core of an interagency task force during mission execution.[27] Pasquarett and Kievit state that these changes would "establish interagency operations as a focal point throughout the training, planning, and execution cycles" of US activities and operations in the region.[28]

After the 2001 establishment of JIACGs at the combatant commands, several military officers—including LCDR Chris Herr, USN, Col Matthew Bogdanos, USMC, and MAJ David Doyle, USA, as well as Neyla Arnas et al., at the National Defense University's Center for Technology and National Security Policy—either argued that the JIACG is already sufficient or proposed further strengthening it to serve as the combatant commander's primary tool to lead interagency coordination.[29] However, it is clear that the JIACGs as currently structured are not able to achieve full interagency coordination at the regional level. Neither the combatant commanders nor their JIACGs currently have the authority to compel interagency participation in coordinated planning or execution, nor can the interagency members of the JIACG commit their agencies to any particular position or course of action.[30] Furthermore, the existence of the JIACGs can leave the impression that the military is (or wants to be) responsible for all executive branch coordination for planning and executing interagency operations in the region.[31]

In 2006, Lt Col Christopher Naler, USMC, proposed an "interagency combatant command"[32] which looks similar to the structures now used by AFRICOM, EUCOM, and SOUTHCOM. In Naler's model, the combatant command would be a civil-military organization with interagency representatives integrated into key leadership and staff positions. It would have both a military and a civilian deputy commander, with the civilian deputy drawn from the State Department. The civilian deputy would be both the ranking State representative and the JIACG director. Interagency representatives on the staff would provide their perspective throughout planning, operations, and exercises and would also communicate relevant information between the combatant command and their parent agencies.[33] Naler's model is shown in figure 13.

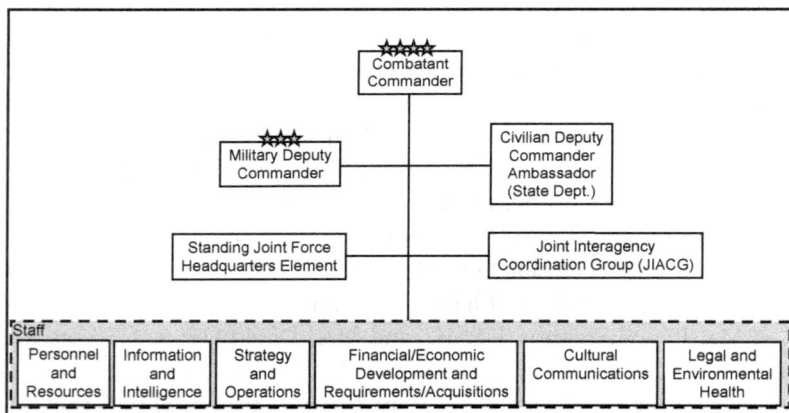

Figure 13. Regional military-led model—the interagency COCOM. (*Adapted from* Christopher L. Naler, "Are We Ready for an Interagency Combatant Command?" *Joint Force Quarterly* 41 [2nd Quarter 2006]: 28.)

LCDR William Whitsitt, USN, proposed a more unified, whole-of-government reorganization of AFRICOM in 2007 which might be extended to the other GCCs. In his model, AFRICOM would continue to be led by a military officer. However, unlike the current structure which has a military flag officer serving as a second deputy, the command would have a single deputy commander, a State Department ambassador.[34] Below the command section, the staff would be inherently interagency and organized more like a JIACG, with the military J-staff working in a supporting role to the main interagency staff.[35]

Finally, in 2009, Maj Brian Schafer, USAF, proposed a more robust planning organization for the geographic combatant commander. This organization, called a "joint planning group" (JPG), would combine the command's J-5 plans directorate, the JIACG, and a multinational planning augmentation team (MPAT), bringing together the GCC's standard military planning organization (the J-5) with the interagency (through the JIACG) and foreign partners in the AOR (through the MPAT).[36] In this construct, Schafer proposed that the J-5 director would lead all planning efforts across the interagency and with coalition partners. The JIACG would be led by a military officer "so the military can guide the interagency partners through the military planning cycle and expertly inject their civilian expertise into the planning process as needed," while a deputy director from a non-DOD agency "would have the necessary authority over its members to make things happen with no legal issues arising." Within the combined organization, the J-5 would take the lead for combat operations, the JIACG would take the lead for interagency-heavy noncombat contingency operations, and the MPAT would take the lead for multinational crises and humanitarian operations, in each case with the other two parts of the organization in support.[37]

A Parallel Regional Structure

Some reformers propose a fourth model consisting of both a GCC and a regional civilian interagency organization with neither having authority over the other and each reporting to different agencies in Washington. Like the military-centric model above, all proponents of this reform proposal found in the literature were members of the military. They tend to view the combatant command as a successful template and look to the civilian side of government to create something similar to balance power and capabilities between the military and civilian sides at the regional level without diminishing the effectiveness or independence of the GCC. However, it is not clear that any of these proposed models produce regional unity of effort, since the parallel civilian and military organizations report to separate bosses in Washington.

In 2005, LCDR Darin Liston, USN, proposed creating an operational level of government for all US civilian agencies equivalent to the military's GCCs. The State Department's regional assistant secretaries and staffs would relocate and become the equivalent of a civilian government "commander" for the region, with all nonmilitary US agencies in the region falling under their authority, including the ambassadors. The regional bureau chief (RBC) and staff would collocate with the geographic combatant commander to facilitate civil-military coordination and a close working relationship, but the RBC and GCC would be peers, with neither having authority over the other and each reporting to their separate agencies in Washington.[38]

That same year, Maj Sunil Desai, USMC, noted that while the military has effective regional structures, the State Department expects nearly 200 ambassadors to report directly to Washington. To enhance the power of the State Department at the regional level, where the combatant commander currently has the most prominent role, and create a more manageable span of control over ambassadors, Desai recommends creating US regional ambassadors who would be senior to country ambassadors, providing a strong parallel State Department chain of command to coordinate with the regional leaders of other US agencies.[39] Like Liston's model, the regional ambassador and geographic combatant commander would be peers, with neither having the authority or responsibility to achieve civil-military unity of effort.

Also in 2005, Lt Col Harold Van Opdorp, USMC, proposed creating a "Regional JIACG Headquarters" (JIACG HQ) to centralize all nonmilitary US agencies in the region.[40] This organization's director would be appointed by the NSC, likely be from the State Department, and report directly to the NSC rather than a lead agency. The regional JIACG HQ director would integrate planning at the regional level across the interagency, including the geographic combatant commander, though the relationship between the regional JIACG HQ and the COCOM would again be that of equals, with neither having directive authority over the other.[41]

Further developing this model in a 2008 article, Lt Col Shannon Caudill, USAF, MAJ Andrew Leonard, USA, and Sgt Maj Richard Thresher, USMC, recommend that the State Department create a regional chief of mission (RCM) in each area to lead nonmilitary elements of US power, be responsible for developing an interagency strategic plan for the region, integrate interagency activities, and act as the primary American voice in the region. This diplomatic post would be on par with the military's GCC, and a joint interagency planning cell between the RCM and the GCC would facilitate civil-military coordination for planning and execution. These authors argue that this construct would "lower the profile, but not the effectiveness, of the . . . regional combatant command."[42] The regional parallel structure model is shown in figure 14.

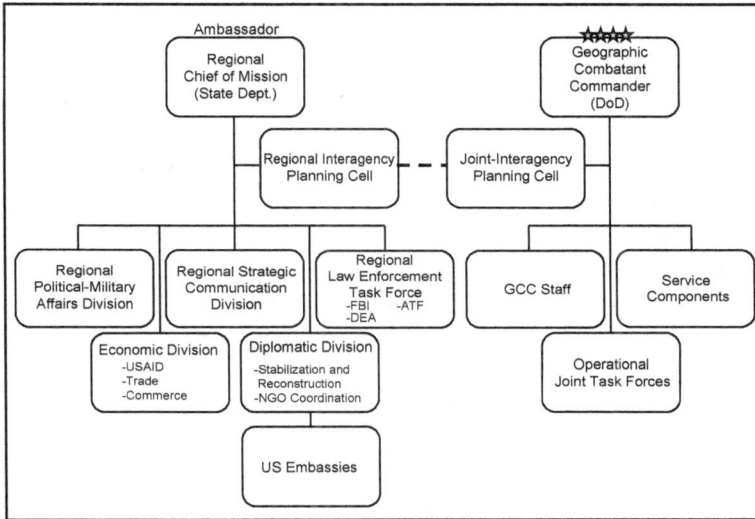

Figure 14. Regional parallel structure model—the regional chief of mission. (*Adapted from* Lt Col Shannon W. Caudill, USAF, MAJ Andrew M. Leonard, USA, and Sgt Maj Richard D. Thresher, USMC, "Interagency Leadership: The Case for Strengthening the Department of State," *American Diplomacy*, April 2008, http://www.unc.edu/depts/diplomat/item/2008 /0406/comm/caudilletal_strength.html.)

Reform Options at the Country Level during Crisis Operations

We next consider models to improve interagency unity of effort at the subregional or country level during crisis operations. In normal peacetime operations, the US ambassador leads the country team of all interagency personnel assigned to the embassy and other missions in the country. Few interagency reform proposals in the literature take issue with this construct.[43] However, many authors note that ambassadors' de facto authority is much weaker than their de jure authority, as expressed in Title 22 *US Code* and their letter of appointment from the president.[44] To enhance the de facto authority of the ambassadors, the "State Department in 2025" working group recommends that the president issue an executive order codifying their authorities, which are currently carried in the presidential letter, and further recommends that the ambassador be the rater for all other agency heads in the country so the other agencies would truly work for the ambassador.[45] Along similar lines, the PNSR study team recommends improving the language in the president's letter "to reinforce the *de jure* authority provided in Title 22 USC Section 3927, and establish procedures for ensuring that country teams are, in fact, true interagency teams rather than a collection of individuals pursuing independent departmental/agency agendas."[46] Additionally, the PNSR team recommends providing each ambassador "control over the assignment, evaluation, and rewards for any official assigned to an embassy or mission staff," including all military personnel not executing missions for the combatant commander under Title 10, who would report to the ambassador through the senior defense official in the embassy as defined in DOD Directive 5105.75, *Department of Defense Operations at U.S. Embassies*, issued 27 December 2007.[47]

More reform is needed for crisis operations, however, and several authors suggest various structures to enhance interagency unity of effort at the country level. Again, we consider four general categories of reform proposals: an integrated interagency organization, an organization led by the State Department, an organization led by the military, or a parallel structure with no single leader or organization in charge. Currently, the closest structures the United States has to interagency organizations at this level are the long-standing JIATFs at SOUTHCOM and PACOM that combine military, law enforcement, and intelligence community personnel in a unified structure. There are no recent examples of State Department–led interagency organizations for contingency operations, though of course the country team led by the ambassador at every US embassy provides a steady-state example of such an organization. On the other hand, recent examples of military-led interagency organizations include the MACV/CORDS structure in Vietnam and the ORHA in Iraq. Finally, a parallel structure exists in Afghanistan (and in Iraq until the end of OND in 2011), with the embassy and the military JTF coordinating with one another but with neither formally subordinate to the other. There have been similar parallel structures during humanitarian response operations with the military and the USAID coordinating as equals, such as the response to the 2004 Asian tsunami.

An Integrated Interagency Structure

The first reform model envisions creating an integrated inter-agency task force for crisis operations, unifying civilian and military efforts and command structures. Many of these proposals are similar to the current JIATFs at PACOM and SOUTHCOM, though with increased command authorities. The most prominent proponents of this reform model include the Defense Science Board's 2004 summer study and the PNRS's 2008 *Forging a New Shield* and 2009 *Turning Ideas into Action* reports.

The Defense Science Board study recommends establishing JI-ATFs composed of the leaders operating in the area of interest—the ambassador, the USAID country director, the CIA chief of station, and other senior agency representatives—augmented with DOD personnel as needed to coordinate planning with higher organizational levels and ensure coordinated action by all US players.[48]

In a 2005 paper, LCDR Darin Liston, USN, recommends establishing joint government task forces (JGTF) for interagency contingency operations led by either the military or a civilian agency, based on which agency's core competency most closely aligned with the primary mission. This means a civilian could have command of assigned military forces.[49] Connecting this to Liston's regional-level parallel structure recommendation described previously, the JGTF would report to either the GCC or the regional bureau depending on whether the commander was military or civilian. His proposed JGTFs would have stronger command arrangements than the current counternarcotics JIATFs at SOUTHCOM and PACOM. In JIATF-S and JIATF-W, the task force commander has only tactical control of participating units while operational control remains with the parent agencies. Liston recommends delegating operational control to JGTF commanders, similar to a military-only joint task force. He would also align the two current JIATFs, and any future standing JIATFs, under the stronger JGTF model.[50]

Maj Sunil Desai, USMC, in a 2005 article, recommends developing interagency task forces as needed for specific missions. A presidential special representative would lead these IATFs, report directly to the president, and have an integrated headquarters staff of representatives from all relevant agencies. Desai does not specifically address how the civilian and military components would relate, but presumably they would all fall under this integrated task force. The major concern with this model is his proposal to have the task force leader report directly to the president; a handful of integrated task forces responding to crises around the globe could quickly overload the president and the NSS.[51]

Another 2005 paper by Lt Col Ted Uchida, USAF, recommends creating and deploying ad hoc interagency task forces (IATF) for crisis operations. These IATFs would be task-organized to accomplish specific missions using the combined capabilities of the interagency and have operational control and command authority over all forces assigned for planning, exercises, and mission execution.[52]

In its 2008 and 2009 reports, the PNSR study team recommends creating integrated interagency crisis task forces (CTF) to conduct crisis operations. Unlike the parallel structure used in US operations in Afghanistan, the CTFs would have an integrated civil-military chain of command (see fig. 15). A CTF would have a single director, a clear mission, and resources and authority commensurate with assigned responsibilities. The CTF director could be either military or civilian, depending on the security situation, and would be supported by an interagency staff.[53] As in other PNSR interagency reform recommendations—which do not envision a significant interagency presence at the regional level—the CTF director would report directly to the president through the national security advisor for "large and important" crises and to the director's respective department (i.e., a lead agency) for less prominent crises. Once again, this reporting structure appears to have the potential to overload the president and the NSS. To ensure the CTF director has the necessary level of authority, the PNSR study team says CTFs should be authorized by Congress and chartered by the president.[54]

Most recently, Buchanan, Davis, and Wight suggest establishing JIATFs that would be subordinate to their proposed regional interagency organization. This type of structure would make operational-level crisis operations both joint and interagency. Moreover, it would provide command authority over all assigned interagency forces from the tactical level, through the JIATF commander, to the regional JIACOM commander (per their regional-level proposal), to the president through the NSC, supported by the NSS.[55]

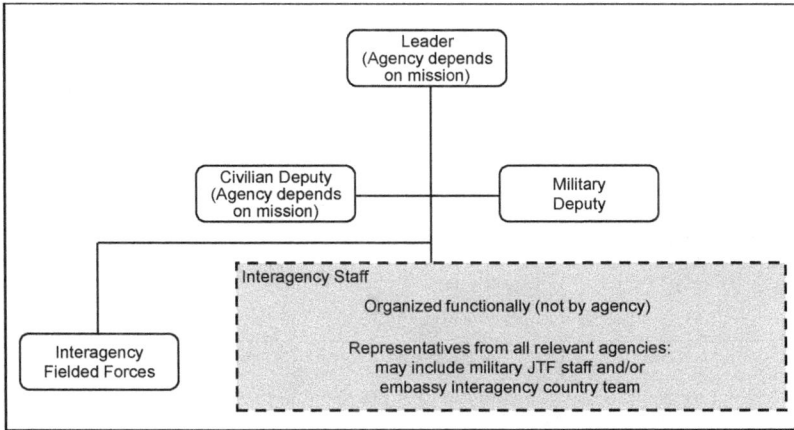

Figure 15. **Integrated interagency crisis task force**. (*Adapted from* PNSR, *Forging a New Shield* [Arlington, VA: Center for the Study of the Presidency, November 2008], 526.)

State Leads

The second model for interagency crisis operations reform would put the State Department in charge of the task force. Interestingly, an exhaustive literature search identified no proposals of this model in the past two decades, not even by State Department–affiliated authors. However, interagency country teams led by the ambassador are standard for steady-state operations at all US embassies, so the model is worth considering for contingencies as well.

In a State Department lead-agency model, the USG would create an interagency task force similar to those described previously, but the leader of the IATF would always be from the State Department. In countries with a functioning US embassy and ambassador, the ambassador would be the logical choice to lead the IATF, since he or she already has responsibility for all US interagency activities in the country except major military operations. Where no functioning US embassy is in place—as is often the case immediately after an invasion or in a failed state with no diplomatic relations with the United States—the president could designate a special representative who would then report through State Department channels rather than directly to the president or national security advisor. This model is shown in figure 16.

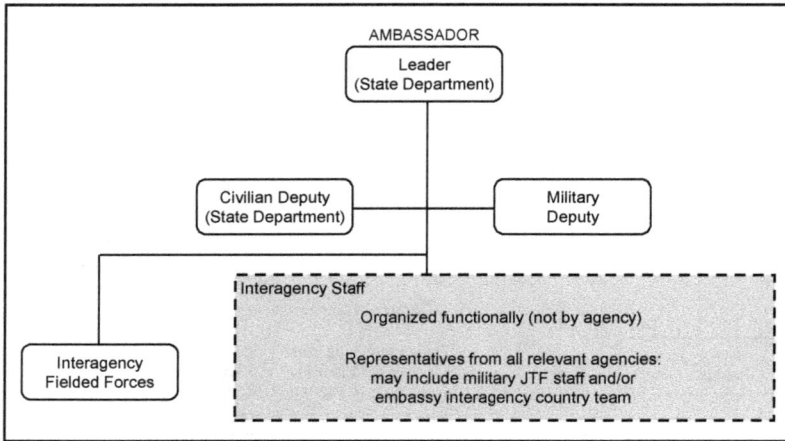

Figure 16. State-led interagency task force

Using this model, the MACV/CORDS model would have been reversed, with the civilian CORDS director in charge of the overall US effort in Vietnam and the MACV commander subordinate and providing military support. Similarly, in the first year after the 2003 invasion of Iraq, Ambassador Bremer, the CPA administrator and presidential special representative, would have been in charge of the overall US effort, with the military JTF in support rather than the uncoordinated parallel structure that existed. The rationale for this proposal is that in complex operations, such as counterinsurgencies or postconflict stabilization and reconstruction, the desired end state is political, not military. While security is a necessary part of the overall campaign, the years of frustration during US operations in Vietnam, Panama, Iraq, and Afghanistan demonstrate that substantial military effort achieves little in the way of overall strategic goals if it is not firmly directed toward larger strategic goals. This model would attempt to put the right senior civilian with the right understanding of broad US goals in charge of the response.

Military Leads

The third reform model for interagency crisis operations would put the military in charge of an interagency task force, much like the MACV/CORDS structure in Vietnam. Again, it is interesting that the literature mentions little about using this model despite praise from many historians and military analysts for the CORDS structure.

The only identified published proposal of this type comes from a 2006 SAMS paper by MAJ Ross Coffey, USA, who states that a CORDS-like construct is still a good model. Coffey recommends that the State Department's S/CRS create a CORDS-type civilian organization that would be a subordinate element of a military JTF like the MACV/CORDS construct in Vietnam. The military-led structure is shown in figure 17. Coffey contends that this would be better than the current JIACG and JIATF models, which try to achieve unity of effort without unity of command, and also better than the parallel structure frequently used today. He argues that the latter mirrors the unsuccessful structure the United States used in Vietnam prior to establishment of the CORDS.[56]

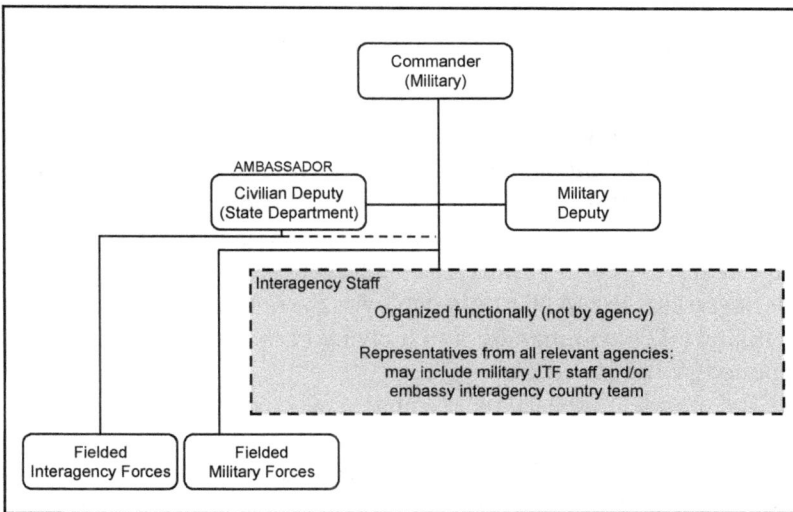

Figure 17. Military-led interagency task force

A Parallel Structure

The fourth and final model for interagency crisis operations would use a parallel civil-military structure with neither in charge of the overall effort. Currently, when the United States has both an embassy and a large military presence in a country, the formal chain of command is usually split, with the ambassador supervising non-DOD personnel while the JTF commander commands DOD personnel. The most significant proponent of this structure is the CSIS Beyond

Goldwater-Nichols study team; few others have proposed such a model. The PNSR study team contends that these "dual civilian and military chains of command in the field complicate unity of purpose and effort."[57]

Lt Col Harold Van Opdorp, USMC, proposed a classic parallel structure in 2005—creating a "deployable JIACG" that would unify the civilian interagency presence in a country under a single organization operating in parallel with the military's JTF.[58] Depending on the situation, either the deployable JIACG or the JTF would be the supported command, with the other acting in support. During major combat operations, the JTF would be the supported command; however, during a humanitarian response, the deployable JIACG would most likely be the supported command. Van Opdorp notes that many operational plans incorporate phases, and the supported/supporting relationship could change as campaign phases change, for instance, passing the lead from the JTF to the deployable JIACG during the transition to postconflict stabilization and reconstruction operations.[59]

The CSIS study team proposes a much more integrated task force structure but maintains two leaders reporting in two separate chains of command, albeit with an integrated staff and a great deal of coordination. It recommends establishing an interagency task force to integrate the day-to-day efforts of all US agencies participating in a crisis operation. The IATF would deploy to the field and be jointly led by a military JTF commander and a civilian special representative appointed by the president.

The president's special representative, who could be the US ambassador to the country or another senior civilian of comparable stature, would be responsible for achieving overall US objectives for the mission and would have directive authority over all US government civilians deployed to the field. The special representative would report to the president through the secretary of state. The JTF commander, a senior military officer, would be responsible for military operations—with operational control over all US military forces—and report to the geographic combatant commander, leaving the traditional military chain of command unbroken. While the special representative would have no direct authority over the JTF commander, he or she would be able to raise disagreements to the NSC or the president for resolution.

Both the special representative and the JTF commander would be supported by a single, integrated, interagency staff composed largely of military personnel under the JTF commander, plus civilian personnel detailed from various agencies to work for the special representative. Where a functioning US embassy exists, the integrated staff would augment the existing country team, which would then become the support staff for the operation.[60] The parallel structure proposed by the CSIS team is shown in figure 18.

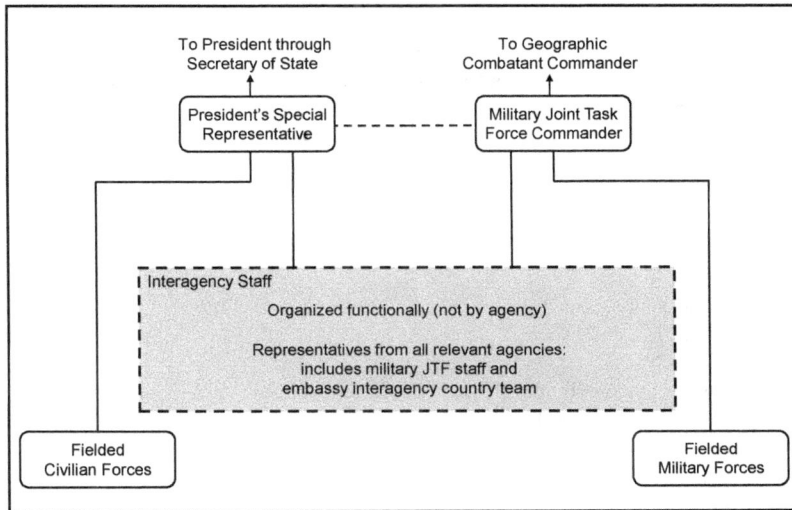

Figure 18. Parallel structure—the interagency task force. (*Adapted from* Clark A. Murdock and Michèle A. Flournoy, *Beyond Goldwater-Nichols: U.S. Government and Defense Reform for a New Strategic Era,* Phase 2 Report [Washington, DC: Center for Strategic and International Studies, July 2005], 49.)

Notes

1. The bibliography to this study has more than 100 such references.

2. One of the two CSIS lead investigators for the 2005 *Beyond Goldwater-Nichols* phase 2 study was Michèle Flournoy, who later served as the undersecretary of defense for policy from February 2009 to February 2012.

3. LT Peter Halvorsen, USN, "Reforming the Interagency at the Operational Level," research report (Newport, RI: Naval War College, February 2005), 2.

4. Ibid., 14–16.

5. Maj J. D. York, USMC, "Militarizing the Interagency," research report (Newport, RI: Naval War College, February 2005), 16.

6. Arnas, Barry, and Oakley, *Harnessing the Interagency*, 16.

7. Charles A. Murdock and Michèle A. Flournoy, *Beyond Goldwater-Nichols: U.S. Government and Defense Reform for a New Strategic Era*, Phase 2 Report (Washington, DC: Center for Strategic and International Studies, July 2005), 20, 37–38.

8. Jeffrey V. Gardner, "Fight the 'Away Game' as a Team: Organizing for Regional Interagency Policy Implementation," *American Intelligence Journal* (Autumn/Winter 2005): 57.

9. Mitchell J. Thompson, "Breaking the Proconsulate: A New Design for National Power," *Parameters* (Winter 2005/06): 63, 72–73.

10. James Jay Carafano, "Managing Mayhem: The Future of Interagency Reform," *Joint Force Quarterly* 49 (2nd Quarter 2008): 136–37.

11. BG Jeffrey Buchanan, USA, CAPT Maxie Y. Davis, USN, and Col Lee T. Wight, USAF, "Death of the Combatant Command? Toward a Joint Interagency Approach," *Joint Force Quarterly* 52 (1st Quarter 2009): 94.

12. Dennis R. J. Penn, "USAFRICOM: The Militarization of U.S. Foreign Policy?," *Joint Force Quarterly* 51 (4th Quarter 2008): 77–78.

13. PNSR, *Forging a New Shield*, 517–18.

14. Ibid., 441, 492–93, 500.

15. Ibid., 498–99, 501.

16. Ibid., 493, 501–2.

17. Ibid., 442.

18. Ibid., 492, 496–97.

19. Ibid., 501.

20. Buchanan, Davis, and Wight, "Death of the Combatant Command?" At the time of their 2009 article, Brigadier General Buchanan was deputy commander for operations, Multi-National Division Center, Iraq; Captain Davis was deputy, Information Technology and Information Resource Management for the deputy chief of naval operations, communication networks; and Colonel Wight was commander, 52nd Fighter Wing, Spangdahlem AB, Germany. An even more recent, though very brief, description of a reform proposal along these lines comes from Patrick Cronin and Kristin Lord, who advocate for "civilian-led equivalents of military combatant commands that can unify our diplomatic, development, public engagement and defense efforts," which "may mean creating regional or subregional hubs, regional equivalents of embassy country teams." Cronin is a senior advisor and senior director at the Washington, DC, think tank called the Center for a New American Security (CNAS) and a former assistant administrator for policy and program coordination at the USAID. Lord is vice president and director of studies at the CNAS and a former special advisor to the US undersecretary of state for democracy and global affairs. Patrick Cronin and Kristin Lord, "Deploying Soft Power: Restructured, Larger Civilian Force Needed for Crises," *Defense News*, 12 April 2010, 53.

21. Buchanan, Davis, and Wight, "Death of the Combatant Command?," 94–95.

22. Barry M. Blechman, Thomas R. Pickering, and Newt Gingrich, *Advisory Committee on Transformational Diplomacy: Final Report of the State Department in 2025 Working Group* (2007), http://2001-2009.state.gov/documents/organization/99879.pdf. The working group was headed by Dr. Barry Blechman, the Stimson Center's cofounder; Amb. Thomas Pickering; and the Honorable Newt Gingrich, former speaker of the House of Representatives.

23. Curry, "Interagency Process in Regional Foreign Policy," 35–36.

24. *Consulate* is the wrong word to use for Sylvia's regional construct. According to the 1963 Vienna Convention on Consular Relations, consular functions generally consist of protecting the interests of (in this case US) persons and corporations in the host country and furthering commercial and economic relations between the two countries. The construct Sylvia describes would be better termed a regional interagency mission. See UN, Vienna Convention on Consular Relations, 24 April 1963, in *Treaty Series*, vol. 596, 261; and UN, Vienna Convention on Diplomatic Relations, 18 April 1961, in *Treaty Series*, vol. 500, 95.

25. Sylvia, "Empowering Interagency Capabilities," 54–59.

26. Blechman, Pickering, and Gingrich, *Advisory Committee on Transformational Diplomacy*, 20–21.

27. Michael Pasquarett and James Kievit, *A Blueprint for a Bold Restructuring of the Organization for National Security: The Military Combatant Commands and State Department Regional Bureaus* (Carlisle Barracks, PA: Center for Strategic Leadership, Army War College, 1997), 24–25.

28. Ibid., 35.

29. LCDR Christopher H. Herr, USN, "Joint Interagency at the Combatant Commands: Making it Real; Making It Work," research report (Newport, RI: Naval War College, 13 February 2006), 11–13; Col Matthew F. Bogdanos, USMC, "Joint Interagency Cooperation: The First Step," *Joint Force Quarterly* 37 (2nd Quarter 2005): 17; David S. Doyle, *Interagency Cooperation for Irregular Warfare at the Combatant Command* (Fort Leavenworth, KS: School of Advanced Military Studies, 14 April 2009), 56–57; and Arnas, Barry, and Oakley, *Harnessing the Interagency*, 16.

30. Thompson, "Breaking the Proconsulate," 67; and Buchanan, Davis, and Wight, "Death of the Combatant Command?," 94.

31. Maj Karen D. Stoff, USAF, "Strategic Planning and Joint Interagency Coordination Groups (JIACGs)," research report (Maxwell AFB, AL: Air Command and Staff College, April 2006), 4–5.

32. Christopher L. Naler, "Are We Ready for an Interagency Combatant Command?," *Joint Force Quarterly* 41 (2nd Quarter 2006): 26.

33. Ibid., 26–28.

34. This COCOM construct with a civilian deputy commander and no military deputy commander would require that the civilian deputy have the authority to command military forces in the combatant commander's absence. The United States already practices civilian control of the military, with the president and secretary of defense in charge of the military during both peace and war, and the civilian secretaries of the military services in charge of each service's organize, train, and equip (i.e., peacetime) mission. Therefore, placing a civilian in charge of the military at the regional level is not without precedent but would probably require congressional legislation. Absent such legislation, AFRICOM, SOUTHCOM, and EUCOM have a military deputy commander as well as the civilian deputy to preserve the military chain of command.

35. LCDR William C. Whitsitt, USN, "U.S. Africa Command: An Opportunity for Effective Interagency Coordination," research report (Newport, RI: Naval War College, 10 May 2007), 6–7.

36. Maj Brian M. Schafer, USAF, "DIME Considerations: A New PACOM Planning Pyramid," research report (Maxwell AFB, AL: Air Command and Staff College, April 2009), 12–15.

37. Ibid., 13–14.

38. LCDR Darin M. Liston, USN, "In the Interagency Process, Mere Coordination Is Not Enough: Toward Joint Government," research report (Newport, RI: Naval War College, 14 February 2005), 7, 12.

39. Sunil B. Desai, "Solving the Interagency Puzzle," *Policy Review* no. 129 (1 February 2005), http://www.hoover.org/publications/policyreview/3431461.html#.

40. Harold Van Opdorp, "The Joint Interagency Coordination Group: The Operationalization of DIME," *Small Wars Journal*, July 2005, 4.

41. Ibid., 4–5.

42. Lt Col Shannon W. Caudill, USAF, MAJ Andrew M. Leonard, USA, and Sgt Maj Richard D. Thresher, USMC, "Interagency Leadership: The Case for Strengthening the Department of State," *American Diplomacy*, 15 April 2008, http://www.unc.edu/depts/diplomat/item/2008/0406/comm/caudilletal_strength.html.

43. The only study I found in the literature focusing on problems and proposed solutions for the embassy country team for both normal and crisis operations is Amb. Robert B. Oakley and Michael Casey Jr., "The Country Team: Restructuring America's First Line of Engagement," *Joint Force Quarterly* 47 (4th Quarter 2007): 146–54. They argue that the country team needs to be improved by enhancing the de facto authority of the ambassador, giving ambassadors the latitude to restructure the embassy country team as they see fit, and creating a better interagency personnel system to develop better ambassadors and agency heads.

44. PNSR, *Turning Ideas into Action*, 28. See also Oakley and Casey, "Country Team," 150, 152.

45. Blechman, Pickering, and Gingrich, *Advisory Committee on Transformational Diplomacy*, 22.

46. PNSR, *Turning Ideas into Action*, 29.

47. Ibid., 20, 29.

48. OSD/ATL, *Defense Science Board 2004 Summer Study on Transition to and from Hostilities* (Washington, DC: OSD, December 2004), v, 32.

49. As stated in note 34, this would likely require legislation.

50. Liston, "In the Interagency Process, Mere Coordination Is Not Enough," 13, 15–16.

51. Desai, "Solving the Interagency Puzzle."

52. Lt Col Ted T. Uchida, USAF, "Reforming the Interagency Process," Air Force Fellows research report (Maxwell AFB, AL: Air Force Fellows Program, May 2005), 97.

53. PNSR, *Turning Ideas into Action*, 56; and PNSR, *Forging a New Shield*, 538–39.

54. PNSR, *Turning Ideas into Action*, 57.

55. Buchanan, Davis, and Wight, "Death of the Combatant Command?," 95.

56. Coffey, "Improving Interagency Integration at the Operational Level," 40–42.

57. PNSR, *Forging a New Shield*, 243.

58. Van Opdorp, "Joint Interagency Coordination Group," 4–5.

59. Ibid., 6.

60. Murdock and Flournoy, *Beyond Goldwater-Nichols*, 48, 51–52.

Chapter 6

Analysis and Recommendation

From the many criticisms against current interagency structures and the problems identified in recent and ongoing operations, this study identified 13 objectives by which to evaluate proposed interagency reforms. It then applied these 13 criteria to national-level interagency reform models proposed in the literature and discussed herein. While this evaluation did not produce a clear recommendation for national-level reform, the details of proposed models and their analysis, albeit inconclusive, appear herein as an appendix.

Objectives

First and foremost, many observers argue that the military's role in interagency foreign policy is too large and that a reform must be found that enables the State Department to lead US foreign policy across the interagency. Having the State Department play the primary role in foreign policy is particularly important externally, where several potential partners would like to engage with the United States at various levels but are wary of being associated with the US military.[1] It is also a key element of strategic communication—the United States cannot easily promote strong civilian-led democracy abroad if the message is delivered by a military officer.

Second, the reform must produce better-coordinated planning at the strategic and operational levels. The US interventions in Panama, Haiti, and Iraq are some illustrations of how lack of coordination between agencies during the planning phase led to significant problems during execution—particularly when the military perceived it was time to hand over responsibility for the operation to another agency.

Third, the reform must produce interagency unity of effort during execution. Uncoordinated actions waste time and resources and can make US goals more difficult to accomplish. For example, if the Army Corps of Engineers builds a school but USAID does not assist with funding for teacher training, the effort to build the school was wasted and may even be counterproductive if it leads the local population to doubt US abilities or commitment.

Fourth, any reorganization of interagency structures and processes must not only lead to a more effective and, ideally, more efficient system than various agencies working alone but also reduce bureaucratic and resource overhead often associated with interagency coordination.[2] Without increased effectiveness, reform is counterproductive. Improved efficiency, while not required, is desirable. The PNSR study team notes that the current system "militate[s] against efficiency and effectiveness by undermining cooperation and collaboration . . . [in which competition] and information hoarding between agencies and their personnel is often standard behavior."[3]

Fifth, the reform should task leaders with clear responsibilities and give them the necessary authority to carry out those responsibilities. Prominent management theorist Lyndall Urwick defined the principle of authority as having a clear line of control from the top of a management structure to every individual and the principle of correspondence as giving leaders authority commensurate with assigned responsibility. He argued that these principles should be observed regardless of an organization's complexity.[4] Too often, today's system of interagency coordination assigns responsibility but does not clearly define a chain of command or provide a leader with the needed level of authority over personnel, resources, or processes of other agencies.

Sixth, participants outside the leader's home agency must perceive decisions that leaders make as legitimate. Michael Donley notes, "Lack of complete authority and murky, unclear divisions of responsibility mean that legitimacy in decision making will be challenged."[5] This is often the case today, as one agency may not perceive a leader's decisions from another executive-branch agency as binding.

Seventh, leaders of the interagency process must have access to the necessary financial, personnel, and material resources from other agencies to be successful in their assigned mission. For example, the State Department or USAID is often tasked to accomplish a diplomatic or developmental mission that it cannot achieve without military logistical or security resources. Avoiding this scenario will in some cases require congressional changes since Congress provides budgets to individual agencies and the executive branch has limited authority to realign resources among agencies.

Eighth, the leader and organization must have a clear chain of command to the president, the ultimate decision maker on foreign policy and national security issues. This is again Urwick's principle of authority, which requires a clear line from the top of a management structure to every individual. Structures reporting generically to "the NSC" or having multiple leaders in the field report to different leaders in Washington contribute to either undefined or multiple competing chains of authority to the president, violating this principle.

Ninth, the structure must not overburden the president and the national security advisory team whose focus needs to be strategic goals and policies rather than crisis decision making. The PNSR study team notes, "White House centralization of interagency missions . . . risks creating an untenable span of control over policy implementation." This "tends to burn out National Security Council staff, which impedes timely, disciplined, and integrated decision formulation and option assessment . . . [and] almost guarantees an inability to do deliberate, careful strategy formulation."[6] Any reform of the interagency system "must free the president and his advisors for strategic direction by providing effective mechanisms for decentralizing national security issue management."[7]

Tenth, the reform should fix the imbalance of bureaucratic power and prestige between the Departments of State and Defense. Additional power is required to ensure State's voice is heard during interagency deliberations, and additional prestige is required for the DOS to obtain the necessary levels of funding and personnel from Congress. Even former defense secretary Robert Gates has argued that the State Department needs additional resources and capacity to participate in the interagency process, saying whole-of-government approaches "can only be done if the State Department is given resources befitting the scope of its mission."[8]

Eleventh, for the coordinated interagency system to improve its capabilities over time, personnel from across the participating agencies need both training and experience working with other agencies. Reform options that routinely place working-level personnel from different agencies in contact with each other are more likely to achieve this objective than stovepiped agencies working in parallel or coordinating only through small interagency cells.

Twelfth, any changes to the interagency system should minimize the financial, personnel, and material costs required to establish a new system. The federal budget has limits, and advocating any reforms to Congress and the various interests in Washington will be much easier if costs are minimized.

Finally, changes to the interagency system should attempt to minimize culture shock in the participating agencies. Much has been written about the different cultures in the various organizations, particularly between the military and the State Department.[9] Reforms will be easier to advocate and implement if working-level personnel in the participating agencies do not perceive the new procedures as threats to their careers or their sense of self. Cultures can be transformed, but it takes a great deal of time and effort.

In summary, interagency reform should fulfill the following 13 evaluation criteria:

1. Provide a nonmilitary voice and face for US foreign policy.
2. Produce fully coordinated planning.
3. Create unity of effort during execution.
4. Be more efficient and effective than agencies working alone.
5. Give leaders authority commensurate with their responsibility.[10]
6. Provide legitimacy to the leader's decisions.
7. Enable the leader to access necessary resources.
8. Offer a clear chain of command to the president.
9. Avoid overburdening the president with operational or crisis matters.
10. Balance the power and prestige of the Departments of State and Defense.[11]
11. Develop interagency expertise among working-level personnel.
12. Minimize the financial, personnel, and material costs of reform.
13. Reduce agency culture shocks resulting from the reform.

Analysis

We will now apply these evaluation criteria to the proposed interagency structures at the regional and crisis levels. In the analysis, each of the four organizational structures is assigned a plus (+), a zero (0), or a minus (–) based on whether it is assessed as beneficial, neutral, or detrimental in meeting each criterion. Then the plusses are added and the minuses subtracted for each model to reach a final score. While this evaluation scheme is qualitative and subjective, it provides a helpful method to compare the models and determine which ones most closely satisfy the evaluation criteria. We first consider the crisis operations models and then the regional models.

Crisis Operations Models

As noted previously, the four general types of structures to reform the interagency for crisis operations are (1) an interagency organization, (2) a State Department–led organization, (3) a military-led organization, or (4) a parallel structure. To evaluate these models, we consider the most robust versions of each structure—the interagency model described by the PNSR study team, Liston, and Buchanan et al.; the State-led model described by this author; the military-led model described by Coffey; and the parallel structure model described by the CSIS study team. Table 1 summarizes the assessment. Based on this analysis, the interagency task force is the best structural model for crisis operations. A brief description of the analysis of each criterion follows.

Table 1. Analysis of crisis-level reform models

Evaluation Criteria	Interagency Organization	State Leads	Military Leads	Parallel Structure
Nonmilitary voice and face for US foreign policy	0	+	–	0
Fully coordinated planning	+	+	+	0
Unity of effort during execution	+	+	+	0
More efficient and effective than agencies working alone	+	+	+	0
Leader's authority commensurate with responsibility	+	0	0	–
Legitimacy of leader's decision making	+	0	0	+
Leader can access necessary resources	+	0	0	0
Clear chain of command to the president	+	+	+	–
Does not overburden the president	+	0	0	–
Balance of power and prestige between DOD and DOS	0	+	–	–
Develops interagency expertise	+	+	+	0
Minimizes cost in money, personnel, and material	0	0	0	+
Minimizes agency culture shocks	0	–	0	+
Totals	+9	+6	+3	–1

The State Department–led interagency task force is best able to guarantee that a nonmilitary voice and face would lead the subregional task force. The interagency organization was judged as neutral since this structure permits either a military or a civilian task force leader. Similarly, the parallel structure has both a civilian- and a military-led structure so it is also neutral against this measure. Finally, the military-led task force is detrimental since it will never have a nonmilitary leader.

The interagency, State-led, and military-led organizations are each able to produce fully coordinated interagency plans at the subregional level. The parallel structure was judged as neutral. With separate military and civilian leaders and no mandate for collaboration, this model would produce coordination when enforced by the two leaders. However, it could drift into uncoordinated stovepipes if the leaders and their staffs choose to work in traditional, comfortable channels rather than coordinating. These arguments are similar for the four models' ability to produce unity of effort during execution and to be more efficient and effective than the various agencies working separately.

The interagency organization is able to provide the leader with authority commensurate with responsibility, but this authority would need to be spelled out when establishing the task force. The leaders of the State- and military-led models would likely have slightly less authority delegated to them since they would report to a lead agency, potentially limiting some of their authority over resources from other agencies. The parallel structure does not provide authority commensurate with responsibility because, while each of the leaders would have authority over their piece of the organization, no one has overall charge of the mission with the ability to enforce decisions on the other side of the organization.

The interagency organization provides the leader with the greatest legitimacy since specifically the president would grant authority and should not be seen as partial to any particular agency. Subordinates will see the decisions of leaders as legitimate in the parallel structure since the military works for a military officer while civilians work in a traditional country-team structure. The State- and military-led task forces are judged as neutral on this measure because—despite enhanced authority vested in these individuals—some personnel from other agencies may still perceive decisions as biased toward the leader's parent agency.

The interagency organization is best able to access the necessary resources from other agencies, again due to the leader's status as a presidential representative. The State-led, military-led, and parallel structures, with proper authority granted to their leaders, should all do reasonably well in accessing interagency resources. However, the agency-specific nature of the leaders would probably result in occasional problems in accessing resources from outside the leader's parent agency.

The interagency model and both lead-agency models provide clear, unambiguous chains of command from everyone in the task force, through the task force leader, and up the chain to the president. The parallel structure model is unable to do this because there is no single leader for the crisis operation, resulting in multiple chains of command.

The interagency model is best to avoid nonstrategic decisions being routinely elevated to the presidential level, as the interagency task force leader would have the authority and legitimacy to make most decisions at the lower level. The lead-agency models are assessed as neutral against this measure since their leaders have most of the authority of the interagency leader but slightly less legitimacy, likely leading to more calls for the president to adjudicate interagency disputes. The parallel structure model fares poorly against this measure as the lack of a single decision authority in the region means many more decisions will be elevated to higher levels for adjudication.

The State-led model is best able to balance power and prestige between the Defense and State Departments. The interagency task force is judged as neutral because it may or may not increase State's power and prestige, depending on whether the task force leader and many of the staffers come from State. The military-led and parallel structures are both unhelpful as both either maintain the current balance or shift power further toward the military.

All three single-leader task forces are assessed as likely to expose a sizable number of working-level personnel from different agencies to the interagency environment. The parallel structure is less likely to do so because coordination between the two organizations may be handled only by key leaders or a small coordination cell.

The parallel structure is the least costly to implement as it essentially uses existing elements. The other three are judged as neutral on this criterion because while they will all require some additional staff to implement, they will primarily be formed from personnel and resources the individual agencies would have used in their response to the crisis.

Finally, the parallel structure has the least impact on agency cultures as this is largely the way things are done today. The military-led and interagency structures are judged as neutral against this criterion because they would involve only small shifts from the current way of doing business. However, the State-led model is judged as negative against this criterion since it would require a substantial cultural shift in the State Department to produce leaders for these interagency crisis task forces.

Regional Models

We now consider the four regional-level models: (1) a new regional-level interagency organization, (2) a structure in which the State Department leads at the regional level, (3) a structure in which the military leads at the regional level, and (4) a parallel structure in which the military and the State Department operate as equals in the region, coordinating their activities to some degree but reporting separately to their parent agencies. To evaluate these regional structures, this study again considered the most robust versions of each structure—Buchanan, Davis, and Wight's and Gardner's interagency structures and the PNSR study team's integrated regional center; Sylvia's State-led model; Naler's and Whitsitt's military-led models, and Desai's and Caudill, Leonard, and Thresher's parallel structure models. Table 2 shows the results of this assessment. Based on this analysis, the State Department-led structure is the best model for integrating interagency foreign policy and national security at the regional level, while an integrated interagency model comes in a close second. A brief description of the analysis follows.

Only the State-led model can guarantee a nonmilitary voice and face for US foreign policy at the regional level. The interagency structure is neutral on this measure because the leader could come from State or another agency. The parallel structure was also judged as neutral because, while the creation of a new regional-level State Department organization would certainly raise its profile in the region, the military's geographic combatant command would be engaging in the region at the same time. Finally, the military-led solution was judged as detrimental since, by definition, it puts a military face on US regional engagement, one of the problems this study set out to address.

Table 2. Analysis of regional-level reform models

Evaluation Criteria	Interagency Organization	State Leads	Military Leads	Parallel Structure
Nonmilitary voice and face for US foreign policy	0	+	–	0
Fully coordinated planning	+	+	0	–
Unity of effort during execution	+	+	0	–
More efficient and effective than agencies working alone	+	+	+	0
Leader's authority commensurate with responsibility	+	+	0	–
Legitimacy of leader's decision making	+	0	0	0
Leader can access necessary resources	+	+	0	0
Clear chain of command to the president	+	+	+	–
Does not overburden the president	0	+	0	–
Balance of power and prestige between DOD and DOS	0	+	–	+
Develops interagency expertise	+	+	0	–
Minimizes cost in money, personnel, and material	–	–	+	–
Minimizes agency culture shocks	–	–	0	+
Totals	+6	+8	+1	-5

The interagency organization would be expected to produce fully coordinated planning at the regional level as its leader would have the authority to accomplish this. Similarly, the State-led model would be expected to do well in producing coordinated regional plans because the organization is effectively identical to the proposed interagency regional organization, only with a leader from the State Department. The military-led model is neutral on this measure because the current COCOM-led, JIACG-enabled model has not always produced coordinated regional plans. Finally, the parallel structure is unhelpful because, while the COCOM would have a regional peer with whom to coordinate, no mechanism or single leader exists to enforce coordination between the two headquarters. The arguments are similar for producing regional unity of effort during execution.

All three single-leader models would be more efficient and effective than the agencies working individually, while the parallel structure is judged as neutral because the agencies are less closely tied together.

The interagency and State-led organizations are best able to provide authority commensurate with responsibility since this would be part of the charter for these organizations. This measure is judged neutral for the COCOM. While this study has demonstrated that the COCOM does not have the authority to compel interagency action, it is often able to produce some amount of interagency unity informally. The parallel structure is negative on this measure since neither leader would have the authority to compel action from the other organization.

The interagency organization best endows the leader's decisions with legitimacy as the leader would be perceived as representing the president rather than a specific agency. The other three models are all judged as neutral against this criterion because, while they would all have strong authority, the perception that leaders primarily represent their parent agencies would decrease their legitimacy in the eyes of some personnel from other agencies.

The interagency organization would be able to access the necessary resources across the interagency due to the nature of the organization. The State-led regional organization is assessed similarly as it is effectively an identical interagency organization but headed by a leader from State. The military-led organization is assessed neutral as it is less able to access resources from outside the DOD because the military-heavy structure is seen as inherently less interagency. The parallel structure is also judged as neutral because, while each leader would have access to resources from the agencies in their organization, the ability to share resources between organizations may be less than complete.

The interagency model and the two lead-agency models all have a clear chain of command to the president. The parallel structure fails on this measure because the two leaders would report through separate chains of command in Washington.

The State-led organization, established as a regional-level "country team" and reporting to the secretary of state rather than directly to the White House, would be best able to avoid overburdening the president with regional-level interagency policy disputes. The interagency organization is judged as neutral because it would report directly to the White House rather than to a parent agency, requiring more of the president's attention. The military-led model is also judged neutral because history has shown many agencies appeal to the White House when they dispute the combatant commander's decisions. The parallel structure is judged as worst because no decision maker is in place at the regional level. Thus, interagency decisions are forced back to Washington, with many likely ending up in the White House.

The State-led model and the parallel structure would each enhance the power and prestige of the State Department because each would create a State-led presence currently lacking in the region (or outside the region but focused exclusively on regional issues, as is the case with all the GCCs except EUCOM). The interagency organization is judged as neutral against this criterion because someone from State may or may not lead the organization. The military-led model is detrimental as it would perpetuate the DOD's regional power and prestige.

The regional interagency organization and the State-led organization would each create a new interagency headquarters with both a substantial civilian and military presence, leading to the assessment that these structures would do the most to develop a cadre of personnel with interagency expertise. The military-led model is judged as neutral on this criterion because it creates only a small cadre of non-DOD civilians with experience on the COCOM staffs and a small number of military personnel who routinely work interagency issues with non-DOD personnel. The parallel structure would not be helpful since the civilian and military organizations would exist separately with only minimal contact opportunities, predominately by senior leaders and those in the coordination cell.

Only the military-led model is judged as a low-cost reform option since it has already been implemented across the COCOMs. The other three structures would all involve creating a new headquarters, requiring substantial funding and new personnel resources.

Finally, the parallel structure would least impact agency cultures as it looks very similar to current practice at the country level. The military-led model is judged as neutral because, while it has already been largely implemented, it continues to cause cultural dislocations among some interagency personnel assigned to work with the CO-COMs. The other two models are judged as negative against this measure as both would require a significant change in State Department career paths and the development of personnel capable of leading large regional interagency organizations or directorates within them.

The Recommended Reform Model

Combining the crisis-level and regional analyses, this study recommends a new interagency structure built around regional headquarters led by the State Department. They would, in turn, conduct crisis operations by creating interagency task forces headed by a leader from the department or agency most appropriate to the mission.

Each regional headquarters could be called a US regional mission (USRM)[12] and led by a regional chief of mission (RCOM), who should be either a Foreign Service Officer with prior experience as an ambassador or a specially appointed ambassador.[13] Because of the great deal of power and importance vested in this leader, the president should nominate, and the Senate confirm, this individual. The presidential nomination would endow this individual with the rank of presidential envoy or presidential special representative, as well as ambassador-at-large, to convey the importance of the position and its role as the region's senior diplomat, overall senior executive-branch representative, and personal representative of the president. To ensure unambiguous State Department control over the organization, the deputy chief of this regional mission should also be a senior FSO so that the top leader would always be a State representative, even when the RCOM is away. The RCOM would be supported by a robust interagency staff similar to the interagency country team at an embassy. The geographic combatant commander would remain the senior military officer in the region and report to both the RCOM and through traditional DOD channels. To improve interagency capabilities, parts of the GCC's staff would transfer to the USRM organization, including elements of the J-4 (logistics), J-5 (plans, policy, and strategy), and J-6 (communications) to provide those capabilities. In addition, the GCC's security cooperation program would largely transfer to the USRM, as would the interagency coordination elements, such as the JIACG, since the USRM would now lead interagency coordination for the region.

During crisis operations, the USRM would establish an interagency task force. Each IATF would have a single director, a clear mission, and resources and authority commensurate with assigned responsibilities. The IATF director could be either military or civilian, depending on the security situation and which agency's core competency most closely aligned with the primary mission of the task force. The IATF director would be supported by an interagency staff using an integrated civil-military chain of command. The task force would be provided with the necessary personnel and material resources from across the interagency, including the military, and the IATF director would have operational control over all assigned forces. The recommended model is shown in figure 19. This model could also be used to strengthen the authorities of the existing counternarcotics JIATFs (JIATF-S and JIATF-W) by transforming them into IATFs and providing their directors with operational control over assigned personnel and resources.

Applying the Model

Under this construct, the United States would build on the successes of the GCCs in both bilateral and regional security cooperation activities. However, leadership and oversight of these activities across the region would now fall under the RCOM, placing these engagement programs under the guidance of a senior diplomat, and they would be planned and executed by an interagency USRM staff with representatives from the geographic bureaus under State's undersecretary for political affairs, USAID, and the Defense Security Cooperation Agency, as well as the military. All theater engagements would meet overall US goals and not just military goals. Additionally, participating personnel would come from the correct mix of agencies, ensuring a civilian diplomatic face on a mission when necessary, leveraging USAID developmental expertise when it is important to the engagement, and so on.

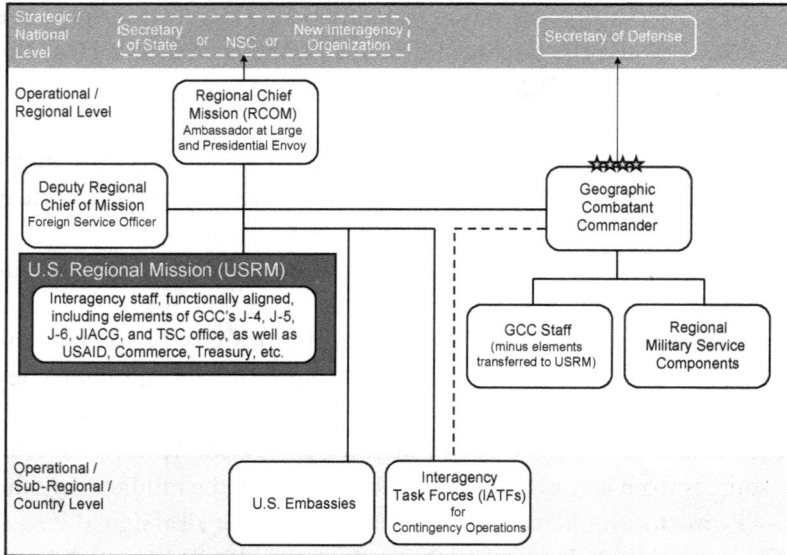

Figure 19. Recommended regional- and crisis-level interagency structure

For regional counterterrorism, moving the oversight of military as well as necessary nonmilitary activities—such as State, the USAID, law enforcement, intelligence, Commerce, and Treasury—from the GCC to the USRM would facilitate interagency participation during operational planning and execution. Enduring regional counter-terrorism engagements, such as the Trans-Sahara Counterterrorism Partnership, could be executed by an IATF established and super-vised by the USRM. In either case, overall authority would fall under a senior diplomat who would be able to harmonize these activities with broader US policies and interests in the region. The centralized interagency planning would reduce the wasted efforts of uncoordi-nated agencies working in parallel, as sometimes happens today. Sim-ilarly, regional counternarcotics initiatives under SOUTHCOM and PACOM should be moved to the corresponding USRMs, recasting JIATF-S and JIATF-W as IATFs with operational control over as-signed assets and working under the supervision of the RCOM and a truly interagency regional headquarters.

For humanitarian responses to disasters such as the Asian tsunami or the Haitian earthquake, the USRM would combine the military's logistical and communication capabilities, as well as its large pool of personnel, with the disaster response expertise of the USAID's Office of Foreign Disaster Assistance and the diplomatic skills of the State Department, both to plan and coordinate the operation and to execute the US response. The response could be conducted as an IATF led by a senior OFDA expert. The task force would initially have a large military component to provide search and rescue, logistics, and communication, but the military component would diminish over time, leaving the OFDA in charge of the remaining interagency response, which could last for months or even years, depending on the magnitude of the disaster and the capacity of the affected areas to recover.

Military actions in which US goals are fulfilled by the military alone—such as the Operation El Dorado Canyon attack on Libya, cruise missile attacks against terrorist targets, hostage rescue missions, and so forth—would be planned and executed by a military-only joint task force under the command of the GCC. The RCOM would be kept informed to ensure that the action was in accordance with US strategic goals, but the overall USRM staff would have little involvement. However, most military missions are more complex and involve US goals much larger than the military can accomplish on its own, such as creating stable, democratic governments in South Vietnam, Panama, Haiti, Iraq, and Afghanistan. The USRM interagency staff should plan and an IATF execute these more involved types of missions.

In Vietnam, the MACV/CORDS organization could have been designated an IATF, with the civilian development element subordinate to the military effort. Or perhaps it could have been better structured with the development director in overall command, while the military commander executed military missions advancing larger US development goals in South Vietnam. Similarly, the USRM staff would have planned the interventions in Panama and Haiti, ensuring interagency involvement from the very beginning rather than after US military forces were on the ground. The missions would then have been executed by an IATF combining the military's JTF headquarters and assigned forces with an ambassador designee for that country from the State Department and an interagency staff. Once a US embassy (re)opened, elements of the IATF would form the ambassador's country team, resulting in an integrated IATF under the overall leadership of the future ambassador.

The model would also work for operations such as Afghanistan and Iraq and would likely have avoided many of the problems the United States has faced in years of often disjointed operations in both countries. In Afghanistan, given the limited time available for the response to the 9/11 attacks, the planning for the initial military operation may not have changed much. However, the USRM staff should have been involved in parallel with interagency planning to determine how to reach the overall desired end state in Afghanistan beyond the military's initial plan to remove the Taliban from power and hunt al-Qaeda terrorists. Once the United States reopened the embassy in Kabul, US forces in Afghanistan would have become an IATF under overall supervision of the US ambassador, with the commander of US military forces in Afghanistan as the ambassador's military deputy. This structure would have produced unity of effort through unity of command rather than personality-driven parallel structures that have existed through most of the US involvement there. Similarly, in Iraq all US elements would have operated under an IATF, with the military deputy initially leading the invasion. Then the civilian director of the task force, Ambassador Bremer, would have taken overall control, ensuring all US actions led toward a coherent end state.

Implementation Considerations

The steps necessary to implement these proposed reforms include overcoming bureaucratic resistance, obtaining diplomatic endorsement from the rest of the world to accept the new construct, choosing locations for the new US regional missions, aligning regional boundaries across the various US departments and agencies, minimizing the cost of the reform while finding a way to pay those costs, addressing issues of agency culture and personnel, and, finally, obtaining congressional support and action.

Bureaucratic Resistance

One issue in implementing any reforms in USG executive agencies is the entrenched power of bureaucracies and their desire to preserve the status quo. While the military has many proponents of various interagency reforms, relatively few of these proposals have come from the State Department. This may indicate that those who hold bureaucratic power at State are not in favor of reform along the lines advocated in this study. For example, while the DOD largely supported the CORDS interagency construct used during the Vietnam

War, non-DOD agencies opposed it and continually tried to reduce the funding, personnel, and mission.[14] Similarly, today there are those in the State Department—particularly in the Bureau of African Affairs and at US embassies across Africa—who did not support the establishment of the military's US Africa Command.[15]

One State Department group that may be particularly resistant to creating a new State-led regional interagency organization is the assistant secretaries who currently direct the six regional bureaus. As the proposed RCOMs assume greater power over interagency planning and execution at the operational level, as well as some authority over the US embassies in their respective regions, the regional assistant secretaries in Washington will almost certainly lose power and resources. To make this reform more palatable, their role in strategic-level foreign policy development and coordination should be maintained and codified. Additionally, if additional resources are directed to the State Department as part of the reform (which would almost certainly be the case), some could go to the regional bureaus to ensure the assistant secretaries have the necessary manpower and funding to fulfill their strategic-level mandate.

DOS leaders also may be concerned that the new IATF construct will divert too many scarce personnel and resources, making it impossible to properly staff and fund existing missions. This concern would be best addressed by increasing the department's budget and staffing, as former defense secretary Gates; former JCS chief, ADM Mike Mullen; and many others have advocated for years.

Another group that may resist this reform is the American Foreign Service Association, the bargaining organization that protects the interests of US Foreign Service Officers. FSOs may have concerns about their career paths, such as whether serving as the US ambassador to a country is as prestigious under the new model, whether service in interagency organizations will derail their careers, or whether interagency service will be required to advance to senior ranks in the Foreign Service. These subjects could be addressed by clearly describing the new career tracks for FSOs and offering suitable promotion, monetary, or other incentives for accepting these career paths.

Other non-DOD agencies may also resist this new construct because their personnel will report to leaders from another agency when serving at the USRMs or IATFs, which many leaders would perceive as a diminution of their power. Addressing the concerns of these non-DOD and non-State leaders could include providing them with additional personnel and funding, clarifying and codifying their roles and authorities under the new system, and clearly delineating career paths leading to senior levels of leadership.

Diplomatic Endorsement

The greatest challenge may come in obtaining diplomatic acceptance and endorsement from the rest of the world for this new foreign affairs construct. Current diplomatic relations around the world are predominantly bilateral, and most countries may prefer to continue this arrangement with the United States via reciprocal embassies in each nation's capital rather than by relating to a new regional construct. The USRMs will not change how other countries engage with the United States, however, because the US embassies will still be in place and US ambassadors will still have plenipotentiary powers to directly represent the United States in that nation. Indeed, the USRMs should actually improve bilateral relations because the country-level ambassadors would be supported by a regional-level pool of interagency resources to aid in their activities. The RCOM would only be expected to redirect the actions of a country-level US ambassador when broader regional or global interests require a different approach at the country level. Because of today's rapid global communication, US ambassadors are no longer truly independent and isolated representatives of the United States—the secretary of state provides guidance as needed—so occasional inputs from the new RCOM should not fundamentally affect their latitude to execute bilateral diplomatic functions.

The United States would need to exercise caution to ensure countries do not bypass the US ambassador to their country in favor of the new RCOM. In the same way that some foreign leaders "follow the money" and choose to deal increasingly with the geographic combatant commander rather than their local US ambassador, the presence of a new RCOM could produce a similar temptation. One way to minimize this problem would be for the RCOM to have relatively little direct interaction with senior foreign leaders, instead working primarily with US actors in the region and in Washington.

The US regional missions are not envisioned to be accredited diplomatic representatives to any particular multilateral counterpart. Consequently, the regions would not be expected to create an equivalent organization to the USRM or to provide a reciprocal regional representation in Washington. The regional chief of mission would be an ambassador-at-large and presidential envoy, meaning the RCOM would represent the president and US interests in the region but would not be accredited to any particular foreign government or multilateral organization.

The new US regional missions would not replace current multilateral US missions to the EU, OSCE, OAS, AU, ASEAN, and NATO, which would continue to be led by US ambassadors accredited to these organizations. Instead, the USRMs would provide additional support, when required, to these multilateral missions in the same way they support bilateral US embassies.

When establishing these USRMs, the United States would need to ensure they are not perceived as imperial proconsulates or neocolonial entities by exercising energetic diplomacy, strategic communication, and judicious choice of location. These civilian-led regional organizations are intended to be more acceptable to local entities than the current military GCCs with their areas of responsibility spanning the globe. As the USRM coordinates US interagency activities in the region, the GCCs should become less visible, placing a diplomatic rather than a military face on US actions in the region.

At the crisis-action level, achieving diplomatic acceptance of the new IATF structure should be much less challenging. When the United States conducts noncombat actions, such as disaster relief, many host nations should prefer to work with an IATF headed by a senior USAID OFDA representative, for example, than one headed by a military officer. Similarly, in complex reconstruction and stabilization operations, host nations would probably perceive an IATF headed by a senior diplomat or reconstruction and stabilization specialist—rather than a military officer—as more of an offer of assistance and less of a threat to their sovereignty. In cases involving US military action in a nonpermissive environment, a military officer would likely lead the IATF, at least initially. Threatened governments in the region would welcome this arrangement, while the perceptions of the target nation would be largely irrelevant.

Locating the US Regional Missions

Choosing suitable locations for US regional missions would be an important factor in both their diplomatic acceptance and effectiveness. Locating USRMs in their respective regions, while desirable, is not required. Currently only one GCC is in its respective region—EUCOM in Stuttgart, Germany—while the others are headquartered elsewhere (i.e., AFRICOM is also in Stuttgart; CENTCOM is in Tampa, FL; SOUTHCOM is in Miami, FL; and PACOM is in Honolulu, HI). The USRMs corresponding to CENTCOM, SOUTHCOM, and PACOM could be collocated with the GCCs, avoiding the need to find a willing host nation and also making it easier for the RCOM to leverage the GCC's logistical, planning, communication, and personnel resources.

It is possible that countries in one or more regions would be interested in hosting USRMs, perhaps for a stronger relationship with the United States or for regional prestige, or because it makes sense to collocate the USRMs near other multilateral diplomatic entities. For example, the USRM for Europe might find a suitable home in Brussels (along with NATO and the European Council) or Vienna (home of many IGOs under the auspices of the UN). The USRM for Africa might be invited to locate in Addis Ababa, Ethiopia, near the headquarters of the African Union, or perhaps Vienna, the location of many Africa-focused UN agencies. Similarly, the USRM for the Pacific region might one day be invited to locate in Jakarta, Indonesia, near the ASEAN headquarters (though the history of US-Indonesian relations makes this unlikely anytime soon). By such reasoning, the USRM for the Americas and the Caribbean might best be located in Washington to be near the headquarters of the OAS. For the Middle East and Central Asia, a minimal US footprint probably best suits US diplomatic goals in the region, so the USRM would probably be best located near CENTCOM headquarters in Tampa or elsewhere in the United States. Ultimately, the locations of these regional missions are less important than their existence and their acceptability to nations in the region.

Regional Boundaries

The major agencies involved in foreign policy each draw different regional boundaries. While the military currently divides the world into six regions (including NORTHCOM), none of the other agencies and departments involved in foreign policy divides the world the same way, making direct coordination at times challenging.[16] The State Department divides the world into six regions with different boundaries. The CIA uses seven regions. Even the OSD divides the world into four regions, choosing a scheme different from its combatant commands.[17]

If the State Department, the military, and other agencies are to work more closely together at the regional level, agreeing on a common map of regional boundaries would make sense. Indeed, without such consensus, it is difficult to imagine USRMs with subordinate GCCs and personnel from other agencies—all supported by various staff structures in Washington—working at all. For example, using current boundaries, the USRM for South and Central Asian Affairs (aligned with the State Department's regional bureau of the same name) would have to supervise the work of two combatant commands—PACOM and CENTCOM. However, PACOM would report as well to the USRM for East Asia and Pacific Affairs, and CENTCOM would also report to the USRM for Near Eastern Affairs. Similar problems exist elsewhere between State Department and GCC regional maps, and the problem gets worse once the regional maps of other agencies are considered. Diplomacy may account for a small number of exceptions (e.g., Canada for many years wanted the State Department to include it in its Bureau of European and Eurasian Affairs rather than its Bureau of Western Hemisphere Affairs),[18] but they should not be made for the convenience of various US agencies.

Several of the reform proposals—including the Project for National Security Reform and the CSIS Beyond Goldwater-Nichols studies—have recognized this problem and recommended establishing a common regional map across the interagency. Several other authors have addressed this issue, including one student in the Army's School of Advanced Military Studies who devoted an entire paper to the topic.[19] President Obama's former national security advisor, retired general James L. Jones, affirmed the need for unified regional boundaries across the interagency, saying, "We are going to reflect in the NSC all the regions of the world along some map line we can all agree on,"[20] though no moves have yet been made in this direction.

Cost

Any reform of the interagency system becomes more difficult, or even impossible, as the projected cost increases. While conducting a detailed assessment of the costs of this reform is beyond the scope of this study, some ballpark estimates can be offered for the country-level IATFs and the regional-level USRMs.

The crisis-level reforms would cost relatively little since the envisioned IATFs would consist mostly of military-heavy organizations like today's JTFs and JIATFs, with the addition of interagency personnel from embassy country teams or other ad hoc groups that currently often operate in parallel with the military structure. Thus, the IATF would use largely the same personnel and resources but in a more integrated structure. However, a modest number of additional personnel from other agencies would be required—as few as 10 or 20 for a small operation to as many as a few hundred for a large, complex operation like the CPA in Iraq prior to returning sovereignty to the Iraqi government. At any given time, probably two to 10 IATFs would be active around the world, leading to a surge requirement of perhaps 100–1,000 non-DOD personnel across the interagency—costing in the neighborhood of $10–100 million in annual salaries, plus training, pensions, and other expenses.[21] However, if legislation shifted these billets from the DOD to the other agencies, additional personnel requirements could be cost-neutral except for additional training. Moving the billets would make sense since the increased presence of the interagency in these operations would be expected to reduce the workload on the military, and 1,000 DOD billets is less than 0.10 percent of its three million personnel.

The US regional missions, on the other hand, could potentially drive a much larger bill. Each USRM would require a headquarters building, office equipment, and an operating budget, as well as perhaps 200–500 staff personnel from across the interagency. This could cost perhaps $5–25 million for each facility,[22] $10–30 million for the operating budget,[23] and $20–50 million for personnel. Assuming five regions, this would require five headquarters buildings, five operating budgets, and 1,000–5,000 personnel; perhaps an upfront cost of $25–125 million and annual personnel and operating costs of $150–400 million. Some of the USRM staff would be military personnel reassigned from the combatant command or elsewhere in the DOD. The other staffers would have to come from non-DOD agencies, but billets could again be transferred from the military to nonmilitary agencies, potentially reducing the costs. If the USRMs were collocated with the current GCCs, they might even be able to share office space (because the GCC staff should shrink as the USRM assumes some of its functions), driving down some or all of the facility costs.

The USRMs may achieve some modest savings in personnel cost by centralizing some of the low-density, high-demand interagency personnel from some of the country teams, making these scarce experts available for use across the region. The regional chief of mission, the US bilateral ambassadors, and the various executive branch agencies would have to carefully examine each case and determine whether the individual would be best used in a regional or bilateral capacity.

Personnel and Culture

While funding for the new model may not be difficult to arrange, actually recruiting and training the necessary 1,100–6,000 new personnel for the non-DOD agencies could be much more challenging, since the skill sets in these agencies tend to require much more initial education than the average entry-level military or DOD civilian position. It might take several years to recruit the necessary personnel and run them through the Foreign Service Institute, National Defense University, or other interagency schools. In the interim, the new organizations could be temporarily staffed with military personnel and DOD civilians, who would be returned to the DOD as non-DOD personnel become available.

Even more important than recruiting and training new personnel is the development of a true interagency career path. The 2006 *Quadrennial Defense Review (QDR)* concurs, saying that interagency operations would be strengthened by establishing a National Security Officer career path.[24] The 2010 *QDR* also addresses this issue, recommending that the USG "allocate additional resources across the government and fully implement the National Security Professional (NSP) program to improve cross-agency training, education, and professional experience opportunities."[25]

The Goldwater-Nichols Act created the joint military, in part by requiring that all flag-rank personnel have experience in a qualifying joint position. The combatant commands, joint staff, and many JTFs provide ample opportunities for military officers to gain experience working in the joint military environment at multiple points in their careers. While mandated interagency experience may not be required to qualify for senior non-DOD leadership positions, the new system would have to offer opportunities at several points in an individual's career—at the working, line supervisory, and senior leadership levels. Doing so would allow the USG to create a cadre of seasoned interagency professionals. These individuals would also benefit from opportunities to attend professional interagency education, analogous to professional military education, at one or more points in their career. This would require funding for the cost of a school and instructors and for enough surplus personnel in the small agencies to ensure all critical billets remain filled.

A further step is making service in interagency organizations an acceptable and even valued part of each participating agency's culture. Today, many professionals in non-DOD agencies are strongly partial to their agency's culture and would prefer to work only within that agency. Over time, this cultural isolation would need to change. Although a defined interagency career path and opportunities to attend school with personnel from other agencies would help, cultural change requires above all simply time to evolve.

Congressional Support and Legislation

Large-scale reforms to the national security system above the level of a single agency or department would require the action of both the president and Congress. Some argue that a presidential executive order would be sufficient to enact the proposed reforms, but this is almost certainly not the case.[26] While an executive order might serve to change the interagency system during that administration, history indicates it would not likely remain the same under the next president.[27] For example, President Clinton's process for interagency reconstruction and stabilization operations, described in Presidential Decision Directive-56 (PDD-56), neither outlasted his presidency nor was generally followed while he was in office.[28] Additionally, an executive order does not presuppose support from Congress, which funds the executive-branch agencies. Because political power in Congress is often strongly tied to the large sums of money associated with the defense budget, Congress will certainly want to be involved in any reforms that change the national security structure. The CSIS Beyond Goldwater-Nichols study team notes that "the role of Congress in the process is the most crucial determinant of the prospects for a reform effort. The recommendations that flow from congressionally-mandated groups, commissions, or blue ribbon panels are more likely to lead to lasting changes than efforts launched exclusively at the executive branch level."[29]

Enduring change comes from legislation. Examples include the 1947 National Security Act that established, among other things, the National Security Council and the Department of Defense; the 1986

Goldwater-Nichols Act that created the joint military; the 2002 act that resulted in the Department of Homeland Security; and the 2004 act that founded the Office of the Director of National Intelligence and the National Counterterrorism Center.

Proper resourcing also comes from legislation. Michael Donley argues that if a new interagency structure is established in statute, "Congress has a more visible obligation to provide supporting institutional resources."[30] The CSIS study team states that "legislation could also provide the basis for realigning agency authorities and resources to ensure that each agency has the capabilities it needs to execute its assigned tasks."[31] Budgeting for the new USRMs would be fairly stable and predictable from year to year. However, because the complex operations that IATFs execute involve unpredictable crises, their funding would require both Congress and executive-branch agencies to exercise some guesswork and flexibility. The State Department and USAID budgets could include additional funds in anticipation of a certain number of IATF operations each year, or funds could be provided to participating agencies through supplemental appropriations for particular crisis operations, as Congress has done for operations in Iraq and Afghanistan. To facilitate unity of effort, the legislation authorizing these funds should include language that facilitates the transfer of funds between agencies and provides the IATF leader with some ability to prioritize efforts and direct interagency funding transfers when necessary and within specified limits. To ensure oversight, the legislation could require congressional notification of any transfers in excess of a specified amount.

While allowing IATF leaders to direct the interagency transfer of funds would be new, the process of interagency funding transfer itself is not without precedent. For example, Section 1207 of the FY 06 National Defense Authorization Act permits the DOD to transfer to the State Department "up to $100 million in defense articles, services, training, or other support for reconstruction, stabilization, and security activities in foreign countries." Also, the Pakistan Counterinsurgency Capability Fund (PCCF)—established by the FY 09 Supplemental Appropriations Act—permits the State Department to transfer all monies appropriated to this fund to the DOD or other federal agencies for building and maintaining the capability of Pakistani COIN forces.[32] In a significant step forward, Congress in FY 12 established the Global Security Contingency Fund (GSCF), a pooled account from both Defense and State for executing contingency operations. Initially funded with $50 million transferred from the PCCF, it is envisioned to grow to as much as $2 billion per year. A director from State and a deputy director from Defense will manage the fund.[33]

Finally, legislation would be required to place interagency civilian leaders, such as the regional chief of mission or a USAID OFDA expert leading a disaster-response IATF, in command of participating military forces and assigned personnel from other US agencies. The United States already practices civilian control of the military, with the president and secretary of defense in charge during both peace and war and the civilian secretaries in charge of each service's organize, train, and equip (i.e., peacetime) missions. Additionally, US ambassadors direct interagency country teams—generally comprising some military personnel—at their respective embassies. Thus, placing civilians in charge of military personnel or placing personnel from one agency in charge of personnel from another is not without precedent. As with interagency funding transfers, Congress could specify authorities and limitations in legislation and provide oversight through the congressional hearing process. Participating executive-branch agencies could also elevate concerns and disputes to the National Security Staff and National Security Council process for resolution, when necessary, though these disputes should decrease in both intensity and frequency as participating agencies become more comfortable with the new construct.

Obtaining legislation for the new reforms would not be easy. Previous ones have largely resulted from significant lessons learned from World War II, the failed hostage rescue mission in Iran, and the 9/11 attacks. The noteworthy lessons learned over the more than two decades since Goldwater-Nichols could serve to motivate the necessary reforms, but they have not yet been enough to influence the president or Congress to devote political capital to a reform effort. Changes across multiple agencies are particularly difficult to get through Congress because authority is distributed across multiple committees in the House and Senate, requiring not only action by those different committees but also the understanding that committee power may shift based on the reform. For example, the proposed reforms would likely appreciably strengthen the House Foreign Affairs and the Senate Foreign Relations Committees while diminishing some of the power of the armed services committees.[34]

There is at least some interest in Congress in assessing and addressing the lack of interagency unity of effort. On 30 April 2009,

Rep. Randy Forbes (R-VA) sponsored the Interagency Cooperation Commission Act (H. R. 2207) that would "establish a commission to examine the long-term global challenges facing the United States and develop legislative and administrative proposals to improve interagency cooperation."[35] However, the bill has no co-sponsors and has been stalled in the House Oversight and Government Reform Committee's Subcommittee on Government Management, Organization, and Procurement since June 2009, with no plans for further action on the bill.[36]

In June 2011, Senator Joe Lieberman introduced the Interagency Personnel Rotation Act of 2011 (S. Res. 1268; HR 2314) to develop national security professionals with interagency experience. The act would establish a committee on national security personnel within the Executive Office of the President. It would produce a strategy to develop personnel to accomplish objectives requiring integration of national security and homeland security personnel, as well as activities from multiple executive-branch agencies, to maximize mission success and minimize cost. The act would also create a system of interagency rotational service to develop expertise in working with personnel from other agencies and would make this service a requirement for promotion to senior executive service. Finally, the act would create an interagency training course. The bill was referred to the Senate Committee on Homeland Security and Governmental Affairs in October 2011, which ordered it "to be reported with an amendment in the nature of a substitute favorably."[37]

More recently, in December 2011, Rep. Russ Carnahan (D-MO) introduced the Contingency Operations Oversight and Interagency Enhancement Act of 2011 (HR 3660). It would institute a new stabilization and reconstruction fund and create a new interagency organization—the US Office for Contingency Operations (USOCO). Charged with planning and executing overseas contingency operations, it would report both to the DOD and State. Specifically, this office would

> (1) monitor political and economic instability worldwide in order to anticipate the need for mobilizing US and international assistance for the stabilization and reconstruction of a foreign country or region that is at risk of, in, or in transition from, conflict or civil strife in the wake of violence or cataclysmic disaster; (2) develop contingency plans and procedures to mobilize and deploy civilian and military personnel to conduct appropriate foreign stabilization and reconstruction operations (operations); (3) execute, administer, and enforce laws, rules,

and regulations relating to the preparation, coordination, and execution of operations; and (4) evaluate, and report to Congress on, the impact of operations.[38]

In December 2011, the bill was referred to the House Foreign Affairs Committee as well as to the House Armed Services Committee and the House Committee on Oversight and Government Reform.[39]

These bills demonstrate that some congressmen are thinking about the need to reform the interagency national security and foreign policy apparatus. Nonetheless—given the many other significant issues facing Congress at the time of this writing, coupled with various election cycles—there may simply not be enough congressional attention or interest to move any of these bills forward or to tackle an interagency reform of this magnitude in the near future.

What If There Is No Appetite for Interagency Reform?

Absent the will (or funds) to establish US regional missions, Congress could still mandate the much more modest step of requiring that contingency operations be conducted by an interagency task force headed by a leader from the organization whose portfolio most closely aligns with the mission. This may be the necessary first step before tackling change at the regional level. Assuming Congress is unwilling or unable to address interagency reform and that reform by executive order would have no lasting effect, can individual agencies do anything within their existing budgets and authorities that would help?

The State Department is very small, both in budget and personnel, and is already struggling to meet its current taskings. Thus, there is little chance it can or will take the initiative to implement the parts of this model that would fall within its jurisdiction.

The Defense Department, on the other hand, has a much larger budget and personnel pool. It also has more motivation to improve interagency coordination since the military is often asked to take on inherently interagency tasks when no one else in government can get the job done.[40] However, the military has already done much of what it can do by itself to create interagency coordination and unity of effort. Additional, feasible steps in this direction could include continuing to evolve the geographic combatant commands along the lines of SOUTHCOM, AFRICOM, and EUCOM, with civilian deputies from the State Department and robust partnering structures in their headquarters, though this will do nothing to put a civilian face on these activities. Increased use of the JIATF construct in areas like the Horn of Africa, Iraq, and Afghanistan would bring more interagency unity of effort and coordination to subregional missions. The DOD could also increase its current personnel exchange programs with the interagency, placing more officers in the State Department, USAID, and other agencies where civil-military contact will enhance working relationships and understanding on both sides. Finally, the DOD could fund additional billets at its PME schools—such as the command and staff colleges, the war colleges, and the National Defense University—to provide more opportunities for interagency personnel to get to know their military counterparts and experience a common national-security curriculum. However, all of these DOD-only actions fall short of the goal of true interagency unity of effort.

Notes

1. Edward Marks, "Why USAFRICOM?," *Joint Force Quarterly* 52 (1st Quarter 2009): 148–49; Robert Munson, "Do We Want to 'Kill People and Break Things' in Africa?," *Strategic Studies Quarterly* 2, no. 1 (Spring 2008): 97–110; and Sylvia, "Empowering Interagency Capabilities," 25.

2. COL Albert Zaccor, USA, *Security Cooperation and Non-State Threats: A Call for an Integrated Strategy*, occasional paper (Washington, DC: Atlantic Council of the United States, August 2005), 24–25.

3. PNSR, *Forging a New Shield*, 95.

4. Derek S. Pugh and David J. Hickson, *Great Writers on Organizations*, 3rd omnibus ed. (Hampshire, UK: Ashgate Publishing, 2007), 149. Lyndall F. Urwick (1891–1983) had the experience of both industry and the British army, was director of the International Management Institute in Geneva, and subsequently devoted himself to lecturing and writing about management.

5. Donley, *Rethinking the Interagency System*, pt. 2, 9.

6. PNSR, *Forging a New Shield*, viii.

7. Ibid., 445.

8. Secretary of Defense Robert M. Gates, quoted in William I. Bacchus, "Regaining Relevance: Five Steps to Strengthen State," *Foreign Service Journal* 86, no. 7–8 (July/August 2009): 14.

9. See LTC Rickey L. Rife, USA, and Rosemary Hansen, FSO, "Defense Is from Mars, State Is from Venus: Improving Communications and Promoting National Security," strategy research project (Carlisle Barracks, PA: Army War College, June 1998).

10. *Leaders* here refers to the leader of whatever organizations are constructed at the regional or subregional levels.

11. Increasing the prestige of the State Department relative to the Defense Department could also increase the relative prestige of other agencies, such as Commerce, Treasury, etc., but that is beyond the scope of this study.

12. The author proposes the term *US regional mission* to replace Sylvia's misnamed "regional interagency consulate," which requires a new name since the proposed organization does not perform a consular function as defined by the Vienna Convention on Consular Relations. UN, Vienna Convention on Consular Relations, 24 April 1963, 261.

13. The deputy chief of mission (DCM) is the number two diplomat assigned to an embassy or mission and serves as the deputy to the ambassador. While the ambassador is often a political appointee with no background in the Foreign Service, the DCM is almost always a career FSO.

14. Stewart, "Winning Hearts and Minds," in *Mismanaging Mayhem*, ed. James Jay Carafano and Richard Weitz, 106.

15. US DOS and the Broadcasting Board of Governors, Office of Inspector General, *Report of Inspection: The Bureau of African Affairs*, report no. ISP-I-09-63, August 2009, 13.

16. Murdock and Flournoy, *Beyond Goldwater-Nichols*, 37.

17. Ibid.

18. Dr. Edwina Campbell (professor of national security studies, Air Command and Staff College, and former FSO), correspondence with the author, 16 April 2010.

19. MAJ David A. Meyer, USA, "Normalizing Executive Department Boundaries: A Timely First Step to Improving Interagency Coordination," monograph (Fort Leavenworth, KS: School of Advanced Military Studies, US Army Command and General Staff College, 21 March 2007). See also Sunil B. Desai, "Solving the Interagency Puzzle," *Policy Review*, no. 129 (February/March 2005): 57–71, http://www.hoover.org/publications/policyreview/3431461.html#; Uchida, "Reforming the Interagency Process," 75; Pasquarett and Kievit, *Blueprint for a Bold Restructuring of the Organization for National Security*, xiii, 24; and Sylvia, "Empowering Interagency Capabilities," 62.

20. The national security advisor, retired general James L. Jones, quoted in PNSR, *Turning Ideas into Action* (Arlington, VA: Center for the Study of the Presidency, September 2009), 59, http://www.pnsr.org/data/files/pnsr_turning_ideas_into_action.pdf.

21. Based on a rough order of magnitude (ROM) cost of $100,000 in salary per person.

22. ROM cost based on an Internet survey of office buildings 20,000–75,000 square feet for sale in Miami and Honolulu, two of the current regional combatant command locations.

23. ROM cost based on SOUTHCOM's average annual operating budget prior to FY 98. "U.S. Military Facilities: U.S. Southern Command," informal weblog for the US military's airborne Spanish linguists, http://www.beanerbanner.org/ussouthcom.htm.

24. DOD, *Quadrennial Defense Review Report* (Washington, DC: DOD, 6 February 2006), 79.

25. Ibid., February 2010, 71. Pres. George W. Bush initiated the National Security Professional Development (NSPD) program by executive order (EO) in 2007. See Bush, EO 13434, NSPD, 22 May 2007. According to the CRS, the NSPD program has accomplished little, and EO 13434 excludes the military, the Foreign Service, and the intelligence community, citing concerns the program would detract from these agencies' already-established education and training paths. The CRS recommends congressional legislation and oversight to improve the NSPD program. See Cathe-

rine Dale, *Building an Interagency Cadre of National Security Professionals: Proposals, Recent Experience, and Issues for Congress*, CRS Report for Congress RL34565 (Washington, DC: CRS, 8 July 2008).

26. PNSR, *Turning Ideas into Action*, 19.

27. Murdock and Flournoy, *Beyond Goldwater-Nichols*, 147. "Executive-driven reforms often lack staying power. . . . The executive branch in the 1990s often sought to use existing agencies for new purposes through the exercise of executive fiat rather than seeking broad, bipartisan reforms. The result was the 'bending' of legacy institutions to new missions, often using Presidential directives and executive findings. . . . These executive-driven innovations had their uses . . . but rarely carried over into successive administrations." York, "Militarizing the Interagency," 13.

28. MAJ Thomas M. Lafleur, USA, "Interagency Efficacy at the Operational Level," monograph (Fort Leavenworth, KS: School of Advanced Military Studies, US Army Command and General Staff College, 26 May 2005), 17–22; and Donley, *Rethinking the Interagency System*, pt. 2, 5.

29. Murdock and Flournoy, *Beyond Goldwater-Nichols*, 146.

30. Donley, *Rethinking the Interagency System*, pt. 2, 8.

31. Murdock and Flournoy, *Beyond Goldwater-Nichols*, 34.

32. Nina M. Serafino, *Department of Defense "Section 1207" Security and Stabilization Assistance: A Fact Sheet*, CRS Report RS22871 (Washington, DC: CRS, 7 May 2008), 1; and *Supplemental Appropriations Act*, Public Law 111-32, 123 Stat. 1895, 111th Cong., 1st sess., 24 June 2009.

33. Josh Rogin, "State Department and Pentagon Creating Joint Office for Funding Emergency Response," The Cable, *Foreign Policy*, 27 December 2011, http://the cable.foreignpolicy.com/posts/2011/12/27/state_department_and_pentagon_creating _joint_office_for_funding_emergency_response.

34. Ben Lieberman, "Crisis! What Crisis? America's Response to the Energy Crisis," in *Mismanaging Mayhem*, 125.

35. US House Armed Services Committee, Oversight and Investigations Subcommittee, Interagency Cooperation Commission Act, 111th Cong., 1st sess., H. R. 2207, 30 April 2009, 1.

36. Library of Congress (LOC), THOMAS, "Status of H. R. 2207," 110th Congress, http://thomas.loc.gov.

37. LOC, THOMAS, "Status of S.1268," 111th Cong.; and LOC, THOMAS, "Status of H. R. 2314," 111th Cong..

38. LOC, THOMAS, "Status of H. R. 3660," 111th Cong.

39. Ibid.

40. RAND and the Army also note the prudence of this approach. In their "Integrating the Interagency in Planning for Army Stability Operations" project, the RAND team writes, "The Army has a great interest in . . . a 'whole-of-government' approach to [stabilization, security, transition, and reconstruction] operations, but the Army also has low leverage over the process. In addition, the DoD and the Army are in a position of trying to move the interagency collaboration process forward and simultaneously planning in case it fails." Thomas S. Szayna et al., *Integrating Civilian Agencies in Stability Operations* (Santa Monica, CA: RAND Corporation, 2009), xiv.

Appendix

Interagency Reform at the National Level

While this study focused on the regional and crisis action levels of US interagency foreign policy planning and operations, many authors have proposed interagency system reforms at the strategic or national level. This study applied the 13 reform analysis criteria to three major categories of national-level reform proposals but found them insufficient to select any one of the three structures. Thus, it makes no recommendations for interagency reform at the national level.

Reform Options at the National Level

The literature proposes three general types of national-level interagency reform models. Authority and responsibility for leading interagency planning and coordinating execution of foreign policy and national security missions could be assigned to a new interagency organization (1) outside the National Security Council (NSC), (2) within the NSC under expanded authorities, or (3) with a lead cabinet-level agency (most likely either the State or Defense Department) operating within the current NSC structure.

A National Interagency Organization outside the NSC

This national-level interagency reform proposal envisions creating a new interagency organization in Washington with the responsibility and authority to coordinate interagency planning and execution, task cabinet-level agencies and other executive-branch departments, and resolve interagency disputes. Proponents of this reform option include both the 9/11 Commission and Gen Anthony Zinni, USMC, retired, a former combatant commander and presidential envoy to Israel and the Palestinian Authority.

This new organization could be created either inside or outside the executive office of the president (EOP). Creating it within the EOP would keep the interagency coordination function close to the president and provide additional capacity for interagency planning and direction, while leaving the NSS free to concentrate on its role of developing policy and advising the president. However, this approach would create two similar national security staffs in the EOP, potentially complicating both coordination and oversight. If the new strategic-level interagency organization were created outside the EOP, it would have some independence from the White House, potentially distancing the organization from politics.[1]

Whether inside or outside the EOP, the new organization would have the authority and resources necessary to lead integrated interagency planning and coordination for both steady-state and crisis activities rather than relying on ad hoc or personality-driven arrangements. However, it would be expensive in personnel from across the relevant executive-branch agencies, requiring the manning of a second national security–related staff. It could also be financially very expensive; for example the new Department of Homeland Security costs $30 billion annually in administrative overhead above the cost of running the 22 previously separate entities centralized under the new department.[2] Additionally, this new organization would create a new layer of government between the president and national security–related agencies and departments, which could create additional bureaucratic costs. Finally, unless establishing the new organization under a suitably strong statute, the very powerful secretaries of defense and state, as well as others, might simply choose to work around it.[3]

In one of the earliest proposals of this type, Lt Col James Bartran, USA, in a 2000 paper proposed creating a national interagency emergency operations center (NIEOC) in Washington with responsibility to execute coordinated US interagency responses to crises around the world. This organization would have a standing professional staff representing all relevant members of the interagency community and be run by a presidential appointee having direct tasking authority over all government agencies designated in support of a crisis response. According to Bartran, the NIEOC director could either report directly to the president (which puts the model in this outside-the-NSC category), or it could potentially fall under the NSC.[4]

In 2004 the 9/11 Commission's report identified the failure of interagency coordination as one of the causes of the terrorist attacks and recommended creating new interagency institutions inside the EOP but separate from the NSC, which would be empowered to coordinate interagency information sharing, jointly plan operations, and oversee the execution of interagency operations. The commission believed this structure would put a leader in charge to ensure unity of effort and improve efficiency while leaving the NSC to focus on policy direction and advising the president. These recommendations led to the creation of the National Counterterrorism Center (NCTC) and the Office of the Director of National Intelligence (ODNI), which perform the interagency information sharing and oversight functions for counterterrorism and intelligence, though the NCTC lacks formal authority over the participating agencies and the ODNI is located outside the EOP.[5]

Also in 2004, General Zinni—who served as both US Central Command commander and presidential envoy—proposed creating an independent interagency organization to coordinate civil-military planning for complex contingency operations, saying, "The new organization should not be at the Cabinet level or within an existing government body, but instead should have representatives from different departments and agencies and make recommendations to the National Security Council."[6]

In a 2005 paper, Maj J. D. York, USMC, proposed the creation of a unified interagency authority analogous to the establishment of the joint military by the Goldwater-Nichols legislation. In York's model, this new agency would replace the NSC and be led by a Senate-confirmed director with a staff representing all government agencies active in foreign policy. This director would replace the national security advisor as the principal advisor to the president for interagency foreign policy, review interagency contingency plans, and provide oversight of interagency operations.[7] However, since the NSC no longer exists in this model—with its policy formulation and presidential advisory functions subsumed by the new organization—one could argue that this is actually a model that places interagency coordination under the NSC, albeit with increased authority and a new name. Capt Timothy Hsia, USA, made a similar recommendation in a 2008 article, calling for the establishment of a foreign policy director, unaligned with either the State or Defense Departments, to be analogous to the chairman of the Joint Chiefs of Staff for the interagency to "orchestrate all the instruments of national policy."[8]

In perhaps the most thorough description of this model, the Project on National Security Reform (PNSR) in 2008 recommended creating within the EOP a director for national security (DNS) with "super-cabinet" authority.[9] The national security advisor and NSS would remain, but the staff would be reduced to 40–50 people and would only provide advice to the president. The DNS would help the president determine which issues should be assigned to lead agencies and which are inherently interagency. For interagency issues, the DNS staff would have the legal authority to supervise interagency teams working the issues and providing direction to all other executive-branch agencies and departments, including directing mission execution. Under the supervision of the DNS, the PNSR study team recommends creating "empowered interagency teams" as needed to work on specific issues and which would have the authority to direct the activities of executive-branch departments and agencies within the scope of their mandate.[10] However, in 2009, the PNSR study team issued a new report backing away from creating an interagency organization separate from the NSC and instead recommending performing the function within an NSS with expanded authorities and capabilities; this new recommendation is described in the next section.[11]

The NSC Leads

In the second type of strategic-level interagency reform structure—the NSC-centric model—the NSC itself coordinates interagency planning and unity of effort. Proposals to strengthen the NSC's authority and capability to provide strategic-level interagency coordination are the most common reform recommendations. This model includes structures in the NSC and staff to directly conduct interagency coordination in a permanent office subordinate to the NSC or in ad hoc organizations created for short-term issues or crisis operations. Prominent proponents of this model include the Defense Science Board, the Beyond Goldwater-Nichols study team, and the PNSR 2009 study.

Broadening the NSC's responsibility to include coordination of operational-level planning and execution would make its existing interagency committees responsible for these roles in addition to policy development and strategic-level coordination. This approach has a couple of key advantages. First, if policy developers also oversee operations, then addressing operational requirements, resources, command arrangements, and other implementation issues will become a natural extension of policy development. Consequently, the NSC would not only produce a better executable policy but also be equipped to more fully advise the president on the implications of various courses of action. Additionally, this model provides an unambiguous chain of authority to the president. However, it could divert the NSC's attention from its primary policy development and presidential advisory functions as urgent operational issues crowd out strategy development.[12] The Hart/Rudman Commission agreed, recommending that the national security advisor and NSS focus on coordinating policy and avoid planning and oversight of execution functions or becoming operators.[13] Echoing this finding, the 9/11 Commission determined that operational planning and direction at the NSC overwhelms the staff and causes it to focus too much on day-to-day issues at the expense of advising the president on larger policy issues—another failure the commission says contributed to the 9/11 attacks.[14]

In 1993 the commander of US Atlantic Command, ADM Paul David Miller, proposed the creation of ad hoc interagency action groups (IAG) under the NSC to coordinate interagency planning and execution for specific missions, such as counternarcotics or humanitarian assistance.[15] IAGs would implement policy, facilitate and expedite interagency coordination, and adjudicate interagency issues during execution. They would be established by presidential decision and report to the NSC. Each IAG would operate under the sponsorship of a lead agency, and the director of an IAG would be the deputy director of the lead agency or an immediate subordinate. A committee of senior representatives from the member agencies would advise and assist the director, and relevant executive-branch agencies would contribute working-level personnel. The IAG director would determine the capabilities and functions required, including personnel and budget from participating agencies, to meet the policy objective and task the organizations possessing the needed capabilities. Each participating department or agency would then use its own established procedures to execute its assigned functions. The IAG would be disbanded upon mission completion.[16] This model contains many of the elements of today's joint interagency task forces (JIATF), though Miller's IAGs operate at both the strategic and operational levels while JIATFs today exist only at the operational level.

In 1997 the US government came close to implementing an NSC-led process at the strategic level when President Clinton issued Presidential Decision Directive 56 (PDD-56), codifying a process by which the NSC would lead interagency coordination, planning, and the monitoring of execution for "complex contingency operations." As a result of interagency friction during the planning and execution of Operation Restore Hope in Somalia in 1992–93 and Operation Uphold Democracy in Haiti in 1994, Clinton saw the need for a more systematic approach to interagency planning and execution for these types of multifaceted operations.[17] Under PDD-56, once a crisis was declared, the NSC's Deputies Committee would task the appropriate functional or regional policy coordination committee (PCC, renamed an integration planning cell [IPC] in the Obama administration) to lead the interagency coordination process for the contingency. The tasked PCC would then develop the political-military ("pol-mil") plan—the strategic-level, interagency blueprint for the contingency—and the director of the PCC (an individual at the deputy assistant secretary level) would become responsible for policy development, planning, day-to-day oversight, and implementation of the pol-mil plan across all executive-branch agencies. However, President Clinton never used the PDD-56 process, instead preferring a less formal process,[18] and in 2001 Pres. George W. Bush rescinded PDD-56, so the NSC-centric process it described was never used.[19]

In 1998 RAND analyst Bruce Pirnie described an NSC-led process specifically focused on interagency coordination of complex contingency operations that shares many features with PDD-56. In Pirnie's model, the NSC's standard system of committees would work together with a presidentially appointed special representative or presidential envoy to provide leadership for the mission. The NSC's Principals Committee would set the policy and strategy for the mission and the Deputies Committee would task a mission-specific NSC executive committee and the special representative to develop and coordinate an integrated pol-mil plan to meet the policy goals. The national security advisor would authenticate the completed pol-mil plan, the special representative would then lead the US government's execution of the plan, and the NSC's tiered system of committees and interagency meetings would continue to revise policy and make day-to-day policy decisions.[20] Pirnie's addition of the presidentially appointed special representative to provide sustained, personal leadership for the mission below the level of the president is a significant new feature over the PDD-56 model. This new role could circumvent not only overloading the advisor but also creating the appearance that the advisor has a vested interest in the mission and is thus less of an honest broker during ongoing interagency policy development and any interagency disputes about the mission that the NSC would need to resolve.[21]

In 2004 the Defense Science Board (DSB) recommended another variation of the NSC-centric model, this time focused on stabilization and reconstruction operations. The DSB stated that "the management discipline used by the military services to plan and prepare for combat operations must be extended to peacetime activities . . . across the government."[22] It recommended creating a set of contingency planning and integration task forces (CPITF) under the NSC to direct the interagency planning effort and ensure interagency unity of effort for stabilization and reconstruction operations. Instead of waiting for a crisis to occur requiring stabilization and reconstruction operations, CPITFs would be proactively established for all countries the NSC assessed as high risk for US intervention leading to stabilization and reconstruction operations. The DSB estimated that anywhere from two to 10 CPITFs would exist at a time, each staffed with personnel from all relevant executive-branch agencies and supported by a small permanent cadre on the NSC staff to provide continuity and expertise.[23]

Also in 2004, Hans Binnendijk and Stuart Johnson at the National Defense University's Center for Technology and National Security Policy proposed a model similar to that in the 2004 DSB summer study. They advocate the creation of national interagency contingency coordinating groups (NIACCG) under the NSC to plan and coordinate postconflict operations. Each NIACCG would have representatives from relevant executive-branch departments and would provide strategic guidance and coordinate planning for a postconflict operation. The NIACCGs would use the JIACGs at each geographic combatant command (GCC) to coordinate national-level interagency planning with regional-level military planning conducted by the combatant commands.[24]

In a 2005 paper, Lt Col Ted Uchida, USAF, recommended creating an interagency headquarters (IAHQ) in Washington.[25] In this model, the NSC would organize and staff a single, national-level IAHQ with representatives from all executive-branch agencies having a role in overseas crisis operations. This IAHQ would consist of both geographic and functional subdirectorates representing, as the Defense Science Board said, areas "where US interests are very important and the risk of intervention is high." The leader of the IAHQ would be nominated by the president, not require Senate confirmation, and report directly to the president and national security advisor. The IAHQ could create and deploy ad hoc interagency task forces (IATF) as needed, which would be task-organized to accomplish specific missions using the combined capabilities of the interagency.[26]

Also in 2005, the Center for Strategic and International Studies (CSIS) released phase 2 of its Beyond Goldwater-Nichols study, led by Clark Murdock and Michèle Flournoy (who served as Obama's undersecretary of defense for policy from 2009 to 2012 and in the Clinton administration as both the principal deputy assistant secretary of defense for strategy and threat reduction and the deputy assistant secretary of defense for strategy), which offered one of the most comprehensive descriptions of the NSC-centric model, though again their model is specific to complex contingency operations. The CSIS team recommended broadening the NSC beyond its traditional role of preparing policy decisions for the president to include a more active coordination and oversight role, ensuring presidential intent is reflected in US government actions, particularly for complex contingency operations. However, the CSIS team cautioned that the NSC should not get involved in the actual conduct of operations and that no NSC staffer should have directive authority over any executive-branch agency or department.[27]

To implement the NSC's expanded role, the study team recommended making more use of the NSS by establishing a new senior director for strategic planning and a senior director for complex contingency planning, each with support offices.[28] In the CSIS model, like PDD-56, the strategic-level interagency process for a complex contingency operation would begin with a decision by the NSC Principals Committee or Deputies Committee, which would task the deputy national security advisor to guide the development of planning guidance and oversee interagency planning. An NSC executive committee—composed of undersecretaries or assistant secretaries from the relevant departments, chaired by the new NSC senior director for complex contingency planning, and supported by the Office of Complex Contingency Planning—would determine the desired strategic end state, the roles and responsibilities of the participating agencies, and the mechanisms to be used to achieve interagency unity of effort and oversee the operation on a day-to-day basis, while the NSC Deputies Committee would be the primary interagency decision-making body.[29]

To connect the strategic-level interagency planning and coordination in Washington with operational-level military planning at the GCC, the NSC executive committee for the operation would assign personnel from its respective agencies to serve on an interagency crisis planning team (ICPT), led by the NSC senior director for that region (positions currently exist on the NSC staff). The ICPT would deploy to the GCC headquarters as early as possible in the planning process to integrate civilian planning at the NSC with military planning at the GCC, reaching back to the NSC and its respective agencies as needed. The ICPT would be the supported planning agency, with the GCC planners supporting its efforts. Any disagreements between the ICPT and military planners would be elevated directly to the national security advisor, who would act as an honest broker and could further elevate issues to the Deputies Committee as the "court of appeals."[30]

In a 2007 article, Nora Bensahel at RAND and Col Anne Moisan, USAF, at the Institute for Strategic Studies at the National Defense University proposed another NSC-centric model for interagency coordination of stabilization and reconstruction operations. They recommended creating a prevention, reconstruction, and stabilization cell (PRSC) under the NSC to monitor potential conflicts around the world which might require a US stabilization and reconstruction mission, to develop coordinated interagency plans for those conflicts which emerge, and to build international coalitions with potential future partners for stabilization and reconstruction operations. The director would report to the national security advisor, and the PRSC would be staffed with 10–15 core personnel from State and Defense who would be permanent NSC staff employees rather than detailees whose loyalties might lie with their parent agencies. The NSC would designate a lead agency for mission execution, but policy oversight and strategic direction would remain in the PRSC.[31]

Finally, PNSR's 2009 report rejected its 2008 recommendation to establish an interagency coordinating body outside the NSC and ultimately decided in favor of an interagency coordination system under NSC leadership. In the revised proposal, the national security advisor would remain as advisor to the president and would receive additional authority to manage the end-to-end national security interagency process but would not have the authority to direct the actions of executive-branch agencies and departments. The interagency teams from the 2008 proposal would report to the national security advisor, preserving several of the features of the earlier recommendation but significantly reducing the authority of the interagency leader below the president.[32]

A Lead Agency

The third type of interagency reform at the strategic level is the lead-agency model in which the National Security Council would retain its traditional policy coordination and presidential advisory functions and would delegate strategic-level planning and inter-agency coordination of foreign policy and national security issues to an existing cabinet-level agency. Depending on the model, the NSC might assign all planning and coordination to the same agency, or the lead agency might change depending on the issue addressed.

The lead-agency model has two key advantages. First, it "builds on the fact that departments and agencies have operational responsibili-ties, capabilities and resources that policy making bodies such as the NSC do not." Second, it "frees the NSC staff to concentrate on high level policy issues." However, there are also some disadvantages. First, while the Department of Defense (DOD) has robust capabilities to lead an interagency process, it is not clear other agencies, such as the State Department, have the resources or institutional culture to be an effective lead agency. Second, it is not certain other executive-branch agencies would follow the lead of a peer agency, which may be per-ceived to have different agency priorities and goals. The 9/11 Com-mission expressed concerns over the lead-agency model, saying that coordination during execution often suffers because the lead agency lacks the authority to direct the activities of other executive-branch agencies.[33] Additionally, the CSIS study team considered both the NSC-centric and lead-agency approach to strategic-level interagency coordination and assessed the NSC-centric model to be superior. It found the lead-agency approach is often insufficient because bureau-cratic agencies resist taking direction from one another and "only the NSC can play the role of the honest broker in coordinating the plan-ning and oversight of interagency operations at the strategic level."[34]

Fewer strategic-level lead-agency reform proposals are found in the literature than for the other two options. The most prominent of these are the Hart/Rudman Commission and the State Department in 2025 Working Group studies, both proposing designating the State Department as lead agency. While the DOD is often either the desig-nated or de facto lead agency for several issues at the strategic level, the literature identifies no reform proposals assigning the DOD as lead agency for foreign policy.

In a 1994 paper, Maj Mark Curry, USA, suggests giving the re-gional assistant secretaries of state directive authority for all inter-agency programs in their region, including peacetime engagements by the combatant commander but excluding combat operations. They would also have formal authority over the ambassadors in the region, preventing them from reporting directly to the secretary of state or the president (though this is highly unrealistic).[35] While the regional assistant secretaries are technically chartered to issue direction to US embassies in their region, the ambassadors leading these embassies are appointed by the president with plenipotentiary powers to represent the United States in their assigned country and generally prefer to deal directly with the secretary of state or the president, bypassing the regional assistant secretary.[36]

In 2001 the Hart/Rudman Commission recommended increasing the importance and authorities of the regional bureau leaders at the State Department by upgrading the positions from assistant secretaries to undersecretaries.[37] These more senior strategic-level leaders of regional foreign policy would then chair interagency working groups within the NSC "to develop regional strategies and coordinated government-wide plans for their implementation." This would "position the State Department to play a leadership role in the making and implementation of US foreign policy."[38] Additionally, the Hart/Rudman Commission recommended the State Department regional undersecretaries meet at least twice a year with the ambassadors and military combatant commanders in their regions to improve coordination between the strategic and operational levels.[39]

The 2007 report from the State Department in 2025 Working Group also recommended casting the State Department as the lead foreign affairs agency within the interagency structure. In this model, the State Department, working in support of the NSC, would lead the periodic interagency development of a global affairs strategic plan, translating the US National Security Strategy into a set of specific interagency goals and plans, with the designation of a lead agency to accomplish each goal and performance objectives to assess attainment of the goals. This State-led planning process would provide strategic coherence to US engagement and operations overseas, "create close collaboration on key strategic issues, highlight vulnerable gaps and seams, and foster a culture of unity across the government."[40] The working group believed the State Department was the correct lead agency for this task because State "is already accountable to the President for ensuring that all USG [US government] efforts overseas support American foreign policy objectives."[41]

Analysis

We now apply the 13 evaluation criteria to the three general structures for interagency reform at the national level. To evaluate these structures, we consider the most robust versions of each—the PNSR super-cabinet model for a new interagency organization, the CSIS description of the NSC-centric model, and the lead-agency description offered by Curry and the Hart/Rudman Commission. Table 3 shows the results of the analysis. The lead-agency model with the State Department in charge comes out slightly ahead. However, the scores for the other two models are very close, so this study does not offer a national-level reform recommendation. A brief description of the analysis follows.

Table 3. Analysis of national-level reform models

Evaluation Criteria	Non-NSC Interagency Organization	NSC Leads	Lead Agency
Nonmilitary voice and face for US foreign policy	0	0	+
Fully coordinated planning	+	+	+
Unity of effort during execution	+	0	0
More efficient and effective than agencies working alone	+	+	+
Leader's authority commensurate with responsibility	+	+	0
Legitimacy of leader's decision making	+	+	0
Leader can access necessary resources	+	+	0
Clear chain of command to the president	+	+	+
Does not overburden the president	0	–	+
Balance of power and prestige between DOD and DOS	0	0	+
Develops interagency expertise	+	0	0
Reform minimizes cost in money, personnel, and material	–	0	+
Reform minimizes agency culture shocks	–	0	0
Totals	+6	+5	+7

The lead-agency model with State in charge would slightly improve State's role as the nonmilitary voice and face for US foreign policy, though this has never been a major shortfall at the national level. The other two models do less to enhance State's role as the foreign policy lead, but they would not really put the military more in charge either. All three reforms are equally likely to provide fully coordinated interagency planning at the national level because this is precisely what these models were designed to do.

The non-NSC interagency model is best able to produce interagency unity of effort during execution for two reasons. First, since the organization is independent of all cabinet agencies, it would be viewed as an honest broker by the participating agencies. Second, because the organization is outside the NSC and would presumably have a robust staff focused on interagency planning, execution, and assessment, it is more likely than the NSC process itself to focus the necessary time and personnel on achieving unity of effort. The other two models are assessed as weaker against this criterion but not negative. All three models are equally likely to be more efficient and effective than the cabinet agencies working without any coordination.

The lead-agency model is slightly weaker than the other two in its ability to provide the leader a level of authority commensurate with responsibility, provide legitimacy to the leader's decisions, and facilitate the leader's access to resources because of the perceived biases that come from a lead agency directing the efforts of other cabinet agencies. The interagency and NSC-centric models are equally likely to produce good results in these areas.

All three models produce an equally clear chain of command to the president. However, the cabinet-level lead-agency model is the least likely to overburden the president as most decisions would be made outside the White House. The interagency organization is judged as neutral against this criterion as its closeness to the White House may or may not drive increased presidential attention. The NSC-centric model is worst against this measure since it would raise many more decisions to the president and occupy much of the NSC staff's time that could otherwise be spent formulating policy and advising the president. The State-Department-as-lead-agency model would enhance the power and prestige of the State Department, while the other two models would have neither a positive nor a negative effect.

The interagency organization would offer the most opportunities to develop personnel with interagency experience as this new structure would require a robust staff to do its job. The other two models are judged as neutral against this criterion because fewer new personnel would be exposed to the interagency environment.

The lead-agency model is the least costly to implement since it would require only a modest augmentation of the State Department's staff. The NSC-centric model is assessed as neutral because it would take several more staffers to enable the NSC to fulfill the interagency coordination role for planning and execution. The new interagency organization is the most costly option because not only would a large staff have to be created from scratch but also a new facility would likely be required.

Finally, the lead-agency and NSC-centric models are judged as having a minimal impact on agency cultures. The new interagency organization, though, would have a relatively large impact as it was staffed from across the interagency and as career paths were altered to staff it.

Notes

1. Michael Donley, *Rethinking the Interagency System*, pt. 2, Occasional Paper no. 05-02 (McLean, VA: Hicks & Associates, May 2005), 8.

2. MAJ David A. Meyer, USA, "Normalizing Executive Department Boundaries: A Timely First Step to Improving Interagency Coordination," monograph (Fort Leavenworth, KS: School of Advanced Military Studies, US Army Command and General Staff College, 21 March 2007), 15.

3. Donley, *Rethinking the Interagency System*, pt. 2, 9; Clark A. Murdock and Michèle A. Flournoy, *Beyond Goldwater-Nichols: U.S. Government and Defense Reform for a New Strategic Era*, Phase 2 Report (Washington, DC: Center for Strategic and International Studies, July 2005), 21.

4. LTC James R. Bartran, USA, "PDD-56-1: Synchronizing Effects; Beyond the Pol/Mil Plan," strategy research project (Carlisle Barracks, PA: Army War College, 10 April 2000), 12–14.

5. *The 9/11 Commission Report*, 22 July 2004, 399–400, http://www.9-11commission.gov/report/911Report; and Michael Donley, *Rethinking the Interagency System*, pt. 1, Occasional Paper no. 05-01 (McLean, VA: Hicks & Associates, March 2005), 7.

6. Chris Strohm, "Former Commander Calls for New Military-Civilian Planning Organization," *GovernmentExecutive.com*, 7 December 2004, http://www.govexec.com/defense/2004/12/former-commander-calls-for-new-military-civilian-planning-organization/8156.

7. Maj J. D. York, USMC, "Militarizing the Interagency," research report (Newport, RI: Naval War College, 14 February 2005), 14–15.

8. Timothy K. Hsia, "Building on the Goldwater-Nichols Act," *Foreign Service Journal*, June 2008, 48.

9. PNSR, *Forging a New Shield* (Arlington, VA: Center for the Study of the Presidency, November 2008), 384, http://pnsr.org/data/files/pnsr%20forging%20a%20new%20shield.pdf. This report "represents the culmination of more than two years of work by more than three hundred dedicated U.S. national security executives, professionals, and scholars" (ibid.).

10. Ibid., xi, xii, 441, 482, 516, 599.

11. PNSR, *Turning Ideas into Action* (Arlington, VA: Center for the Study of the Presidency, September 2009), 18, 23, http://www.pnsr.org/data/files/pnsr_turning_ideas_into_action.pdf.

12. Donley, *Rethinking the Interagency System*, pt. 2, 6–7.

13. US Commission on National Security/21st Century (Hart/Rudman Commission), *Road Map for National Security: Imperative for Change*, Phase III Report, 15 February 2001, xi.

14. *The 9/11 Commission Report*, 402.

15. Admiral Miller was the combatant commander of the US Atlantic Command, later renamed the US Joint Forces Command and disestablished in August 2011.

16. ADM Paul David Miller, *The Interagency Process: Engaging America's Full National Security Capabilities*, National Security Paper 11 (Cambridge, MA: Institute for Foreign Policy Analysis, 1993), 16–18, 45.

17. MAJ Thomas M. Lafleur, USA, "Interagency Efficacy at the Operational Level," monograph (Fort Leavenworth, KS: School of Advanced Military Studies, US Army Command and General Staff College, 26 May 2005), 17.

18. Ibid., 18–22.

19. Donley, *Rethinking the Interagency System*, pt. 2, 5.

20. Bruce R. Pirnie, *Civilians and Soldiers: Achieving Better Coordination* (Santa Monica, CA: RAND National Security Research Division, 1998), xv–xvi, 45.

21. Ibid., 43.

22. Office of the Undersecretary of Defense for Acquisition, Technology, and Logistics (OSD/ATL), *Defense Science Board 2004 Summer Study on Transition to and from Hostilities* (Washington, DC: OSD/ATL, December, 2004), transmittal letter from board chairman William Schneider Jr.

23. Ibid., transmittal letter from summer study co-chairs, 29.

24. Hans Binnendijk and Stuart E. Johnson, *Transforming for Stabilization and Reconstruction Operations* (Washington, DC: National Defense University, 2004), 110–11.

25. Lt Col Ted T. Uchida, USAF, "Reforming the Interagency Process," Air Force Fellows research report (Maxwell AFB, AL: Air Force Fellows Program, May 2005), 13. This recommendation builds on the *Defense Science Board 2004 Summer Study*.

26. Ibid., 96–97.

27. Murdock and Flournoy, *Beyond Goldwater-Nichols*, Phase 2 Report, 7, 50.

28. Ibid.

29. Ibid., 45–46.

30. Ibid., 20, 46–47.

31. Nora Bensahel and Anne M. Moisan, "Repairing the Interagency Process," *Joint Force Quarterly* 44 (1st Quarter 2007): 107–8. Dr. Bensahel is a senior political scientist at RAND. US Air Force colonel Moisan at the time of this writing was a

senior research fellow in the Institute for National Strategic Studies at the National Defense University.

32. PNSR, *Turning Ideas into Action*, 16, 18, 23.

33. Donley, *Rethinking the Interagency System*, pt. 2, 7–10.

34. Murdock and Flournoy, *Beyond Goldwater-Nichols*, Phase 2 Report, 20.

35. MAJ Mark L. Curry, USA, "The Interagency Process in Regional Foreign Policy," monograph (Fort Leavenworth, KS: School of Advanced Military Studies, US Army Command and General Staff College, 5 May 1994), 34–35.

36. Ibid., 9, 17.

37. Hart/Rudman Commission, *Road Map for National Security*, xi.

38. Ibid., 59, 62.

39. Ibid., 63.

40. Barry M. Blechman, Thomas R. Pickering, and Newt Gingrich, *Advisory Committee on Transformational Diplomacy: Final Report of the State Department in 2025 Working Group*, 2007, ii, 19–22, http://2001-2009.state.gov/documents/organization/99879.pdf.

41. Ibid., 19.

Abbreviations

ACT	advance civilian team
AF	Bureau of African Affairs
AFF	Air Force Fellows
AFRICOM	US Africa Command
AOR	area of responsibility
ASEAN	Association of Southeast Asian Nations
ASFF	Afghanistan Security Forces Fund
ATF	Bureau of Alcohol, Tobacco, and Firearms
AU	African Union
C4I	command, control, communications, computers, and intelligence
CBP	Customs and Border Protection
CCF	command collaborative forum
CENTCOM	US Central Command
CERP	Commander's Emergency Response Program
CETO	Center for Emerging Threats and Opportunities
CFLCC	combined forces land component commander
CIA	Central Intelligence Agency
CIEG	commander's interagency engagement group
CJCMOTF	coalition joint civil-military operations task force
CJTF–HOA	Combined Joint Task Force–Horn of Africa
CJIATF	combined joint interagency task force
CMG	crisis management group
COCOM	combatant command
COIN	counterinsurgency
CORDS	Office of Civil Operations and Revolutionary (or "Rural") Development Support
CPA	Coalition Provisional Authority
CPITF	contingency planning and integration task force
CRC	Civilian Response Corps
CRC-A	Civilian Response Corps–Active
CRC-R	Civilian Response Corps–Reserve
CRC-S	Civilian Response Corps–Standby
CRSG	country reconstruction and stabilization group
CSF	combined support force
CSG	combined support group
CSIS	Center for Strategic and International Studies

CT	counterterrorism
CTF	crisis task force
DART	disaster assistance response team
DC	Deputies Committee
DCM	deputy chief of mission
DCMA	deputy to the commander for civil-military activities
DCMO	deputy to the commander for military operations
DEA	Drug Enforcement Administration
DHS	Department of Homeland Security
DISA	Defense Information Systems Agency
DOD	Department of Defense
DOE	Department of Energy
DOS	Department of State
DSB	Defense Science Board
DSCA	Defense Security Cooperation Agency
DSS	Diplomatic Security Service
DTRA	Defense Threat Reduction Agency
EAP	Bureau of East Asian and Pacific Affairs
ECCD	US European Command civilian deputy
EOP	executive office of the president
EU	European Union
EUCOM	US European Command
EUR	Bureau of European and Eurasian Affairs
EWG	executive working group
FBI	Federal Bureau of Investigation
FMF	foreign military financing
FMS	foreign military sales
FPA	foreign policy advisor
FSO	foreign service officer
GAO	Government Accountability Office
GCC	geographic combatant command
GPOI	global peace operations initiative
GSCF	global security contingency fund
HQ	headquarters
IA	interagency
IACG	interagency coordination group
IAG	interagency action group
IAHQ	interagency headquarters

IATF	interagency task force
IAWG	interagency working group
ICE	Immigration and Customs Enforcement
ICMAG	integrated civilian military action group
ICPT	interagency crisis planning team
IGO	intergovernmental organization
IMET	international military education and training
IMS	interagency management system
IPC	integration planning cell
IPC	interagency policy committee
IRC	integrated regional center
ISAF	International Security Assistance Force
J-1	joint staff directorate of manpower and personnel
J-2	joint staff directorate of intelligence
J-3	joint staff directorate of operations
J-4	joint staff directorate of logistics
J-5	joint staff directorate of plans, policy, and strategy
J-6	joint staff directorate of communications
J-7	joint staff directorate of training, exercises, and engagement
J-8	joint staff directorate of resources and assessments
J-9	joint staff directorate of partnering or outreach
JCP	joint campaign plan
JCS	Joint Chiefs of Staff
JFCOM	US Joint Forces Command
JGTF	joint government task force
JIACG	joint interagency coordination group
JIACG/CT	Joint Interagency Coordination Group for Counterterrorism
JIACOM	joint interagency command
JIATF	joint interagency task force
JIATF-CTAP	Joint Interagency Task Force for Counterterrorism in the Asia-Pacific Region
JIATF-I	Joint Interagency Task Force–Iraq
JIATF-S	Joint Interagency Task Force–South
JIATF-W	Joint Interagency Task Force–West
JOC	joint operations center
JP	joint publication
JPG	joint planning group

JTF	joint task force
JTF-5	Joint Task Force–5
MACV	Military Assistance Command–Vietnam
MNF-I	Multinational Force–Iraq
MPAT	multinational planning augmentation team
MSG	military support group
NATO	North Atlantic Treaty Organization
NCTC	National Counterterrorism Center
NEA	Bureau of Near Eastern Affairs
NGO	nongovernmental organization
NIACCG	national interagency contingency coordinating group
NIEOC	national interagency emergency operations center
NORTHCOM	US Northern Command
NSA	National Security Agency
NSC	National Security Council
NSP	national security professional
NSPD	national security professional development
NSS	national security staff
OAS	Organization of American States
ODNI	Office of the Director of National Intelligence
OEF	Operation Enduring Freedom
OFAC	Office of Foreign Assets Control
OFDA	Office of Foreign Disaster Assistance
OIF	Operation Iraqi Freedom
OMA	Office of Military Affairs
OMB	Office of Management and Budget
OND	Operation New Dawn
OPG	operational planning group
OPLAN	operational plan
ORHA	Office of Reconstruction and Humanitarian Assistance
OSCE	Organization for Security and Cooperation in Europe
OSD	Office of the Secretary of Defense
OTI	Office of Transition Initiatives
PACOM	US Pacific Command
PC	Principals Committee

PCC	policy coordination committee
PCCF	Pakistan Counterinsurgency Capability Fund
PDD	Presidential Decision Directive
PM	Bureau of Political-Military Affairs
PME	professional military education
PNSR	Project on National Security Reform
POLAD	political advisor
PRSC	prevention, reconstruction, and stabilization cell
PRT	provincial reconstruction team
QDR	*Quadrennial Defense Review*
RBC	regional bureau chief
RCM	regional chief of mission
RCOM	regional chief of mission
RIB	regional interest bureau
RID	regional interagency directors
SACEUR	Supreme Allied Commander Europe
SAMS	School of Advanced Military Studies
SCA	Bureau of South and Central Asian Affairs
S/CRS	Office of the Coordinator for Reconstruction and Stabilization
SDE	senior developmental education
SES	senior executive service
SJFHQ	standing joint force headquarters
SOUTHCOM	US Southern Command
TSB	target synchronization board
UK	United Kingdom
UN	United Nations
USA	US Army
USAF	US Air Force
USAID	US Agency for International Development
USFOR-A	US Forces–Afghanistan
USG	US government
USN	US Navy
USRM	US regional mission
WHA	Bureau of Western Hemisphere Affairs
WMD	weapon of mass destruction

Bibliography

The 9/11 Commission Report, 22 July 2004. http://www.9-11commission
.gov/report/911Report.pdf.

Adams, Gordon. "The Role of Civilian and Military Agencies in the Advancement of America's Diplomatic and Developmental Objectives." Testimony before the Subcommittee on State, Foreign Operations, and Related Programs of the House Committee on Appropriations, 5 March 2009.

Amend, Kurt. "The Diplomat as Counterinsurgent." *Foreign Service Journal,* Summer 2009, 21–27.

Anderson, Gary W. " 'Interagency Overseas': Responding to the 2004 Indian Ocean Tsunami." In *Mismanaging Mayhem,* edited by James Jay Carafano and Richard Weitz, 192–210.

Arnas, Neyla, Charles Barry, and Robert B. Oakley. *Harnessing the Interagency for Complex Operations.* Washington, DC: Center for Technology and National Security Policy, National Defense University, August 2005.

ASEAN Secretariat. "US to Open Mission to ASEAN in Jakarta." Press release. Phuket, Thailand, 22 July 2009.

Bacchus, William I. "Regaining Relevance: Five Steps to Strengthen State." *Foreign Service Journal* 86, no. 7–8 (July/August 2009): 14–17.

Barnett, Thomas P. M. *The Pentagon's New Map: War and Peace in the Twenty-First Century.* New York: G. P. Putnam's Sons, 2004.

Bartran, LTC James R., USA. "PDD-56-1: Synchronizing Effects; Beyond the Pol/Mil Plan." Strategy research project. Carlisle Barracks, PA: Army War College, 10 April 2000.

Bensahel, Nora, and Anne M. Moisan. "Repairing the Interagency Process." *Joint Force Quarterly* 44 (1st Quarter 2007): 106–8.

Binnendijk, Hans, and Stuart E. Johnson. *Transforming for Stabilization and Reconstruction Operations.* Washington, DC: Center for Technology and National Security Policy, National Defense University, 2004.

Birkenes, Robert M. "Interagency Cooperation: The JIATF in Iraq." *Foreign Service Journal* 86, no. 9 (September 2009): 28–34.

Blechman, Barry M., Thomas R. Pickering, and Newt Gingrich. *Advisory Committee on Transformational Diplomacy: Final Report of the State Department in 2025 Working Group.* http://2001-2009
.state.gov/documents/organization/99879.pdf.

Bogdanos, Col Matthew F., USMC. "Joint Interagency Cooperation: The First Step." *Joint Force Quarterly* 37 (2nd Quarter 2005): 10–18.
———. *Transforming Joint Interagency Coordination: The Missing Link between National Strategy and Operational Success.* Washington, DC: Center for Technology and National Security Policy, National Defense University, August 2007.

Bremer, Amb. L. Paul, III. *My Year in Iraq: The Struggle to Build a Future of Hope.* New York: Threshold Editions, 2006.

Bruno, Greg. "Afghanistan's National Security Forces." Council on Foreign Relations backgrounder, 16 April 2009. http://www.cfr.org/publication/19122/afghanistans_national_security_forces.html?breadcrumb=%2Fpublication%2Fby_type%2Fbackgrounder#2.

Buchanan, BG Jeffrey, USA; CAPT Maxie Y. Davis, USN; and Col Lee T. Wight, USAF. "Death of the Combatant Command? Toward a Joint Interagency Approach." *Joint Force Quarterly* 52 (1st Quarter 2009): 92–96.

Bullock, Todd. "USAID Announces New Office of Military Affairs." *The Washington File*, Bureau of International Information Programs, US Department of State, 24 October 2005. http://usinfo.state.gov.

Bush, George W. Executive Order 13434. National Security Professional Development, 22 May 2007.

Carafano, James Jay. "Managing Mayhem: The Future of Interagency Reform." *Joint Force Quarterly* 49 (2nd Quarter 2008): 135–37.

Carafano, James Jay, and Richard Weitz, eds. *Mismanaging Mayhem: How Washington Responds to Crisis.* Westport, CT: Praeger Security International, 2008.

Cardinal, Charles N., Timber P. Pagonas, and Edward Marks. "The Global War on Terrorism: A Regional Approach to Coordination." *Joint Force Quarterly* 32 (Autumn 2002): 49–53.

Caudill, Lt Col Shannon W., USAF, MAJ Andrew M. Leonard, USA, and Sgt Maj Richard D. Thresher, USMC. "Interagency Leadership: The Case for Strengthening the Department of State." *American Diplomacy*, April 2008. http://www.unc.edu/depts/diplomat/item/2008/0406/comm/caudilletal_strength.html.

Chun, Clayton K. S., and Frank L. Jones. "Learning to Play the Game: The National Security Policymaking Process." In *Affairs of State*, edited by Gabriel Marcella, 171–214.

Clark, Maj Stephen A., USAF. "Interagency Coordination: Strengthening the Link between Operational Art and the Desired End

State." Research report. Newport, RI: Naval War College, 8 February 1999.

Clinton, Secretary of State Hillary Rodham. "President's Proposed Budget Request for Fiscal Year 2011 for the Department of State and Foreign Operations." Testimony before the Senate Appropriations Subcommittee on State, Foreign Operations, and Related Programs, Washington, DC, 24 February 2010.

———. "Remarks on Development in the 21st Century." Peterson Institute for International Economics, Washington, DC, 6 January 2010.

Cloud, David, and Greg Jaffe. *The Fourth Star: Four Generals and the Epic Struggle for the Future of the United States Army.* New York: Crown Publishers, 2009.

Coffey, MAJ Ross M., USA. "Improving Interagency Integration at the Operational Level: CORDS—A Model for the Advanced Civilian Team." Monograph. Fort Leavenworth, KS: School of Advanced Military Studies, US Army Command and General Staff College, 25 May 2006.

Cohen, Craig, and Noam Unger. *Surveying the Civilian Reform Landscape.* Project brief. Muscatine, IA: Stanley Foundation Center for a New American Security, 2008.

Cohen, Eliot A. "History and Hyperpower." *Foreign Affairs* 83, no. 4 (July/August 2004): 49–63.

Cole, Beth, and Emily Hsu. "Guiding Principles for Stability and Reconstruction: Introducing a Roadmap for Peace." *Military Review* 90, no. 1 (January/February 2010): 7–15.

Coordinator for Reconstruction and Stabilization. *2009 Year in Review: Smart Power in Action.* Washington, DC: Department of State, 1 March 2010.

Cronin, Patrick, and Kristin Lord. "Deploying Soft Power: Restructured, Larger Civilian Force Needed for Crises." *Defense News,* 12 April 2010, 53.

Curry, MAJ Mark L., USA. "The Interagency Process in Regional Foreign Policy." Monograph. Fort Leavenworth, KS: School of Advanced Military Studies, US Army Command and General Staff College, 5 May 1994.

Dale, Catherine. *Building an Interagency Cadre of National Security Professionals: Proposals, Recent Experience, and Issues for Congress.* Congressional Research Service (CRS) Report for Congress RL34565. Washington, DC: CRS, 8 July 2008.

Dana, Michael G. "The JIATF Fusion Center: A Next-Generation Operations Cell for Consequence Management." *Marine Corps Gazette* 84, no. 2 (February 2000): 38–41.

Daniels, Mitchell E., Jr., director, US Office of Management and Budget (OMB). "Report to Congress Pursuant to Section 1506 of the Emergency Wartime Supplemental Appropriations Act, 2003 (Public Law 108-11)." Washington, DC: OMB, 2 June 2003.

David, G. J. "The Interagency Abroad: The New Paradigm's Progress." *Military Review* (January/February 2010): 58–62.

David, G. John, and Paul S. Reinhart. "A Joint Staff to Believe In." *Joint Force Quarterly* 56 (1st Quarter 2010): 128–33.

Desai, Sunil B. "Solving the Interagency Puzzle." *Policy Review*, no. 129 (February/March 2005): 57–71. http://www.hoover.org/publications /policyreview/3431461.html#.

Dodaro, Gene L. "Maximizing DOD's Potential to Face New Fiscal Challenges and Strengthen Interagency Partnerships." Speech before the National Defense University, Washington, DC, 6 January 2010.

Donley, Michael. *Rethinking the Interagency System.* Pt. 1. Occasional Paper no. 05-01. McLean, VA: Hicks & Associates, March 2005.

———. *Rethinking the Interagency System.* Pt. 2. Occasional Paper no. 05-02. McLean, VA: Hicks & Associates, May 2005.

Doyle, MAJ David S., USA. "Interagency Cooperation for Irregular Warfare at the Combatant Command." Monograph. Fort Leavenworth, KS: School of Advanced Military Studies, US Army Command and General Staff College, 14 April 2009.

Eckhardt, MG George S., USA. *Vietnam Studies: Command and Control, 1950–1969.* Washington, DC: Department of the Army, 1991.

Eikenberry, Karl W., and GEN Stanley McChrystal, USA. *United States Government Integrated Civilian-Military Campaign Plan for Support to Afghanistan.* Kabul, Afghanistan: Embassy of the United States of America and US Forces Afghanistan, 10 August 2009. http://www.comw.org/qdr/fulltext/0908eikenberryandmc chrystal.pdf.

Embassy of the United States of America, Bangkok. "United States Moves on New Mission to ASEAN." Press release. Bangkok, Thailand, 25 January 2010.

Fallows, James. "Blind into Baghdad." *Atlantic Monthly* 293, no. 1 (January/February 2004): 52–74.

Finney, John D., and Alphonse F. La Porta. "Integrating National Security Strategy at the Operational Level: The Role of the State

Department Political Advisors." In *Affairs of State*, edited by Gabriel Marcella, 281–320.

———. "Maximizing the Value of the Political Adviser Function." *Foreign Service Journal* 85, no. 10 (October 2008): 16–19.

Fishel, John T. "The Interagency Arena at the Operational Level: The Cases Now Known as Stability Operations." In *Affairs of State*, edited by Gabriel Marcella, 409–46.

Folmsbee, Paul. "From Pinstripes to Khaki: Governance under Fire." *Foreign Service Journal*, September 2009, 35–39.

"A Foreign Affairs Budget for the 21st Century." *Foreign Service Journal*, December 2008, 53–57.

Galvin, LTC Thomas P., USA. "Extending the Phase Zero Campaign Mindset: Ensuring Unity of Effort." *Joint Force Quarterly* 45 (2nd Quarter 2007): 46–51.

Gantz, Peter H. "Peacebuilding: A New National Security Imperative." *Foreign Service Journal*, February 2006, 33–38.

Garamone, Jim. "Discussion Needed to Change Interagency Process, Pace Says." American Forces Press Service, 17 September 2004. http://www.defenselink.mil/news.

Gardner, Jeffrey V. "Fight the 'Away Game' as a Team: Organizing for Regional Interagency Policy Implementation." *American Intelligence Journal* (Autumn/Winter 2005): 51–60.

Gribbin, Robert E. "Implementing AFRICOM: Tread Carefully." *Foreign Service Journal*, May 2008, 25–31.

Halvorsen, LT Peter, USN. "Reforming the Interagency at the Operational Level." Research report. Newport, RI: Naval War College, 14 February 2005.

Heiniger, Lt Col Penny A., USAF. "Regional Engagement from Phase 0: A Joint Interagency Task Force for the Trans-Sahel." Research report. Newport, RI: Naval War College, 16 May 2006.

Herbst, John. "Ambassador John Herbst, Coordinator for Reconstruction and Stabilization on S/CRS 2009 Year in Review," Press briefing, Washington, DC, 1 March 2010.

Herr, LCDR Christopher H., USN. "Joint Interagency at the Combatant Commands: Making It Real; Making It Work." Research report. Newport, RI: Naval War College, 13 February 2006.

Hillen, John, assistant secretary of state for political-military affairs. "The Changing Nature of the Political-Military Interface." Remarks. Joint Worldwide Planning Conference, Garmisch, Germany, 30 November 2005. http://2001-2009.state.gov/t/pm/rls/othr/misc/58492.htm.

Holbrooke, Richard. *To End a War*. New York: Random House, 1998.

Holmes, Brig Gen Robert H., USAF. *Statement of Brigadier General Robert H. Holmes, Deputy Director of Operations, United States Central Command, before the House Armed Services Committee Subcommittee on Terrorism, Unconventional Threats and Capabilities*. Prepared statement. Washington, DC. 110th Cong., 2d sess., 26 February 2008. http://www.dod.mil/dodgc/olc/docs/testHolmes080226.pdf.

Hsia, CPT Timothy K., USA. "Building on the Goldwater-Nichols Act." *Foreign Service Journal*, June 2008, 47–50.

Johnson, Thomas E., Jr. "Working It Out with the Military: The View from Kabul." *Foreign Service Journal* 84, no. 6 (June 2007): 15–19.

Joint Publication 3-0. *Doctrine for Joint Operations*, 10 September 2001.

———. *Doctrine for Joint Operations*, 17 September 2006 (incorporating change 1, 13 February 2008).

Joint Publication 3-05.1. *Joint Special Operations Task Force Operations*, 26 April 2007.

Joint Publication 3-07.4. *Joint Counterdrug Operations*, 13 June 2007.

Joint Publication 3-08. *Interagency, Intergovernmental Organization, and Nongovernmental Organization Coordination during Joint Operations*. Vol. 1, 17 March 2006.

Joint Publication 3-40. *Combating Weapons of Mass Destruction*, 10 June 2009.

Jones, James L. *The 21st Century Interagency Process*. Washington, DC: The White House, 18 March 2009.

Jones, Seth. *In the Graveyard of Empires: America's War in Afghanistan*. New York: W. W. Norton, 2009.

Kaufmann, COL Greg, USA. "Orchestrating Foreign Policy: US Interagency Decisions Post–September 11." *Harvard International Review* 24, no. 2 (Summer 2002): 20–25.

Keen, Judy. "Rice Will Manage Iraq's 'New Phase.'" *USA Today*, 6 October 2003. http://www.usatoday.com/news/world/iraq/2003-10-06-rice-iraq_x.htm.

Kelleher, Patrick N. "Crossing Boundaries: Interagency Cooperation and the Military." *Joint Force Quarterly* 32 (Autumn 2002): 104–10.

Kfir, Isaac. "The Challenge That Is USAFRICOM." *Joint Force Quarterly* 49 (2nd Quarter 2008): 110–13.

Kiehl, William P. "Seduced and Abandoned: Strategic Information and the National Security Council Process." In *Affairs of State*, edited by Gabriel Marcella, 321–70.

Kopp, Harry W., and Charles A. Gillespie. *Life and Work in the U.S. Foreign Service*. Washington, DC: Georgetown University Press, 2008.

Lafleur, MAJ Thomas M., USA. "Interagency Efficacy at the Operational Level." Monograph. Fort Leavenworth, KS: School of Advanced Military Studies, US Army Command and General Staff College, 26 May 2005.

Lamb, Christopher J., and Martin Cinnamond. "Unified Effort: Key to Special Operations and Irregular Warfare in Afghanistan." *Joint Force Quarterly* 56 (1st Quarter 2010): 40–53.

Lieberman, Ben. "Crisis! What Crisis? America's Response to the Energy Crisis." In *Mismanaging Mayhem*, edited by James Jay Carafano and Richard Weitz, 113–29.

Liston, LCDR Darin M., USN. "In the Interagency Process, Mere Coordination Is Not Enough: Toward Joint Government." Research report. Newport, RI: Naval War College, 14 February 2005.

Litt, David C. "New Directions for U.S. Foreign Policy in the Greater Middle East." In *American Foreign Policy*, edited by Richmond M. Lloyd, 169–78.

Lloyd, Richmond M., ed. *American Foreign Policy: Regional Perspectives*. Proceedings of a Ruger Chair Workshop, 13–15 May 2009. Newport, RI: Naval War College, 2009.

Loftus, Gerald. "Expeditionary Sidekicks? The Military-Diplomatic Dynamic." *Foreign Service Journal* 84, no. 12 (December 2007): 15–17.

Loxterkamp, Lt Col Edward W., USAF, Lt Col Michael F. Welch, USAF, and CDR Richard M. Gomez, USN. "The Interagency Process: The Need for New Legislation." Research report. Norfolk, VA: Joint Forces Staff College, 27 September 2003.

Marcella, Gabriel, ed. *Affairs of State: The Interagency and National Security*. Carlisle, PA: Strategic Studies Institute, US Army War College, December 2008.

———. "Understanding the Interagency Process: The Challenge of Adaptation." In *Affairs of State*, edited by Gabriel Marcella, 1–52.

Marks, Edward. "PACOM, JIACG, and the War on Terror." Camber Corporation on contract to the Joint Interagency Coordinating Group on Counterterrorism, PACOM, 18 August 2005. http://www.ndu.edu/itea/storage/678/PACOM%20JIACG%20and%20the%20War%20on%20Terror.pdf.

———. "Why USAFRICOM?" *Joint Force Quarterly* 52 (1st Quarter 2009): 148–51.

McCabe, Laurence L. "Panel II: Western Hemisphere—Summary of Discussion." In *American Foreign Policy*, edited by Richmond M. Lloyd, 95–98.

McComas, Lesa, John Benson, Christopher Cook, Druso Daubon, and William McDaniel. "Interagency Teaming to Counter Irregular Threats." Coordinating draft. Laurel, MD: Johns Hopkins University Applied Physics Laboratory, 19 October 2009.

McGeary, Johanna. "Looking beyond Saddam." *Time* 161, no. 10 (10 March 2003): 26–33.

Mendel, William W., and Lt Col David G. Bradford, USAF. *Interagency Cooperation: A Regional Model for Overseas Operations*. McNair Paper 37. Washington, DC: National Defense University, Institute for National Strategic Studies, March 1995.

Meyer, MAJ David A., USA. "Normalizing Executive Department Boundaries: A Timely First Step to Improving Interagency Coordination." Monograph. Fort Leavenworth, KS: School of Advanced Military Studies, US Army Command and General Staff College, 21 March 2007.

Miller, Paul David. *The Interagency Process: Engaging America's Full National Security Capabilities*. National Security Paper 11. Cambridge, MA: Institute for Foreign Policy Analysis, 1993.

Miles, Donna. "SOUTHCOM Transformation Promotes New Approach to Regional Challenges." American Forces Press Service, 28 August 2008. http://www.defense.gov/News/NewsArticle.aspx?ID=50936.

Mines, Keith W. "A Horizontal Model for Transformational Diplomacy." *Foreign Service Journal*, March 2006, 50–54.

Moeller, Robert T., and Mary C. Yates. "The Road to a New Unified Command." *Joint Force Quarterly* 51 (4th Quarter 2008): 67–73.

Munson, Robert. "Do We Want to 'Kill People and Break Things' in Africa?" *Strategic Studies Quarterly* 2, no. 1 (Spring 2008): 97–110.

Murdock, Clark A., and Michèle A. Flournoy. *Beyond Goldwater-Nichols: U.S. Government and Defense Reform for a New Strategic Era*. Phase 2 Report. Washington, DC: Center for Strategic and International Studies, July 2005.

Nakamura, Kennon H., and Susan B. Epstein. *Diplomacy for the 21st Century: Transformational Diplomacy*. CRS Report for Congress. Washington, DC: CRS, 23 August 2007.

Naler, Lt Col Christopher L., USMC. "Are We Ready for an Interagency Combatant Command?" *Joint Force Quarterly* 41 (2nd Quarter 2006): 26–31.

Nigro, Louis J., Jr. "The Department of State and Strategic Integration: How Reinforcing State as an Institution Will Improve America's Engagement with the World in the 21st Century." In *Affairs of State*, edited by Gabriel Marcella, 255–80.

Oakley, Robert B., and Michael Casey Jr. "The Country Team: Restructuring America's First Line of Engagement." *Joint Force Quarterly* 47 (4th Quarter 2007): 146–54.

Office of the Federal Register, National Archives and Records Administration. *The United States Government Manual 2009/2010*. Washington, DC: Government Printing Office (GPO), 2009. http://www.gpoaccess.gov/gmanual/index.html.

Office of the National Counterintelligence Executive. "About Us." http://www.ncix.gov/about/about.php.

Office of the Undersecretary of Defense for Acquisition, Technology, and Logistics (OSD/ATL). *Defense Science Board 2004 Summer Study on Transition to and from Hostilities*. Washington, DC: OSD/ATL, December 2004.

———. *Defense Science Board 2004 Summer Study on Transition to and from Hostilities: Supporting Papers*. Washington, DC: OSD/ATL, January 2005.

Office of U.S. Foreign Disaster Assistance. *Annual Report for Fiscal Year 2008*. Washington, DC: USAID, 2009. http://pdf.usaid.gov/pdf_docs/PDACM965.pdf.

Olson, William J. "Interagency Coordination: The Normal Accident or the Essence of Indecision." In *Affairs of State*, edited by Gabriel Marcella, 215–54.

Packer, George. "War after the War: Letter from Baghdad." *New Yorker*, 24 November 2003, 59–85. http://www.newyorker.com/fact/content/?031124fa_fact1.

Palmer, Jeffrey S. "Legal Impediments to USAFRICOM Operationalization." *Joint Force Quarterly* 51 (4th Quarter 2008): 79–85.

Pasquarett, COL Michael, USA, and James Kievit. *A Blueprint for a Bold Restructuring of the Organization for National Security: The Military Combatant Commands and State Department Regional Bureaus*. Carlisle Barracks, PA: Center for Strategic Leadership, Army War College, 1997.

Penn, Dennis R. J. "USAFRICOM: The Militarization of U.S. Foreign Policy?" *Joint Force Quarterly* 51 (4th Quarter 2008): 74–78.

Pirnie, Bruce R. *Civilians and Soldiers: Achieving Better Coordination.* Santa Monica, CA: RAND National Security Research Division, 1998.

Pope, Maj Robert S., USAF. "Interagency Planning and Coordination for Stabilization and Reconstruction Operations." Research report. Maxwell AFB, AL: Air Command and Staff College, April 2004.

Priest, Dana. *The Mission: Waging War and Keeping Peace with America's Military.* New York: W. W. Norton, 2003.

Project on National Security Reform. *Forging a New Shield.* Arlington, VA: Center for the Study of the Presidency, November 2008.

———. *Turning Ideas into Action.* Arlington, VA: Center for the Study of the Presidency, September 2009.

Pugh, Derek S., and David J. Hickson. *Great Writers on Organizations,* 3rd omnibus ed. Hampshire, UK: Ashgate Publishing, 2007.

Reed, Maj Clifton D., USAF. "The Battle Within: DOD and Interagency Coordination for Regional Conflicts—AFRICOM and the Interagency Management System as Models." Research report. Maxwell AFB, AL: Air Command and Staff College, April 2008.

Rhatican, COL Thomas M., USAR. "Redefining Security Cooperation: New Limits on Phase Zero and 'Shaping.'" Strategy research project. Carlisle Barracks, PA: Army War College, 15 March 2008.

Reighard, Lt Col Robert D., USAF. "Security Cooperation: Integrating Strategies to Secure National Goals." Strategy research project. Carlisle Barracks, PA: Army War College, 15 March 2006.

Rife, LTC Rickey L., USA, and Rosemary Hansen, Foreign Service officer. "Defense Is from Mars, State Is from Venus: Improving Communications and Promoting National Security." Strategy research project. Carlisle Barracks, PA: Army War College, June 1998.

Rivera, LCDR Reinaldo, USNR. "The Joint Interagency Task Force (JIATF) Conundrum: Cooperation among Competitors: Is Harmony Achievable through Trust and Understanding?" Research report. Newport, RI: Naval War College, 3 February 2003.

Rogin, Josh. "State Department and Pentagon Creating Joint Office for Funding Emergency Response." The Cable. *Foreign Policy,* 27 December 2011. http://thecable.foreignpolicy.com/posts/2011/12/27/state_department_and_pentagon_creating_joint_office_for_funding_emergency_response.

Schafer, Maj Brian M., USAF. "DIME Considerations: A New PACOM Planning Pyramid." Research report. Maxwell AFB, AL: Air Command and Staff College, April 2009.

Schraeder, Peter J. "Great Expectations versus Daunting Challenges: Prospects for U.S. Foreign Policy toward Africa during the Obama Administration." In *American Foreign Policy*, edited by Richmond M. Lloyd, 261–72.

Serafino, Nina M. *Department of Defense "Section 1207" Security and Stabilization Assistance: A Fact Sheet*. CRS Report RS22871. Washington, DC: CRS, 7 May 2008.

———. *Section 1206 of the National Defense Authorization Act for FY2006: A Fact Sheet on Department of Defense Authority to Train and Equip Foreign Military Forces*. CRS Report RS22855. Washington, DC: CRS, 28 September 2009.

Sewall, Sarah, and John P. White. *Parameters of Partnership: U.S. Civil-Military Relations in the 21st Century*. Cambridge, MA: Harvard Kennedy School Project on Civil-Military Relations, 2009.

Shapiro, Andrew J., assistant secretary of state for political-military affairs. "Political-Military Affairs: Smart Power Starts Here." Keynote address. ComDef 2009, Washington, DC, 9 September 2009.

Skocz, Dennis E. "A Front-Line View of 'The' Interagency: The Practice of Policy Coordination inside the Government." In *Affairs of State,* edited by Gabriel Marcella, 371–408.

Smith, CAPT Bradley B., USN. "The CINC's Joint Interagency Coordination Group (JIACG)—Essential to Winning the War on Terrorism." Research report. Newport, RI: Naval War College, 13 May 2002.

Sopher, LTC Terry R., USANG. "Joint Interagency Coordination Groups (JIACGs): A Temporary Solution to a Long Term Requirement." Master of Strategic Studies Degree report. Carlisle Barracks, PA: Army War College, 3 May 2004.

Stahl, Marcy. *Joint Interagency Coordination Group (JIACG) Training and Education Survey Results*. Vienna, VA: Thought Link Inc., 15 January 2004. http://www.thoughtlink.com/ppt/TLI-JIACG Survey-FinalBrief-Revised.ppt.

Steers, Howard J. T. "Bridging the Gaps: Political-Military Coordination at the Operational Level." Research report. Newport, RI: Naval War College, 17 May 2001.

Stephenson, James. "Military-Civilian Cooperation: A Field Perspective." *Foreign Service Journal*, March 2006, 55–62.

Stewart, Richard W. "Winning Hearts and Minds: The Vietnam Experience." In *Mismanaging Mayhem*, edited by James Jay Carafano and Richard Weitz, 89–112.

Stoff, Maj Karen D., USAF. "Strategic Planning and Joint Interagency Coordination Groups (JIACGs)." Research report. Maxwell AFB, AL: Air Command and Staff College, April 2006.

Strohm, Chris. "Former Commander Calls for New Military-Civilian Planning Organization." *Government Executive.com*, 7 December 2004. http://www.govexec.com/defense/2004/12/former-comman der-calls-for-new-military-civilian-planning-organization/18156.

Stuart, Douglas. "Constructing the Iron Cage: The 1947 National Security Act." In *Affairs of State*, edited by Gabriel Marcella, 53–95.

Stuhlreyer, LCDR Tom, US Coast Guard. "The JIATF Organization Model: Bringing the Interagency to Bear in Maritime Homeland Defense and Security." *Campaigning*, Spring 2007, 39–48.

Supplemental Appropriations Act. Public Law 111-32, 123 Stat. 1895. 111th Cong., 1st sess., 24 June 2009.

Sylvia, MAJ Brett G., USA. "Empowering Interagency Capabilities: A Regional Approach." Monograph. Fort Leavenworth, KS: School of Advanced Military Studies, US Army Command and General Staff College, 25 May 2006.

Szayna, Thomas S., Derek Eaton, James E. Barnett II, Brooke Stearns Lawson, Terrence K. Kelly, and Zachary Haldeman. *Integrating Civilian Agencies in Stability Operations*. Santa Monica, CA: RAND Corporation, 2009.

Taylor, Paul D. "The Outlook for U.S. Foreign Policy in Latin America and the Caribbean: The Challenges of Transforming Goodwill into Effective Policy." In *American Foreign Policy*, edited by Richmond M. Lloyd, 85–93.

Thompson, Mitchell J. "Breaking the Proconsulate: A New Design for National Power. *Parameters* 35, no. 4 (Winter 2005/06): 62–75.

———. "CORDS: A Lesson in True Interagency Cooperation." *Foreign Service Journal*, March 2006, 70–71.

Tomlin, COL Harry A., USA. *The Joint Interagency Coordination Group (JIACG): The United States European Command Experience and the Way Ahead*. Syracuse, NY: Maxwell School of Citizenship and Public Affairs, Syracuse University, 1 October 2003.

Tully, Andrew F. "Iraq: New U.S. Plan Seeks to Expedite Reconstruction." *Radio Free Europe/Radio Liberty*, 8 October 2003.

Uchida, Lt Col Ted T., USAF. "Reforming the Interagency Process." Air Force Fellows research report. Maxwell AFB, AL: Air Force Fellows Program, May 2005.

United Nations. Vienna Convention on Consular Relations, 24 April 1963. In United Nations, *Treaty Series*, vol. 596, 261.

———. Vienna Convention on Diplomatic Relations, 18 April 1961. In United Nations, *Treaty Series*, vol. 500, 95.

United States Agency for International Development (USAID), Office of Transition Initiatives. *15 Years: 1994–2009*. Washington, DC: USAID, 2009.

United States Commission on National Security/21st Century (Hart/Rudman Commission). *Road Map for National Security: Imperative for Change*. Phase III Report, 15 February 2001. http://govinfo.library.unt.edu/nssg/PhaseIIIFR.pdf.

"United States European Command (EUCOM) Interagency Partnering Directorate, ECJ9." Briefing, 12 March 2010. Provided to the author by Mike Anderson, deputy director, EUCOM/J-9.

USAFRICOM. "About United States Africa Command." http://www.africom.mil/AfricomFAQs.asp.

———. "CJTF-HOA Factsheet." http://www.hoa.africom.mil/AboutCJTF-HOA.asp.

———. "Organizational Chart, Headquarters U.S. Africa Command," 8 December 2011. http://www.africom.mil/pdfFiles/AFRICOM%20Org%20Chart.pdf.

US Agency for International Development, Office of Transition Initiatives. *15 Years—1994–2009*. http://www.globalcorps.com/sitedocs/oti15yearreport.pdf.

———. *Office of U.S. Foreign Disaster Assistance: Annual Report for Fiscal Year 2008*. http://www.usaid.gov/our_work/ humanitarian_assistance/disaster_assistance/publications/annual_reports/pdf/AR2008.pdf.

———. "Transition Initiatives." http://www.usaid.gov/our-work/cross-cutting_programs/transition_initiatives.

———. *USAID-DOD Relations*. 19 October 2005. http://www.usaid.gov/about_usaid/acvfa/usaid_dod_relations.pdf.

US Air Force. "Biography, Michael B. Donley." http://www.af.mil/information/bios/bio_print.asp?bioID=11336&page=1.

US Central Command. *CENTCOM Posture Statement: Senate Armed Services Committee Statement of General David H. Petraeus, U.S. Army, Commander U.S. Central Command before the Senate Armed Services Committee on the Afghanistan-Pakistan Strategic Review and the Posture of U.S. Central Command*. http://www.centcom.mil/en/about-centcom/posture-statement.

US Department of Defense (DOD). *Quadrennial Defense Review Report*. Washington, DC: DOD, 6 February 2006.

———. *Quadrennial Defense Review Report*. Washington, DC: DOD, February 2010.

———. "Report on Progress toward Security and Stability in Afghanistan." Report to Congress in accordance with section 1230 of the National Defense Authorization Act for Fiscal Year 2008 (Public Law 110-181), as amended, November 2010.

US Department of Homeland Security. *Brief Documentary History of the Department of Homeland Security: 2001–2008*. http://www.dhs .gov/xlibrary/assets/brief_documentary_history_of_dhs_2001 _2008.pdf.

US Department of State. *Afghanistan and Pakistan Regional Stabilization Strategy*, Office of the Special Representative for Afghanistan and Pakistan, January 2010.

———. "Bureau of International Organization Affairs." http://www .state.gov/p/io/other/133723.htm.

———. Bureau of South and Central Asian Affairs, "U.S. Counternarcotics Strategy for Afghanistan," 24 March 2010. http://www .state.gov/p/sca/ci/af/2010/141491.htm.

———. "Bureaus/Offices Reporting Directly to the Secretary." http://www .state.gov/s/.

———. Office of the Spokesman. "Civilian Response Corps Reaches 100 Active Members," 16 April 2010.

———. "Frequently Asked Questions: Office of the Coordinator for Reconstruction and Stabilization," 15 July 2008. http://www.state .gov/s/crs/66427.htm.

———. "Special Envoys and Special Representatives." http://www .state.gov/misc/129676.htm.

———. "Department Organization Chart," May 2012. http://www.state .gov/r/pa/ei/rls/dos/99494.htm.

———. "Under Secretary for Political Affairs." http://www.state.gov/p/.

———. "U.S.-ASEAN Cooperation." http://www.state.gov/r/pa/prs/ps /2011/07/168943.htm.

———. Office of the Coordinator for Reconstruction and Stabilization. "About Us." http://www.state.gov/s/crs/about/index.htm.

———. "Office of Civilian Response Operations." http://www.crs .state.gov/index.cfm?Fuseaction=public.display@shortcut=.

———. "S/CRS Supports Peace Efforts in Darfur." http://www.crs.state .gov/index.cfm?fuseaction-public.display&shortcut=4F5I.

———. "What We Do." http://www.state.gov/j/cso/what/indes.htm.

US Department of State and the Broadcasting Board of Governors, Office of Inspector General. *Report of Inspection: The Bureau of African Affairs.* Report Number ISP-I-09-63, August 2009.

US Department of State and US Agency for International Development. *Strategic Plan: Fiscal Years 2007–2012—Transformational Diplomacy.* Revised 7 May 2007.

———. Bureau of Conflict and Stabilization Operations. "CSO: One-Year Progress Report," 8 March 2013. http://www.state.gov/j/cso/releases/other/2013/206410/htm.

———. Office of the Spokesperson. "U.S. Department of State Launches Bureau of Conflict and Stabilization Operations." Fact sheet, 22 November 2011.

———. US Mission to the African Union. "About Us." http://www.usau.usmission.gov/aboutus.html.

———. US Mission to the African Union. "Key Officers." http://www.usau.usmission.gov/key-officers.html.

———. US Mission to the European Union. "About the Mission." http://useu.usmission.gov/root/about-the-mission.html.

———. US Mission to the Organization of American States. "Introduction." http://www.usoas.usmission.gov/aboutus.html.

———. US Permanent Mission to the OAS. "United States Delegation." http://www.usoas.usmission.gov/aboutus.

US Department of State. "The U.S. Mission to the OSCE [Organization for Security Cooperation in Europe]." http://osce.usmission.gov/info.html.

US European Command. "Biography of Mr. Michael G. Ritchie, Director of Interagency Partnering." http://www.eucom.mil/english/bio2.asp?bioid=DAF6183B-F421-4BDF-839B-94D68C3A38A0.

US Government Accountability Office (GAO). *Interagency Collaboration: Key Issues for Congressional Oversight of National Security Strategies, Organizations, Workforce, and Information Sharing.* GAO-09-904SP. Washington, DC: GAO, September 2009.

US House Armed Services Committee, Oversight and Investigations Subcommittee. *Agency Stovepipes vs. Strategic Agility: Lessons We Need to Learn from Provincial Reconstruction Teams in Iraq and Afghanistan.* Committee print 8. Washington, DC: GPO, 2008.

———. Interagency Cooperation Commission Act. 111th Cong., 1st sess. H. R. 2207, 30 April 2009.

US House of Representatives. *Eliminating Terrorist Sanctuaries: The Role of Security Assistance—Hearing before the Subcommittee on International Terrorism and Nonproliferation of the Committee on International Relations*. 109th Cong., 1st sess., 10 March 2005. Serial no. 109-19.

US Joint Forces Command. *Commander's Handbook for the Joint Interagency Coordination Group*. Norfolk, VA: USJFCOM Joint Warfighting Center, Joint Innovation and Experimentation Directorate, 1 March 2007.

———. *Doctrinal Implications of the Joint Interagency Coordination Group (JIACG)*, Pamphlet 6. Norfolk, VA: Joint Warfighting Center, Joint Doctrine Series, 27 June 2004.

———. *Insights and Best Practices: Interagency, Intergovernmental, and Nongovernmental Coordination: A Joint Force Operational Perspective*, Focus Paper no. 3. Norfolk, VA: Joint Warfighting Center, July 2007. http://jko.cmil.org/file/109/view.

———. *Interagency Working Group E'Newsletter*. September 2004. http://www.ndu.edu/itea/storage/558/September%2004%20 Newsletter.pdf.

———. *Joint Interagency Coordination Group*. Fact sheet. http://www .jfcom.mil/about/facts_prt/JIACG.pdf.

———. "Provincial Reconstruction Teams." Joint Warfighting Center predoctrinal research white paper no. 07-01, 21 November 2007.

US Pacific Command. "Asia-Pacific Area Network." http://www1.apan -info.net/ SecurityCooperation/tabid/4614/Default.aspx.

———. "Joint Interagency Task Force–West." http://www.pacom.mil /staff/JIATFWest/index.shtml.

"U.S. Military Facilities: U.S. Southern Command." Informal weblog for the US military's airborne Spanish linguists. http://www.beaner banner.com/ussouthcom.htm.

US Senate, Committee on Foreign Relations. *Embassies as Command Posts in the Anti-Terror Campaign*. 109th Cong., 2nd sess., 15 December 2006. Senate Print 109-52. Washington, DC: GPO, 2006.

Van Opdorp, Lt Col Harold, USMC. "The Joint Interagency Coordination Group: The Operationalization of DIME." *Small Wars Journal*, July 2005. http://smallwarsjournal.com/documents/swjmag/v2/odie .htm.

Ward, William E., and Thomas P. Galvin. "U.S. Africa Command and the Principle of Active Security." *Joint Force Quarterly* 51 (4th Quarter 2008): 61–66.

Weitz, Richard. "'Interagency Problems and Proposals: A Research Review." In *Mismanaging Mayhem*, edited by James Jay Carafano and Richard Weitz, 235–71.

Welle, Joshua W. Civil-Military Integration in Afghanistan: Creating Unity of Command. *Joint Force Quarterly* 56 (1st Quarter 2010): 54–59.

"White House Establishes Iraq Task Force." *Government Custom Wire*, 6 October 2003.

White House, Office of Management and Budget. "The U.S. Department of Defense 2010 Budget." Fact sheet. http://www.white house.gov/omb/assets/fy2010_factsheets/fy10_defense.pdf.

The White House, Office of the Press Secretary. "Foreign Affairs Reorganization." Fact sheet, 30 December 1998. http://www.fas.org /news/usa/1998/12/98123003_tlt.html.

———. Presidential Policy Directive 1 (PPD-1). *Organization of the National Security Council System*, 13 February 2009.

Whitsitt, LCDR William C., USN. "U.S. Africa Command: An Opportunity for Effective Interagency Cooperation." Research report. Newport, RI: Naval War College, 10 May 2007.

Whittaker, Alan G., Frederick C. Smith, and Elizabeth McKune. "The National Security Policy Process: The National Security Council and Interagency System." In *Affairs of State*, edited by Gabriel Marcella, 97–170.

Yates, Mary C. "U.S. Africa Command: Value Added." *Joint Force Quarterly* 52 (1st Quarter 2009): 152–55.

Yeatman, Richard M. "JIATF-South: Blueprint for Success." *Joint Force Quarterly* 42 (3rd Quarter 2006): 26–27.

York, Maj J. D., USMC. "Militarizing the Interagency." Research report. Newport, RI: Naval War College, 14 February 2005.

Wyler, Liana Sun, and Kenneth Katzman. *Afghanistan: U.S. Rule of Law and Justice Sector Assistance*. Washington, DC: Congressional Research Service, 9 November 2010.

Zaccor, COL Albert, USA. *Security Cooperation and Non-State Threats: A Call for an Integrated Strategy*. Occasional paper. Washington, DC: Atlantic Council of the United States, August 2005.

Zeller, Shawn. "Who's in Charge Here?" *Foreign Service Journal* 84, no. 12 (December 2007): 20–28.

Index